The Political Ideas of the Utopian Socialists

The Political Ideas of the Utopian Socialists

KEITH TAYLOR
Senior Lecturer in Political Science
Coventry (Lanchester) Polytechnic

FRANK CASS

First published in 1982 in Great Britain by
FRANK CASS AND COMPANY LIMITED
Gainsborough House, 11 Gainsborough Road,
London, E11 1RS, England

and in thc United States of America by
FRANK CASS AND COMPANY LIMITED
c/o Biblio Distribution Centre
81 Adams Drive, P.O. Box 327, Totowa, N.J. 07511

British Library Cataloguing in Publication Data

Taylor, Keith
The political idea of the utopian socialists.
1. Utopias
I. Title
321'.07 HX806

ISBN 0-7146-3089-6

Typeset by Macdonald & Evans Ltd, Plymouth

Printed in Great Britain by
Page Bros (Norwich) Ltd

Contents

Preface

The foundations of modern socialist thought were laid during the first half of the nineteenth century in the writings of a number of thinkers, chiefly French, British, and German, who attempted in their various ways to show how a radical improvement in the condition of the working classes could be brought about. In this book I have selected for special attention the work of Saint-Simon and his disciples (the Saint-Simonians), Owen, Fourier, Cabet, and Weitling – those thinkers who did, I believe, make the most important contributions to the development of early socialist theory.

There were, of course, many thinkers besides those dealt with here who played a role in the evolution of pre-Marxian socialism: such men as Babeuf, Dézamy, Blanc, Auguste Blanqui in France; Godwin, Hall, Hodgskin, Bray in England; the so-called 'True Socialists' (Bruno Bauer, Hess, Grün, Lüning, Semmig, Püttman, and others) in Germany. Generally speaking, however, I tend to regard these men as theoreticians of secondary importance – writers of less weight and originality, who are notable more for occasional, isolated insights than for comprehensive systems such as those associated with Saint-Simon and his disciples, Owen, Fourier, Cabet, and Weitling. One need only look at the many commentaries on socialism which appeared during the 1830s and 1840s to see that it was these latter thinkers who were regarded as the representatives *par excellence* of the new movement.

It became a common practice, at this time, to mock the efforts of these early pioneers and dismiss them as expressions of a naive utopianism. Such was the view enunciated with great force, for example, by Proudhon, Marx, and Engels. The designation 'utopian' has since entered into the conventional vocabulary of the history of ideas, and is now used almost without question. These thinkers were certainly utopian in the sense that they sought to describe the structure of an ideal future society – a golden age of happiness – from which major sources of human conflict would be eradicated; but whether they were utopian in the sense of being completely fanciful and unrealistic is a much more complex issue to unravel. They defended themselves vigorously against such charges, and from this point of view they would certainly have not approved of a book which referred to them as utopian socialists. There is no doubt in my own mind that these thinkers often came to hasty and over-optimistic conclusions on the basis of a somewhat superficial investigation of contemporary social trends, and failed in many ways to comprehend the significance of the emerging capitalist system of production. But in other respects, especially in the area of political analysis, I would argue that they proved themselves to be just as perceptive, if not perhaps more so, than Proudhon, Marx, Engels, and other critics who were convinced of their own scientific superiority. Furthermore, these same critics were in fact greatly indebted to the predecessors they so readily mocked, and anyone who cares to undertake a comparative study will soon discover that some of the central ideas of the utopians were assimilated, not rejected, by later theorists.

The ideas of the utopian socialists are not simply of historical importance, however, but are of enduring interest and of direct relevance to the problems which confront men in modern industrial societies, particularly the problems of dehumanisation and powerlessness, problems which, in my own view, are unlikely to be solved unless we are able to develop that same sense of vision, of enthusiasm for an alternative form of social life, which motivated the utopians. The reawakening of interest during the 1960s and 1970s in communitarianism, the emergence of various 'alternative society' movements reacting against both western capitalism and Soviet-style communism, the vigorous debate on possible 'post-industrial' futures: all this suggests that the utopian spirit is still very much alive, and that the theories of the early socialists are still likely to provoke constructive argument.

In my introduction I have drawn upon material originally presented in a paper written for the 1978 annual conference of the Political Studies Association of the United Kingdom: 'Politics as Harmony. Utopian Responses to the Impact of Industrialism, 1830-1848'. This paper formed the basis of an article (with the same title) subsequently published in the journal *Alternative Futures* (vol. 2, no. 1, Winter 1979). In chapter 1 and the first section of chapter 4 I have utilised an analysis which first appeared in the introduction to my book, *Henri Saint-Simon. Selected Writings on Science, Industry and Social Organisation*, Croom Helm, London; Holmes and Meier, New York (1975).

For financial assistance which greatly facilitated my research I am indebted to the Central Research Fund of Lanchester Polytechnic. I should also like to take this opportunity to thank the following: David McLellan, who first stimulated my interest in utopian socialism during my years as an undergraduate at the University of Kent, and with whom I have since discussed many of the views which now appear in this book; Richard Greaves, for whom I worked as a research assistant at the London School of Economics and Political Science during 1973-4, and from whom I learned much about early English socialism; Barbara Goodwin, Henryk Katz, Lyman Sargent, and Bill Stafford, who, often without knowing it, helped me to clarify my ideas; and last, but by no means least, my wife Chris, who provided bibliographical help and that most precious of all aids, encouragement.

Keith Taylor

Introduction

The Utopian Impulse in Early Socialist Thought

The thinkers whose ideas are studied in this book did not belong to a single, homogeneous school of thought. They disagreed with each other over many fundamental issues, and there were pronounced divergencies in their social and political recommendations. However, they shared a common concern for the plight of the poorest sections of society, and they all attempted in their various ways to show how a much greater level of equality could be achieved. In this respect they were collectively responsible for laying the foundations for the development of modern socialist doctrines. Above all they were great pioneers, formulating startlingly new concepts and terminology (the actual words 'socialism' and 'socialist', for example, first gained currency during the 1830s largely as a result of their influence), and either undertaking directly, or at least inspiring, remarkable communitarian experiments in co-operative living, in both Europe and the United States.

Because they lived and worked during an age notable for its optimistic view of history and its romantic faith in unbounded progress through the application of human reasoning, we should not be surprised to find that the notion of social perfectibility underlies much of their thought. In their numerous descriptions of ideal societies all elements of serious human conflict are absent, and the characteristic condition is one of true harmony (to use a favourite term of Owen, Fourier, and Weitling): an earthly paradise is finally established in which man's various needs, both physical and spiritual, find complete satisfaction. Such images of truly harmonious social conditions may suggest that these thinkers belong to the same tradition of western utopianism which has its roots in Plato's *Republic* and Thomas More's *Utopia*. But the early socialists themselves did not like the term 'utopian'; indeed they all made great efforts to show that their theories could not possibly be regarded as 'mere utopias' (this was a common phrase). To them the term suggested a kind of purely speculative theorising – inspirational but ultimately fanciful and hopelessly impracticable – which they were anxious to reject. They preferred to think of themselves as scientists rather than utopians, since they believed they had attained a truly objective understanding of the ways in which western societies were actually developing, and an equally objective insight into how they could be organised in future so as to maximise human happiness. At the same time their conceptions of scientific method and its applicability to the study of man and society varied enormously. Thus, the somewhat crude positivism of Saint-Simon, with its emphasis on the systematic observation of social phenomena, must be distinguished from his disciples' stress on the crucial role of intuitive genius and imagination in the formulation of social theories. Whereas Saint-Simon and Owen were full of admiration for the achievements of the natural sciences, Fourier's attitude was one of deep-rooted cynicism and doubt as to whether anything really important had ever been achieved (apart from one or two notable exceptions!). And in Cabet and Weitling we have two men who tended to pay lip-service to the importance of scientific method, but who were actually much less interested in this question than in the practical problem of creating a socialist movement.

There is thus a certain ambiguity at the heart of early socialist thought. On the one hand utopia, in the sense of an ideal state of social organisation, was the common goal to which all theories were pointing: and, furthermore, proponents of these theories were convinced that they could describe this future state in considerable detail. On the other hand, the ideal state was to be achieved, according to these thinkers, through thoroughly sober and realistic, i.e. non-utopian, methods of analysis based on a new social science. But, of course, this view of science as an agent of transition to an earthly paradise could itself be described as utopian. It is a view which is rooted in a boundless faith in man's capacity to acquire knowledge concerning exceedingly complex social problems, and to apply this knowledge in the movement towards a future golden age – a faith which, in the light of man's experience of scientific development and applications of science since the early nineteenth century, we might now consider to be unacceptable.

The Future as Harmony

The period in which the early socialists were formulating their theories was one of widespread socio-economic upheaval, a period in which the development of capitalist industrialism was causing in all western societies (although at different rates of change) a severe dislocation to the situation of many social groups. Most importantly, it was a period in which a new working class was being created. This class was not an integrated whole, however, but was very clearly divided between different occupations, between the agricultural and manufacturing sectors, and, within manufacturing, between artisans and handicraft workers on the one hand, whose status and livelihood were threatened by new forms of mechanised production, and, on the other hand, the labour force employed in the factories. As a consequence of this process of dislocation, traditional social values associated with an essentially pre-capitalist (perhaps even pre-industrial) society lost much of their relevance, and new norms were called for which were more appropriate to the stage of socio-economic development attained in the western countries. The essential constitutive values of utopian socialism may be seen as a response to this problem. They represent various attempts to formulate new normative systems in a period of upheaval. Inevitably, however, these normative systems retained links with the older, more traditional values which the utopians felt were being lost. This contradiction, if one may call it that, is to be seen first of all in the idea of harmony, already referred to above, which was undoubtedly the key goal towards which all the utopian socialists directed their efforts.

The actual word 'harmony' is encountered in much of the utopian literature and in many utopian schemes during the early nineteenth century, from George Rapp's Harmony Society (a community of German separatists who settled in America in 1803) to the systems of Fourier ('harmonism' was the supreme human passion, and the future social order would be known as Harmony), Weitling (see, for example, his *Guarantees of Harmony and Freedom*), and Owen (whose two major experimental communities were at New Harmony and Harmony Hall, Queenwood). Other thinkers (for example, Saint-Simon, the Saint-Simonians, Cabet) may not have placed quite so much emphasis on the word itself, but the idea for which it stood was clearly implicit in their thought. One might argue that all utopian thinkers throughout history have put forward a vision of social harmony. In the early nineteenth century, however, the concept assumed a new significance with a number of very specific connotations. It derived in part from a Newtonian view of the universe as an orderly, perfectly integrated, system; and there can be little doubt that Saint-Simon and Fourier, both of whom drew analogies between laws of social attraction (which each believed he had discovered) and Newton's law of universal gravitation, were impressed by this scientific argument. Saint-Simon also admired the physiological harmony of the human body, and saw no reason why such an arrangement could not be reproduced in society. (This is an outlook which reappears in the writings of Cabet.) The idea of harmony suggested certain artistic principles, too, especially in music (Fourier, once again, was fond of this analogy); and it even linked up with the economic theories of men such as Adam Smith and Jean-Baptiste Say, who claimed to have discovered a natural harmony of economic interests in society. But perhaps even more important than all these suggestions is the fact that the notion of harmony implied a distinctive view of social relations according to which a great premium was placed on the capacity of members of society to live together without conflict and with common interests, united by ties of true love and affection. One of the most usual ways of presenting future society was in the image of a large, happy family; and in the case of some utopians, notably Owen, Fourier, and the Saint-Simonians, this actually implied superseding the traditional, more limited nuclear family (regarded as a bastion of self-interest, antiquated religious doctrine, and social divisions), and allowing sentiments of love (including, perhaps, feelings of sexual desire) to find expression much more spontaneously and with the minimum of restriction.

The social origins of these ideas are not difficult to discern: the vision of a future state of harmony was born amidst conditions which were quite obviously lacking in harmony. Revolutionary upheaval, socio-economic dislocation caused by new mechanised methods of capitalist production, the decline of traditional sources of legitimacy and authority – these were painful facts of life during the period in question, especially painful for those groups, such as the artisans and handicraft workers, whose life-style and mode of work were threatened most directly by the pressures of change. Any vision of the future, if it was to appeal to those groups suffering most under these conditions of social transformation, had to promise salvation from the worst evils, and salvation was bound to be seen in terms of the opposite of upheaval and instability, in other words as harmony.

In this respect the utopians put forward a radically new view of politics, a view which is one of the central concerns of the present analysis. The idea of politics, traditionally associated with competing interests and the resolution of conflict, was now seen to be in need of reformulation. Politics would be transformed into an activity concerned with rational-scientific questions, especially in the sphere of economics. Harmony would require administration rather than government, a notion emphasised particularly by Saint-Simon and Weitling. It would also involve the rejection of individualism (equated with a conflict of interests) and its replacement by some more collective form of organisation.

This idea of an alternative to individualism can be clarified more precisely by examining three further concepts which were essential ingredients of the theories of the early socialists, and which served as components of the broader notion of harmony: association, community, and co-operation. Association was a particularly important idea. As one commentator has put it, it had the force of a kind of messianic vision during this period.[1] Its power stemmed from the widespread demand voiced by workers in the early nineteenth century to be granted the right to associate for various social and economic purposes. At a time when workers were frequently deprived of this right, the call for association represented very positive, concrete aspirations. In England, for example, the anti-combination laws of 1799 and 1800 were attacked by English utopians such as Owen. Their repeal in 1824 allowed certain kinds of association to be formed, and thus represented a partial realisation of early socialist aims. In France, on the other hand, the 1791 Le Chapelier law (which abolished guilds) and subsequent additions to it made 'anything like the English trade-union movement impossible'.[2] Hence the continuing ferment caused by demands for association in France in the 1830s and 1840s, culminating in the efforts of the revolutionaries in 1848 to use producers' associations as the basis for a new 'democratic and social republic'. In Germany the situation was different again owing to the fact that the traditional guild system still existed. The distinction in status between masters and journeymen was widening, however, and this prompted many groups of journeymen to support demands for the creation of new workers' associations as an alternative to the guilds. Such demands gained much support among the émigré workers in London and Paris, where, for obvious reasons, German workers were influenced directly by the beliefs of their English and French counterparts.

Association promised a variety of future benefits: at least the achievement of better working conditions through increased bargaining power, and perhaps even the ownership of property by workers who could not afford to buy individually. Buchez, who for a time supported the Saint-Simonian movement, believed that in this way one could eliminate the capitalist.[3] It was also argued that if workers stopped competing with one another on the labour market, and replaced competition by association, the downward trend in wages – a trend which was regarded as the inevitable consequence of competition between workers – would be reversed, and there would be greater security of employment. But as well as looking forward to the future, association also hearkened back to the past, to the actual experience of solidarity and combination among workers in guilds, trade and craft clubs, the French *compagnonnages,*[4] and so on. Such experience was important, in particular, for workers with clearly defined skills: the artisans and handicraft workers, the journeymen and apprentices. The consciousness of association in a special trade or craft was here vitally significant, quite different from the position in which the workers employed in the new factories found themselves.

'Association' usually seems to have been used by the utopians to denote a small-scale group organised in a particular occupation or place of work. The Saint-Simonians, however, took great exception to this vision of a society built upon numerous small associations, and they advocated instead 'universal association', a scheme intended to unite entire societies and, ultimately, whole continents and indeed the total population of the world.[5] This is certainly one very important reason why, in the 1830s, the Saint-Simonians came to be widely regarded as advocates of a conspicuously authoritarian, perhaps even the most authoritarian, version of socialism.

After association, another crucial concept for the utopians was community. At first sight it is tempting to dismiss this as a somewhat vague goal, but the notion of community, as part of the total vision of a harmonious society, grew out of certain very real experiences of a sense of common living and common identity shared by persons living in distinct locations, belonging to, say, a friendly society or trade club, pursuing their occupations in the same workplace, or even attending the same church. Many social historians have revealed the importance of this community identity among workers during the Industrial Revolution. Thus, to take just one illustration:

> Another interesting phenomena observable in Lancashire was the perpetuation of semi-independent communities on the outskirts of industrial towns whose members felt a strongly particularistic rather than urban loyalty, and this doubtless inhibited class development in these areas. Similarly, many cotton operatives persisted in feelings of loyalty towards a mill-community and an individual mill-owner, accepting the latter's political tutelage rather than striking out politically on class lines.[6]

In time the idea of community assumed the specific connotation of actually going out to a new location and building a new village, town, or workplace. Hence the mania for experimental communities and deliberate environmental planning associated with many utopian socialists and their followers throughout the nineteenth century.

In France the term *'commune'* had obvious implications in terms of a unit of local government. There was no problem, therefore, about understanding the general meaning of *'communauté.'* A difficulty did arise, however, when *'communauté'* was used by Cabet and others to mean a system based on communal ownership of property, for this was a much more specific meaning than had previously been understood. In this way community became inextricably linked with communism. And this in turn gave rise to an ambiguity, because in France at least communism tended to be associated with insurrectionary methods (as advocated, for instance, by Blanqui), whereas Cabet recommended a strategy rooted firmly in pacifism.

Co-operation was a third crucial idea implicit in the utopians' picture of social harmony. As with association and community, the concept of co-operation tended to suggest both something which had actually been experienced – for example, the co-operation among workers in various clubs and friendly societies, or even the co-operation between masters and apprentices in certain trades and skilled occupations – and also something yet to be attained in other spheres of working life. The small workshop typical of pre- and early capitalist society presented the utopians with a ready-made image of true co-operation. The modern factory, although still in its infancy in the first half of the nineteenth century, threatened to destroy co-operation through its separation of employers and employees, and also its dehumanising effects on the individual worker. Hence the meaning of co-operation became perfectly clear; and indeed the rise of, for example, the co-operative societies in Britain and the *sociétés de secours mutuel* in France[7] showed that co-operation was also a realistic goal.

The co-operative principle was further extended by Owen and Fourier, who believed that it could offer an alternative mode of social organisation to capitalism. According to this more specific view, the co-operative philosophy demanded that a club or community should be controlled by those who made some direct contribution to the production of wealth, and the aim should be to distribute any resulting income among these producers, thus avoiding the employer's profit-margin. This could perhaps be regarded as a new principle. Yet at the same time many advocates of co-operation saw the scheme's virtue in terms of its ability to permit workers collectively to acquire wealth. As was mentioned earlier in relation to the idea of association, the suggestion here was that workers might not be able to afford property individually, but they could when grouped together in co-operation. This would seem to be not so much an attack on ownership as a desire to spread the benefits of ownership to groups of people normally deprived of them. And the fact that Owen came to advocate communism, while Fourier always defended the institution of private property, indicates the ambiguity involved in these early co-operative schemes.

From the above comments it can be seen, I hope, that the emphasis on harmony, with its further suggestions of association, community, and co-operation, was not a totally vague, abstract construction, as might be suspected from many accounts of early socialist thought. It was much more than a romantic vision of the future, for it was derived directly from the actual experiences of men in small-scale groups. Thus the sense of association, community, and co-operation grew out of life in the village, town, *commune*, and workshop, or among members of a particular religious sect. This key idea of attaining social harmony was not, therefore, entirely unrealistic (as the designation 'utopian' is frequently taken to mean), although one might argue that as the capitalist system developed it became increasingly difficult to achieve in practice. In fact, when the utopians came to work out detailed strategies by which to achieve harmony, they often floundered, and disagreements, controversies, and heated disputes became characteristic of the socialist movement in the 1830s and 1840s. Thus, although they might agree on the importance of striving for association, community and co-operation, the thinkers studied in this book could not agree at all on the specific steps required to make these qualities operational. The consequence was a range of what may be called strategic value conflicts, the most important of which will now be considered.

Harmonians in Conflict: Six Strategic Dilemmas

(i) Industrialism versus anti-industrialism Probably the most basic conflict of all concerned the whole question of the desirability of an industrialised society. To the utopians industrial-

ism implied, first and foremost, the advent of mechanisation and factory employment. From one point of view this promised remarkable levels of economic growth and productivity, welcomed unreservedly by Saint-Simon in his enthusiasm for *le système industriel* (an enthusiasm carried on after his death by his disciples), by Cabet, who described his Icarian doctrine as being totally opposed to agrarianism, and also by Owen. But on the other hand it threatened the livelihood and status of artisans and handicraft workers, who faced the prospect of being taken away from their homes and workshops and being either 'proletarianised' (i.e. pushed into factory employment) or made completely redundant as the machines took over. Agricultural workers, too, were likely to see industrialism as a threat to their way of life, although Saint-Simon urged them to regard agriculture as part of industry (he adopted such an outlook because he viewed agriculture as a productive occupation and therefore no different from manufacturing in that specific sense); and Owen foresaw a need for more, not fewer, agricultural workers once the superiority of spade husbandry over the plough was recognised. The strongest defences of agrarianism and handicraft are to be found in the writings of Fourier and Weitling, who were particularly concerned to remove the threat which industrialism posed to more traditional – and in their view, more noble – occupations.[8]

There were economic arguments, also, to support hostility to industrialism. The spread of machinery was widely seen as a cause of over-production, an idea associated particularly with the theories of Sismondi, who accordingly wanted to halt industrialisation. In addition the policy of actually destroying machinery was adopted in practice by many workers' movements in the early nineteenth century, from the Luddites in Britain to the Silesian weavers who revolted in 1844. Even Chartism advocated workers' opposition to mechanisation.

(ii) Private property versus common ownership After the question of industrialism, the next most divisive issue concerned property ownership. Some utopians, notably Saint-Simon and Fourier, saw no need at all to get rid of private property as long as owners were obliged to put their property

to productive use. The Saint-Simonian disciples, also, did not seek to abolish private property, but thought it desirable to put an end to the transfer of property rights through inheritance. Instead the allocation of property was to be determined by the state authorities, acting in the general interests of society. Other thinkers, however, identified private property as the basis of capitalist exploitation and advocated schemes of communism (the later Owen, Cabet, Weitling). Such an identification is not surprising. Under modern working conditions there was a clear physical separation between those who owned property and those who did not. Property ownership brought many advantages apart from the obvious pecuniary ones. Voting rights, for example, were usually related to wealth in the form of property. Furthermore, as has already been mentioned, for workers who could not afford to purchase property as individuals, communism seemed a very realistic alternative. This particular idea motivated many of the founders of experimental communities, especially those in America, where land was readily available for communal purchase. In certain workers' associations, too, principles of common ownership actually operated, for example in some co-operative societies and the French *sociétés de secours mutuel.* Here is yet another instance in which a particular value grew out of experience, an instance which tends to confirm the perceptive point made by Rosabeth Moss Kanter:

> Utopian values may be after-the-fact explanations for social practices that arose accidentally, from expediency alone, to fit the needs of particular individuals, or to help maintain the group. A few nineteenth century groups . . . first began to share property communally as the result of pressing economic circumstances rather than consciously to implement a set of coherent values; utopian ideals were later used to justify the practice.[9]

Communism could not be expected, though, to appeal to all workers. Many artisans placed great emphasis on the virtues of private property. In many skilled occupations workers usually possessed their own tools; and through apprenticeship schemes they could hope one day to achieve the status of master craftsman, employing a number of workers in a workshop. In such circumstances many groups of workers felt that they could legitimately strive to attain ownership of property. If one examines the working-class literature that emerged in the second quarter of the nineteenth century, one finds that private property was frequently seen as a fundamental natural right, and any opposition to private property was accordingly condemned as unnatural. Thus, to take an example, the important French working-class newspaper *Echo de la fabrique* confidently dismissed all schemes for communal ownership as totally unrealistic, preferring to support the more moderate theories of Fourier.[10] And in America the disciples of Fourier, including Albert Brisbane, attacked the Owenites for their rejection of private property.[11] There was a fundamental conflict here between two concepts of economic equality. One emphasised the equal right of all men to own property, a right which, once operational, would inevitably lead to a certain amount of inequality of wealth, because some individuals would put their property to productive use, while others would not have the necessary ability or inclination. The second concept saw equality in terms of a pooling of property rights, a handing over of property to the community as a whole. It is therefore not very helpful simply to say that the early socialists were egalitarians. There were two quite distinct egalitarian traditions, one much more radical than the other.

(iii) Religion versus secularisation The question of religion posed major problems for the utopian socialists. One reaction was to see religion as a thing of the past, belonging to an age of superstition and no longer acceptable in the light of modern science. Such a view characterised much of Fourier's work, although it was modified as Fourier became interested in the possibility of love becoming a new kind of religious bond (an idea presented only very sketchily, and mainly in writings which remained unpublished during the author's lifetime). Owen, too, was associated with an attitude of hostility towards religion until the early 1830s, but he subsequently reconciled rationalism and religion to such an extent that he presented the 'new moral world' as the Second Coming of Christ. Other utopians, very much in the tradition of Rousseau and the French Revolution, remained convinced that religion was a social necessity. One possibility was that

science itself could become the basis for a new religious faith (an idea developed in the early writings of Saint-Simon). Secondly, a new doctrine of social mysticism, more sentimental than scientific, could be formulated (this was the conviction of the Saint-Simonians). A third possibility was that Christianity could be reformed, brought up to date, and made scientific and more radical (this was the proposal of the later Saint-Simon, Cabet, and Weitling).

There were in fact so many versions of new, reformed Christianities and religions of humanity during this period that one must seek some social explanation of the tendency. To begin with, the expectation, shared by all these thinkers, of a completely transformed social existence clearly lent itself to presentation in messianic terms. This was particularly true in the case of France, where utopian socialism often appealed to disillusioned Catholics. In Britain and America the religious ideas of the early socialists were undoubtedly influenced by the great revival of millenarianism – that is, the anticipation of the thousand-year reign of Christ on earth, with its consequent consolidation of peace, justice, and fraternity – that occurred on both sides of the Atlantic at this time, and which found expression in numerous sects and movements of every kind. Many commentators have noted how the spirit and even the vocabulary of millenarianism became increasingly important ingredients in Owen's thinking following his return from the New Harmony community in America, and it is clear that this shift cannot be fully understood without reference to the more general rise of religious millenarianism which was then taking place, and to which Owen had to respond.

Another factor which must be taken into account is that to many working-class groups, especially in France, religion seemed to be as natural an institution as private property, and its demise was therefore unthinkable. Furthermore, the principles of harmony, association, community, and co-operation represented a rejection of selfishness and individualism, and expressed a growing concern for humanity and the common good – values traditionally associated with the inspiration of religion, especially the Christian religion; and it is not surprising that during the period in question these principles appealed particularly to groups who already had some religious, usually Christian, outlook in common. There were, for instance, many religious sects who turned to utopian socialism mainly because their religious rights were not recognised in their own societies. Many of the groups who emigrated from Europe to America in order to form experimental communities did so in an effort to practise their own religions free from persecution. The Judaic element also played a part in the emergence of some socialist schools, most notably the Saint-Simonian movement after 1825. On the other hand, a distinctly anti-semitic attitude marked some aspects of Fourier's teachings, especially his vehement attacks on the commercial classes.[12]

The point is also worth mentioning that religion was often able to serve the crucial function of creating positive commitment to a socialist movement. It was a most effective mechanism for recruiting support and for creating that sense of attachment without which no movement can endure for any length of time. It is true, of course, that none of the new utopian religions was very successful; but what is important is that religion was often decisive in the formative, take-off, stage of modern socialism. Interestingly enough, the most successful early socialist movement, Cabet's Icarianism, was unashamedly based on a doctrine of the new Christianity, a doctrine which stressed, in particular, the primitive communism of the early Christians.

(iv) Revolution versus gradualism It has already been remarked that the utopians' insistence on harmony had certain counter-revolutionary implications. Many of them did indeed reject violence altogether. But one specific strand of the socialist movement persistently advocated revolution: the tradition of insurrection stemming from Babeuf (leader of the Conspiracy of Equals, 1796), further developed by Barbès and Blanqui (who directed the Paris uprising of 1839), and adopted by Weitling. For many years, particularly in France, communism was widely regarded as being synonymous with insurrection, and it was often contrasted with socialism for this reason. Yet Cabet confused matters by putting forward a theory of pacific communism: he wanted his movement to be out in the open, legitimate, and respectable rather than being hidden away underground in the form of a secret society.

It is also the case that revolutionary methods were not in keeping with the experience of certain groups of workers in the early nineteenth century. Many workers, after all, enjoyed reasonably good relations with their employers. The master-apprentice relationship in the workshop was frequently of this nature. In these circumstances revolution seemed inappropriate. Only when the modern factory took over, bringing with it a different set of industrial relations, did revolutionary attitudes gain more widespread support. One of the most valuable insights offered by economic and social historians is that the level of workers' radicalism during the Industrial Revolution varied from area to area and from industry to industry depending on the social structure of the locality in question and the framework of industrial relations.[13] A number of excellent studies of labour unrest in France, dealing particularly with the Revolutions of 1830 and 1848 and the Lyons uprisings of 1831 and 1834, show that it was among fairly specific groups of workers and in distinct locations that revolutionary doctrines had their greatest impact.[14] Often utopian thinkers who normally rejected revolution changed their outlook through their involvement in particular revolutionary situations. Thus the Saint-Simonian disciples, usually advocates of gradualism, became very conscious of the revolutionary fervour of the workers in the 1831 Lyons uprising, and this prompted them to modify their theories accordingly.[15]

There were other reasons, too, why many utopian socialists opposed violent methods of change. There was a strong emphasis in their theories on the social question as opposed to the strictly political, and so political revolution could be dismissed as being somewhat irrelevant. In addition socialism was often viewed as an experimental tradition, an approach which encouraged groups to gradually build a socialist community, usually on a small scale; and this meant that comprehensive revolution, involving the overthrow of an entire society, was quite inappropriate.

(v) Statism versus communitarianism This leads on to another controversial issue. Whereas some thinkers, (for example, Saint-Simon and his disciples, Cabet, Weitling) envisaged their utopias in terms of complete societies under quite a high

degree of centralised control, others (notably Owen and Fourier) emphasised the need for small-scale decentralised, communitarian schemes. Thus there is a striking contrast between, say, Saint-Simon's vision of future industrial society and the Saint-Simonians' conception of 'universal association', on the one hand, and Owen's plan for numerous 'home colonies' or Fourier's Phalanxes on the other. (Fourier was most specific: every Phalanx should have between 1500 and 1800 people.) With Cabet and Weitling it has to be admitted that a contradiction arises, for although they advocated the transformation of whole societies, circumstances eventually persuaded them to put their ideas into operation at the communitarian level in the United States.

This disagreement has remained at the heart of disputes about the proper organisation of socialist society right up to the present day. But it is doubtful whether it has been a source of more tension than during the early nineteenth century. At that time there was a direct and uncompromising opposition between those who urged total societal change and those who wished to achieve change through more modest schemes of experimentation. The latter view linked up most directly with those principles of association, community, and co-operation discussed earlier, for it was at the local level or in a specific group of workers that those principles could be most meaningfully expressed. Also, it was widely seen to be more realistic to strive for social improvement through small communities than through large-scale organisation. In America, of course, it was fairly easy to adopt this approach, since there was every opportunity to start new communities. In Britain and the countries of continental Europe, however, it was less easy. Owen probably had most success with his scheme for 'home colonies' in Britain; but even he considered the prospects to be better in America, in company with many other utopians who shared the view that socialist society could most easily be created on virgin soil.

(vi) Democratic versus authoritarian organisation Linked to this latter issue is the problem of whether the utopian socialists subscribed to basically democratic or authoritarian values. Many commentators have pointed out that the vast

majority of utopian schemes throughout history have tended to be authoritarian, chiefly because of the characteristic utopian emphasis on harmony, consensus, the avoidance of conflict, and the rejection of individualism.[16] As far as the thinkers dealt with here are concerned, it is undoubtedly true that with the exception of Owen the idea of democracy seldom entered into their detailed blueprints for future organisation. On the other hand, there was a general awareness of the importance of certain freedoms, not only those of a legal-constitutional nature but perhaps even more significantly economic and social freedoms, which would nowadays be regarded as central to democracy. The Saint-Simonians, interestingly enough, with their constant emphasis on the need to preserve hierarchy in social and political organisation, were frequently condemned by rival utopian groups for what were considered to be fundamentally illiberal attitudes.[17] In this respect, at least, one might say that there was some concern for democratic values.

Generally speaking, the democratic/authoritarian distinction reflected the communitarian/statist distinction, for it was the thinkers who were interested in small-scale experimentation, such as Owen and Fourier, who seemed to care most for democracy in the sense of individual and group self-determination. But perhaps even more significant is the fact that where there was some concern for democratic participation, this seemed to grow out of the actual experience of democratic methods in workers' associations, clubs, friendly societies, etc. Thus Saint-Simon and his disciples, who had no such experience, placed little emphasis on democracy. Owen, Fourier, and also Weitling, however, whose doctrines were closely linked to the activities of co-operative organisations, had much more of a positive contribution to make.

Factors which conspired against democracy in utopian schemes were numerous and varied. The workers involved in these movements had little or no experience of political democracy at the national level. Their membership of a utopian movement probably represented their first mobilisation in any real action group, and this meant that strong leadership rather than extensive democratisation was likely to be emphasised. Furthermore, democracy was often equated with insurrection and militancy, characteristics which workers frequently wished to avoid. Jones and Anservitz have also shown the importance of charismatic authority in movements during this period, and it is certainly true, as they point out, that at times of social instability large groups of people often exhibit a remarkable willingness to support movements dominated by an individual leader or leaders who display charismatic qualities.[18] In the case of the utopian socialists, this aspect is very important precisely because so many of their doctrines assumed the form of religious instruction. Finally, one might add the sociological observation that any attempt to create a new scheme of social organisation is likely to be more successful if it is carried through under strong leadership. There is abundant evidence to show that the most successful utopian communities in the nineteenth century were also the most authoritarian.[19]

The Roots of Utopian Commitment

A conventional method of analysing the ideas of the utopian socialists would involve looking at those ideas in purely logical terms. Thus, the key questions might be: Were the utopian socialists right? Did they argue sensibly and coherently? Were their conclusions related to valid assumptions and verifiable observations? Such an approach would be in keeping with the way in which the study of social and political ideas has tended to develop in the western world. Major social movements are reduced to systems of ideas to be analysed in terms of their conceptual validity. While this approach is clearly of some use, and is indeed indispensable for certain purposes, it does overlook the fact that ideas often gain acceptance not because they are particularly logical or reasonable, but because they give expression to the deep-rooted aspirations of specific groups in society. There can be little doubt that the essential constitutive values of utopian socialism emerged primarily as the response of certain identifiable groups to the impact of socio-economic upheaval. One is led, therefore, to consider the ways in which utopian values actually mobilised leadership and support during the period in question, thus creating a sense of utopian commitment.[20]

It must be stressed that the whole issue of utopian socialism's significance as an agent of mobilisation is very much a matter of scholarly dispute. Rudolf Heberle, for example, asserts that the utopians 'did not create a real mass movement'.[21] Yet the most recent research suggests that at least one movement, Icarianism, *was* a mass movement; and the Saint-Simonian and Owenite sects, at the height of their appeal, also had large numbers of adherents. Yet even if one decides not to become involved in this rather vague debate on what exactly constitutes a mass movement, one cannot deny that some utopian socialist movements were more successful in mobilising leadership and support than others, and Icarianism stands out as undoubtedly the most successful of all such movements.

Furthermore, not all utopian socialist movements appealed to the same groups in society, and none of them appealed to the newly emergent factory workers, a group still at a relatively undeveloped stage in its growth, especially in the countries of continental Europe and in America. In the first half of the nineteenth century the working class still consisted mainly of artisans and handicraft workers, and this meant that utopian socialism could only draw its numerical strength from this sector. The point has already been made that many of the key values of utopian socialism were derived from artisan experience, and this reinforces the view that the utopian socialists were in an extremely ambiguous position, combining both a consciousness of the old society (pre-capitalist or pre-industrial) and an anticipation of the new, however they might choose to define it.

What has to be stressed is that during this period large numbers of workers were willing to lend their support to movements offering security and salvation in a basically insecure world. Why certain movements attracted more support than others is a fascinating question, especially in relation to France, which was a battle-ground for numerous alternative utopian schemes. It may be useful, therefore, to proceed with some more detailed comments on the French situation. Icarianism deserves to be dealt with first, not only because it was the most successful utopian socialist movement, but also because we know more about Icarianism than about any other movement thanks to the outstanding work of Christopher Johnson.[22]

(i) Icarianism The success of Icarianism is in some ways surprising, for the movement was rooted in the ideas of Cabet, who was one of the least interesting and least original of the utopian socialists. In its most successful phase Icarianism attracted a very large following, somewhere between 100,000 and 200,000.[23] As Johnson shows, it was the most conspicuously working-class of all utopian socialist movements, although 'working-class' here means artisan rather than proletarian. It must be admitted that the term 'artisan' is itself somewhat vague, since it covers a variety of occupations, from master craftsmen to journeymen, apprentices, and ordinary labourers. Johnson accordingly encounters some difficulty in giving a more precise picture of the basis of support for Icarianism. The statistical evidence he presents suggests that most Icarians were of fairly low status; there were more journeymen, apprentices, and labourers than master craftsmen. In other words, the kind of independent artisan who might justifiably be described as 'petty-bourgeois' tended to excluded.[24] Furthermore, Johnson is able to show that Icarianism was particularly popular among such specific groups as tailors, shoemakers, and cabinetmakers.

A number of factors seem to have contributed to Icarianism's success. It was the most deliberately political of the utopian socialist movements, placing a great emphasis on active involvement in political affairs. It was very well organised, had a strongly charismatic leader in Cabet, utilised propaganda brilliantly, and assumed the persuasive form of a Christian sect. The combination of these factors enabled it to appeal most effectively to those artisans who were working in depressed industries and who were most severely threatened by mechanisation and the introduction of capitalist forms of production. This appeal was strongest at times of economic crisis, when the declining position of the lower-placed artisans became most evident. Not surprisingly, support for Icarianism was concentrated in the largest cities (there was hardly any rural following at all). As Johnson points out, it is in the cities during the July Monarchy that 'one can discern the first steps in the "proletarianisation" of the diverse groups of artisans'.[25]

The success of Icarianism confirms a view put forward by Heberle, who states that 'it is generally recognised . . . that the chances of an idea's becoming part of the creed of a mass movement depend not so much upon its intrinsic value as upon its appeal to the interests, sentiments, and resentments of certain social strata and other groups'.[26] In the case of Icarianism, as has already been pointed out, the movement's underlying ideas were hardly original and usually lacked coherence. Yet the movement had a staggering success. It did not survive increasing governmental persecution in the late 1840s, and there were also failures of leadership, most notably Cabet's decision not to continue the struggle in France but to emigrate with a band of followers to America. It may also be argued that Cabet failed to understand the revolutionary potential of certain elements of the working class, and in this sense his emphasis on respectable, pacific communism certainly appeared out of place by 1848. Yet in spite of these failings, Icarianism played a vitally important role in mobilising large groups of workers into an organised movement.

(ii) Saint-Simonism In considering Saint-Simonism we face the problem that we still know very little about the movement's social composition and the sources of its support. However, certain essential facts are established: Saint-Simonism flourished for only a short time as a coherently organised school, from the death of Saint-Simon in 1825 to 1833, when it was declared illegal. Under the Restoration Monarchy (to 1830) it could hardly be expected to enjoy any real success, but its appeal grew after the July Revolution of 1830, when it became associated with the republican cause. It managed to gain some 40,000 or so adherents,[27] and even after it was banned in 1833, it continued to have an influence, certainly up to 1848.

Like Icarianism, the Saint-Simonian movement enjoyed considerable organisational advantages. It was authoritatively and charismatically led, had numerous colleges, churches and missions throughout France and also abroad, and used propaganda with great effectiveness. It was, however, always a movement *for* the working class rather than one *of* the working class, and was thus quite different from Icarianism. There were a number of reasons for this. It was very intellectual in orientation, basing its theories on extremely sophisticated and rarified arguments which must have been difficult for some people to grasp, even though the Saint-Simonian leaders attempted to simplify the message for the uneducated and the less intelligent. The essential doctrine may have been known, as one commentator points out, 'to every educated person in Europe',[28] but then not every person was educated. Much of the doctrine's terminology was quite novel and therefore difficult to understand, and quite often Saint-Simonian ideas appeared extremely eccentric (Saint-Simon himself having been widely dismissed in his lifetime as a bizarre, even mad, thinker!).

Following Saint-Simon's conception of 'the industrial class', the movement attempted to unite all productive workers in society, including labourers, artisans, the 'captains of industry', farmers, artists, and so on. Such an outlook could not be expected to appeal to the working class in the same way that Icarianism was able to do in the 1840s. In fact Saint-Simonism tended to appeal first and foremost to the middle classes, who were most clearly able to identify with the movement's 'bourgeois' notion of progress through industrial development and programmes of government-sponsored public works. A strong technocratic tendency drew many adherents from the ranks of businessmen and engineers, especially those from the Ecole Polytechnique. Industrialists who gained from the economic expansion of the 1830s admired the movement greatly, although the school's growing collectivist sympathies eventually led to a loss of support from this group. To a certain extent, also, the appeal of the movement had a generational basis. Young middle-class radicals were impressed by Saint-Simonism as a way of achieving an alternative society to the strongly conservative France of the 1820s. History furnishes us with many examples of radical movements appealing particularly to alienated youth, and Saint-Simonism was very important in this respect during the late 1820s and early 1830s.[29]

Gradually, after 1830, the Saint-Simonians did attempt to appeal more directly to the working class. Their involvement in working-class communities, and their participation in such upheavals as the Lyons uprising of 1831 encouraged the leaders of the movement to appreciate specifically working-class aspirations and to develop more of a revolutionary awareness. However, such a move came too late, for the movement was now being split through arguments over religious and moral questions. Its rejection of Christianity, its creation of a new religion of humanity, its proposals for a new moral code (including suggestions for a more liberal attitude towards sexual relations and the institution of marriage) – all these were out of touch with mass opinion. Furthermore, there can be no doubt that Saint-Simonism was pointing in the direction of a considerable degree of authoritarianism. As was mentioned earlier, there was a strong body of working-class opinion which believed that Saint-Simonism threatened to put an end to human liberty.

(iii) Fourierism Like Saint-Simonism, the Fourierist movement is difficult to analyse because of the general lack of information concerning its social composition. We can be certain, however, that the movement was never as successful as Icarianism or Saint-Simonism, and this is not too difficult to explain. For one thing, it was the least political of the utopian socialist movements in France during the 1830s and 1840s. It also emphasised small-scale experimentation through a system of 'Phalanxes', and was persistently anti-industrial in its approach to social change, emphasising a hatred of factories and commerce, and a defence of the traditional arts and crafts, agriculture, and horticulture. Such an outlook managed to appeal to certain middle-class elements, to many intellectuals, and also to workers in agriculture (this last element was conspicuously absent in the case of Icarianism and Saint-Simonism), but not to any large sector of the working class. In organisational terms Fourierism had some success in the workers' co-operative movement in France, but generally speaking it was marked by 'petty-bourgeois' characteristics, for it was the more independent, property-owning tradesman or craftsman who was most likely to be attracted to Fourierist doctrine.[30]

The Fourierist movement also suffered from being badly led and organised. Fourier himself was content to sit and wait for benevolent capitalists to come and offer financial help so that his schemes could be put into operation. He was not a great charismatic leader, and his ideas were frequently bizarre, badly presented, indeed often incomprehensible. Propaganda was almost non-existent in the early stages. Only later, with the involvement of new leaders such as Considérant in France and Brisbane and Greely in America, did Fourierism become more of an organisational force. This was particularly the case in America, where a national association was set up to promote the creation of Phalanxes. With improved organisation came a growing emphasis on the messianic qualities of Fourierism. 'First came Jesus Christ, then Fourier' was one slogan.[31] Thus, we have yet another instance of what would seem to be an inevitable tendency for French utopian socialism to merge into religion. In the case of Fourierism, though, the religious element was so artificial that it could not possibly hope to gain as much success as either Cabet's 'true Christianity' or the Saint-Simonians' new religion of humanity.[32] Splits in the Fourierist leadership also contributed to the movement's failure, especially in France. Only in America did it maintain any momentum, possibly because its emphasis on small-scale communitarianism was so acceptable among the pioneers and immigrants who wished to establish a new way of life for themselves.

Ideologically, the virtues of Fourierism derived from two vital ingredients. First, it was not communist, and it thus offered an alternative for those groups who recognised the worth of private property and who believed that communism was bound to be violent and insurrectionary. Secondly, it was always libertarian and anti-authoritarian in outlook, and this served to counteract the undeniable authoritarianism of some movements, most notably of Saint-Simonism. Fourierism was indeed so liberal and moderate that the French Government always tolerated it, and the social basis of support for the movement was also of such modest proportions that the Government never anticipated any Fourierist upheaval.

(iv) Owenism We may now shift our attention from France to Britain, where Owenism was the most important utopian socialist movement in the 1830s and 1840s. Of all early socialist movements Owenism was the one which tried hardest to come to terms with the realities of mechanisation and factory production. Britain, of course, was more industrialised at this stage than France, Germany, or America, and therefore utopian socialism had to respond to a more advanced stage of industrial development. Also, Robert Owen himself formulated his ideas through his experience in the factory situation, and he had a much better understanding of mechanisation

and the relationship between men and machines than most other thinkers.

Nevertheless, for many years Owen's ideas had little or no appeal to ordinary working men. Until the late 1820s his views were associated with paternalism and benevolent managerialism, and his absence in America for most of the period 1824-9 did not help matters. Only after his return to England did Owenism gain significant levels of working-class support, reaching a peak in 1834 after which date the movement declined as Owen broke with trade unionism, and as Chartism offered workers a more radical alternative.[33] Unfortunately, the extent of working-class support during the years 1829-34 is difficult to measure precisely. Thus, while some commentators have seen Owenism as a real mass movement,[34] others have rejected that view.[35] At some Owenite demonstrations there were probably as many as 100,000 participants;[36] yet the number of persons who actively took part in Owenite organisations, clubs, societies, and trade unions was undeniably much smaller.

What is striking about the success of Owenism in the early 1830s, however one tries to measure it statistically, is that the movement appealed to a very broad group of people from the point of view of its social characteristics: middle-class philanthropists, utilitarians, enlightened capitalists, as well as the working class (although as with Icarianism, 'working class' here means primarily artisans and the more highly skilled labourers rather than proletarians). In part, this very broad appeal was due to the essential vagueness of Owenite schemes and also their flexibility. At the same time one must recognise that Owenism was able to direct its energies towards fairly specific institutional forms: co-operatives, trade unions, labour exchanges, 'home colonies', and so on. This gave Owenism a very valuable organisational structure within which to operate, although it also followed that any weakening of the structure (e.g. through the failure of trade unionism) inevitably weakened the movement. It is also important to note that these organisational forms were derived directly from working-class experience. Indeed, Owen frequently came to issue proposals for certain forms of association precisely because he knew that the working class had already demonstrated a willingness to support them. As Thompson has pointed out:

> The germ of most of Owen's ideas can be seen in practices which anticipate or occur independently of his writings. Not only did the benefit societies on occasion extend their activities to the building of social clubs or alms-houses; there are also a number of instances of pre-Owenite trade unions when on strike, employing their own members and marking the product. . . . The covered market, or bazaar, with its hundreds of little stalls, was as old institution: but at the close of the Wars new bazaars were opened, which attracted attention in philanthropic and Owenite circles, where a section of counter was let (by the foot) for the week, the day, or even part of the day. . . . By 1827 a new bazaar was in being, which acted as a centre for the exchange of products made by unemployed members of London trades. . . .
>
> Thus the Equitable Labour Exchanges, founded at London and Birmingham in 1832-3, with their labour notes and exchange of small products, were not conjured out of the air by paranoiac prophets.[37]

Although Owenism was thus based on a body of working-class experience, one might argue that this experience was of more relevance to the older craft occupations than to modern, large-scale industry. The repeal of the combination laws in 1824 assisted Owenism because it permitted precisely the kinds of association which could help to enlist support for the movement; but even so Owenism did not develop any significant proletarian basis. One other important reason for this was that Owenism encouraged a politically moderate approach to social improvement. It followed that politically radical groups could find little of substance in Owenism, and after 1836 another vehicle for workers' demands – Chartism – was thus able to benefit from this weakness and managed to attract widespread support. Owen did not in fact lend any public support to the Charter until the very last year of his life (1858), and this actually made his approach much less convincing. There was the consequent irony that

> while Chartism increasingly drew its support from the casualties of the industrial changes of the period, trade unionism developed either among craftsmen who were little affected by such changes, as for instance those in the service trades of London, or among workers who had actually benefited from change, as in the case of the new engineering tradesmen, the boilermakers, and so on.[38]

One other element in Owenism which deserves mention is the strongly secular basis it retained until the early 1830s. This contrasts greatly with the enthusiasm among French utopian socialists for new versions of Christianity or religions of humanity. Owen's emphasis on rationality up to (and including) the years of success during 1829-34 led him to advocate a thoroughly secular perspective on social affairs. In later life he did become more interested in various forms of mysticism and the possibility of a rational religion, but the fact remains that as an organised movement Owenism derived much of its strength from its original opposition to religion. As Hobsbawm has written, 'the mechanics of the 1820s followed Robert Owen not only for his analysis of capitalism, but for his unbelief, and, long after the collapse of Owenism, their *Halls of Science* spread rationalist propaganda through the cities'.[39]

(v) German utopian socialism Turning now to German utopian socialism, we encounter a new factor: the most important movements were invariably established among émigré workers, particularly in Paris and London, also for a time in Switzerland. While Weitling was undoubtedly the major theoretician, other leaders – for example, Schapper – contributed much in matters of organisation. These German émigré groups were dominated by artisans, and perhaps more than any of the other movements dealt with here their ideas reflected artisan experience of association in particular trades and crafts. Guilds persisted in Germany, and they influenced the German artisans in their approach to socialism. Most importantly, the gap between masters and journeymen in the guilds was seen to be widening, and this encouraged journeymen such as Weitling to urge the creation of new workers' clubs as an alternative to the guilds. During the 1840s the new clubs did

much to stimulate a working-class (i.e. artisan) consciousness which finally came to fruition in the upheavals of 1848-9.[40]

German artisan socialism had a major impact on the development of the League of the Just (known after 1847 as the Communist League), in which a running battle was mounted in the late 1840s between the artisan view of socialism and the Marxist approach. There were many dimensions to this argument. The artisans, for instance, tended to reject large-scale mechanisation, and they believed future society could restore workshop forms of production. Marx rejected this view and urged the necessity of accepting wholesale industrialisation even if it meant the proletarianisation of craft workers. Religion was also a controversial issue. For some artisan leaders, such as Weitling, socialist, and in his case communist, society had to be based on Christian principles. Such a view derived not only from theoretical arguments; it was also based on the experience of artisans in Germany, their existing knowledge of doctrines of millenarianism, and their emphasis on the one book with which they were usually familiar: the Bible. Yet some leaders, including Schapper, rejected this notion of a Christian socialism, and this rejection was also endorsed by Marx.

Another dispute centred on the question of revolution. Many German artisans in France were linked with the insurrectionary movement organised by Blanqui, and their whole approach to change was inspired by revolutionary fervour. This was the attitude of Weitling, but Schapper and others adopted a more moderate approach, believing in the virtues of pacifism in a similar way to Cabet. On this point Marx agreed with Weitling, qualifying it however by insisting that revolution could not be accomplished in the immediate future by artisans but must await the further development of capitalism and the growth of a factory proletariat. Such a warning was directed in particular at the situation in Germany, where, as Marx and Engels frequently pointed out, the attack on feudalism was just beginning, and hence socialist revolution lay far in the future. Not surprisingly, German utopian socialism was mocked as a form of 'petty-bourgeois' nostalgia by Marx and Engels, even though they acknowledged the contribution of such writers as Weitling to the socialist cause.[41]

Possibilities for the development of an effective socialist

movement in Germany itself were continually weakened by emigration. In addition to the groups of workers, often journeymen, who made their way to such cities as Paris and London, thousands emigrated to Russia and America. The movement to America was especially noteworthy after the 1830s and early 1840s. Between 1846 and 1855 more than one million Germans emigrated to America, many of them small farmers who had been ruined by economic change in their native country.[42] This provided a strong basis for utopian socialism in America, but did nothing at all for the progress of workers' movements in Germany.

(vi) Utopian socialism in America The impact of utopian socialism in America is a huge topic, but because of the interest shown in America by many of the thinkers dealt with here a few general comments should be made. To begin with, one should perhaps draw attention to the irony of a situation in which theories formulated in western Europe, against a background of fairly specific social and economic changes, were put into operation in a society which had not undergone the same process of change, and where generally speaking industrialism was not causing the same dislocation that workers were experiencing in France, Britain, and Germany. There were other distinctions too. Mechanisation was generally beneficial to labour in America owing to the shortage of workers in many areas, and hence the opposition to the power of machinery voiced by some socialists was less appropriate. (The absence of any kind of Luddism in America is interesting in this respect.)[43] Communitarianism was more acceptable in America, as the long tradition of community-building since colonial times, much of it remarkably successful, demonstrated, and the availability of land for this purpose greatly assisted utopian schemes. This same factor suggested to many of the utopians that the creation of a new society in America would not necessitate the destruction of the old regime (as it would in Europe), since there was in fact no old regime to destroy. The country was therefore considered to be particularly suitable for a peaceful, orderly approach to social change. It is also noteworthy that small-scale communities were economically viable in America, whereas they might not be in France, Britain, or Germany. To take just one example, George Rapp's

'Harmony' community was widely regarded as an economic showplace.[44] The typical economic unit in America consisted of small, independent producers and property owners.

This combination of socio-economic factors, coupled with the political freedom and religious toleration which America seemed to offer, helps to explain the extraordinary proliferation of utopian experiments in the United States during the early nineteenth century, and it also enables us to understand why certain movements which were not successful in Europe made rapid progress on the other side of the Atlantic. The Fourierist movement, for example, did not meet with much success in France, but it did in America, where some forty Fourierist communities were established in the 1840s. In part, this was due to good organisation and leadership, but perhaps even more important is the fact that the Fourierist view of society coincided with peculiarly American assumptions: the emphasis on small-scale units of production, support for agrarianism, anti-authoritarianism, a defence of private property, and so on. In this respect Fourierism had more in common with the Jeffersonian view of democracy than even Fourier could ever have imagined.

Utopian Socialism's Legacy: The Critical and Constructive Dimensions

The ideas of the utopian socialists may be studied from two distinct points of view. First of all, these ideas constitute a body of essentially critical thinking about what is wrong with certain forms of social organisation. Because the utopian socialists were writing about western societies in the early nineteenth century, it is inevitably the case that some of their criticisms are less striking today than they were when they first appeared. For example, their comments on social evils such as acute poverty, disease, bad housing conditions, unemployment, and illiteracy were regarded in their own day as bold and original, whereas today such views are so well established, and the literature dealing with these problems is so enormous, that the writings of the early socialists now appear to be somewhat immature and lacking in rigour. (At the same time, of course, it must be recognised that the original impetus provided by the utopians in the discussions of these issues was extremely important in stimulating later, more systematic, investigation.) There are other aspects of their critical thought, however, which have lost little of their relevance and which seem to be just as provocative and exciting as when they were put forward in the early 1800s. In particular, there is much discussion in their writings of the problems of dehumanisation, powerlessness, and loss of community, problems which have persisted in western societies as they have gone through successive stages of economic and social development, and of which the utopian socialists were in many respects more aware than most later thinkers. In these areas of analysis their social criticism still deserves to be carefully examined, and one can learn a great deal from reading, say, the ideas of Saint-Simon and his followers on man's sense of spiritual loss in modern society, or Fourier's views on the way in which certain fundamental human 'passions' are stifled.

Throughout history this critical dimension has been central to utopianism and utopian thought. After all, the most incisive method of criticising an existing society is to link one's criticisms to a view of a radically different society, and to contrast the imperfection of the present with the potential of a future improvement or even perfectibility. The utopian thinker might indeed be regarded as the social critic *par excellence.* The point has already been made in this introduction, however, that the early socialists did not see themselves as purely critical thinkers, but were very much concerned with the practical problem of how a better order could be constructed; and in the case of all the thinkers studied in this book, the constructive dimension assumed increasing importance as their literary output grew and their theories developed. Furthermore, the conviction, shared by all the utopian socialists, that their views on social improvement grew out of scientific analysis and a discovery of the laws underlying social evolution meant that for them utopia was always much more than a standard by which to reveal the inadequacies of the present: it was a goal towards which men should direct all their energies, a goal which would one day be achieved.

In many ways this attempt to construct a social future was foolhardy. The early socialists sought to create a science of society, but clearly failed to appreciate the difficulty of the enterprise. They were absolutely self-assured, and never doubted that they could discover social laws quite easily. Each thinker believed that he, and he alone, had reached the correct conclusions and had gained an insight into society which no other thinker in the history of civilisation had ever been granted. (It is one of the common characteristics of utopians that they lack intellectual modesty.) Today, for fairly obvious reasons, the scientific claims of these thinkers are difficult, if not impossible, to sustain in their entirety. This does not mean to say that their arguments lacked all scientific foundation. On the contrary, they often succeeded in perceiving very real tendencies at work in the development of western societies, as can be seen particularly in their judgment of the likely political impact of scientific and industrial modernisation. But what they did not do was to provide us with the kind of total, all-embracing social science, perfectly mature in its analytical methods, which they thought they had been able to formulate.

It is more reasonable, today, to regard the deliberately constructive element in early socialist thought as a combination of scientific observation and social ethics. That is to say, their visions of the future were in some respects based on the methods of a science of society (however primitive and underdeveloped), but, perhaps even more importantly, these visions represented applications of ethical principles to new problems, problems which had in some cases never been dealt with before. Some idea of the range of these problems has already been given in this introduction, and further elaboration is provided in the book's six major sections which follow. What must be emphasised once again is that there were many fundamental disagreements between the early socialists on the subject of how utopia could be constructed, and for many purposes, therefore, it is misleading to group these thinkers together, as is so often done.

It has often been argued that this second, constructive, dimension of early socialist thought was based on a complete lack of realism, and was thus utopian in the particular sense of impracticable. Such a view is indeed so widespread that it is likely to be accepted by modern students of early socialism almost without question. but the student would be well advised to approach this important issue by asking a number of key questions. First, what exactly is meant by realism in this context? Secondly, on the basis of this definition, can it be shown quite conclusively that the early socialists were not realists? And thirdly, even if the answer to the previous question is affirmative, does it necessarily follow that the ideas of an unrealistic thinker are without positive value?

The first question raises some very complicated problems, problems which are frequently overlooked. To say that the proposals of a particular thinker are unrealistic is to say that they are not practicable. The thinker is condemned as an idealist who is advocating the impossible, and hence, it is asserted, there is no point in taking the proposals seriously. But what, we must ask, are the criteria of practicability which are being used to support this case?[45] The critic who regards himself as a realist may be saying that his opponent's scheme is *technically* impossible – that is, society lacks the necessary technical means to implement and maintain the scheme; or alternatively he could be saying that the scheme is *politically* impossible – that is, the scheme cannot be put into operation because it lacks the support of those who occupy appropriate positions of power in society. There is also a third attitude: the critic might believe that even if the scheme is technically and politically possible, it will not lead to the condition of happiness which is being predicted. In this case the scheme is considered to be practicable in the sense that it can be put into practice, but is judged unrealistic as a method of promoting human satisfaction. The point must be stressed that each of the first two objections, if it is to make sense, requires further elaboration. A scheme may be dismissed as technically or politically impossible in all places and at all times – both in the present and in the future; or only in particular places and at particular times. It can be seen, therefore, that there is no one absolute concept of realism. Accordingly, to state that a thinker is lacking in realism begs a number of key questions which the critic must answer if the validity of his argument is to be judged.

Is there any sense, then, in which we can give a definite answer to the question of whether the early socialists were or were not realists? The various strategies put forward in their writings – strategies designed to achieve the ideals of harmony, association, community, and co-operation – contained many elements which, from a purely technical point of view, could be regarded as quite feasible. If one refers again to the list of six major strategic dilemmas facing these thinkers, one there finds twelve policy standpoints (two alternatives on each issue), and it is doubtful whether any of these was technically impossible. The anti-industrial stance of Fourier and, to a lesser extent, Weitling was perhaps the least feasible of the twelve standpoints, since in retrospect one can see that it was an attempt to put a halt to a process which had already developed an apparently irresistible momentum by the early nineteenth century. The student may wish to argue that other aims of the early socialists could not be achieved because of technical obstacles. It cannot be denied that many of the details of Fourier's sexual paradise are wildly extravagant, yet the central aims of free love and unhindered gratification of the senses were really much more serious and a lot less ludicrous than they might appear at first sight. The idea of creating a new social religion, and the intention to transform politics into a thoroughly scientific-rational activity (the replacement of government by administration) also strike many people as futile visions. In each case, however, the goal, although it obviously posed considerable difficulties, was not beyond the bounds of possibility. History furnishes us with many examples of the rise of new religions (such as Christianity itself) or their transformation (as in the Protestant Reformation). Could one really say, then, that in the nineteenth century man did not possess the capacity to inaugurate a new religion, possibly in the form of a revised Christianity? And as far as the desire to place political affairs on a scientific-rational basis is concerned, the main emphasis was on economic planning, the provision of social welfare, and the modification of the natural world through technology – techniques which can hardly be described as impossible, although most people would now hesitate to say that they amounted to administration rather than government. The strategy of peaceful change and class collaboration advocated by most of the early socialists has also been subject to much criticism, especially by Marxists, who have insisted that such a strategy could never be put into operation. In fact the early socialists were not quite so naive on this question as Marxists usually suggest. The strategy was put forward by them in order to avoid certain kinds of class conflict which they considered to be a very real threat. They did not close their eyes to the likelihood of revolution (as Marxists invariably claim), but did believe that revolution could be avoided through a general awareness among different social classes of their common interests. (The exception, of course, was Weitling, who repeatedly called for revolutionary change.) If it was to be effective, this awareness of common interests must be given expression in major structural changes in western societies – changes, for example, in the ownership and/or control of property, in the organisation of work, and in the remuneration of labour. This agenda was bold, adventurous, and posed numerous problems, but it was based on a perfectly feasible proposition: that a new type of society can be created without violent upheaval if there is sufficient commitment to its basic principles among the major constituent groups. (Furthermore, it is demonstrably true if one examines the actual history of western societies since the early nineteenth century, a history which certainly does not confirm the Marxist theory of increasing class antagonism and the growth of revolutionary fervour among the proletariat.)

A case can be made, therefore, for regarding many of the early socialists' schemes as realistic in a strictly technical sense. But what about the political practicability of those schemes? From this point of view one can state quite definitely that the early socialists were not realists, since they lacked a power base through which their policies could be put into operation, and, moreover, they greatly underestimated the difficulties involved in creating such a power base. They all attempted to influence the powerful political and economic leaders of their day, and in retrospect one can find many reasons to mock their efforts to convince kings, emperors, prime ministers, and businessmen of the virtues of their doctrines. Some of them achieved quite large popular followings, particularly Cabet, who in effect founded a spectacular mass movement, yet such successes were not consolidated, and no permanent centre of power was ever established. The nearest they came to practical results in their own day was in the equally short-lived communitarian experiments associated with Owen, Cabet, Weitling, and their followers, and also with the disciples of Fourier after their master's death.

Earlier in this section another perspective on the viability of the early socialists' schemes was suggested, concerned not so much with the practicability of those schemes in technical or political terms, but with the notion of a 'golden age' or state of almost unqualified happiness which was put forward as the chief characteristic of future socialist society. Such optimism or extreme idealism grew naturally out of the Enlightenment's many philosophies of progress and perfectibility, and found its ultimate expression in nineteenth-century romanticism, a tradition to which early socialism undoubtedly belongs. It is interesting to note, also, that there was a close link between this socialist conception of progress and the liberal notion of utilitarianism, with its emphasis on achieving 'the greatest happiness of the greatest number' (as in Bentham's formulation), seen as the pursuit of pleasure and the avoidance of pain. Both socialism and liberalism, therefore, could be viewed as too optimistic in their views of man's capacity for progress. Of course, it is easy to be wise in hindsight. The early socialists could be condemned for their idealism. Yet at the same time their idealism was an essential ingredient in their whole approach to the question of how man could improve his social existence; and without that idealism they would probably not have been stimulated to devote their lives to the solution of such a broad range of problems. Thus, although we may justifiably doubt whether mankind can ever achieve the level of happiness anticipated by the early socialists, their recommendations still deserve to be examined as possible ways of improving society. The degree of improvement may fall short of perfection, but it may still be a movement in the right direction.

This brings us to the last of the three issues raised earlier. Does it matter if we conclude that the early socialists were lacking in political realism? Does it follow that their ideas are without positive value? It could be argued that only ideas which stand some reasonable chance of being put into practice in the very near future are worthy of serious consideration. But this is a very narrow-minded view, and it would surely be more reasonable to accept that ideas also have a long-term value. It may indeed take many years or several decades – perhaps even longer – before certain ideas gain sufficient support and can be backed up by the power which is necessary to secure their practical application. Every politically successful doctrine originates as the doctrine of an individual or a small group, and at first it may appear that the doctrine is doomed to failure. But circumstances can change, and in the course of time that same doctrine may come to exercise a great influence, and may actually emerge as the dominant doctrine in one or more particular countries. Hence the early socialists' ideas should not be regarded as insignificant simply because they failed to win immediate approval among large, powerful groups. A more serious objection would be that from the beginning those ideas stood no chance at all of winning support. But the history of the late nineteenth and twentieth centuries shows us that nothing could be further from the truth. After 1848 numerous socialist movements arose throughout Europe and the rest of the world, some of them eventually becoming large political parties, and their policy goals and programmes embodied many of the aims of the early socialists. These movements and parties exerted direct influence on government, and in due course were able in several countries to form governments of their own. The result is that today a large proportion of the world's population lives under regimes deriving inspiration from doctrines of socialism of one kind or another, and this in effect means that the long-term practical influence of early socialist thought is now firmly established and remarkably widespread. It has to be admitted, of course, that no socialist regime describes itself as Saint-Simonian, Owenite, Fourierist, or Icarian. This is hardly surprising, since after 1848 the ideas of the early socialists were so widely disseminated, and later thinkers and leaders of movements drew upon those ideas in such a synthetic fashion, that the original doctrines became submerged in a vast new range of socialist theories, from democratic socialism to syndicalism, anarchism, and Marxism. (It is interesting to reflect on the fact that today many regimes choose to call themselves Marxist. We are accustomed to this designation, but a century ago the idea would certainly have been dismissed as absurd, even by Marx himself. Was the idea of a Saint-Simonian, Owenite, Fourierist, or Icarian regime any more absurd?)

Today movements, parties, and entire societies willingly refer to themselves as socialist or communist. Yet in the early nineteenth century the goals of socialism and communism were frequently considered to be unattainable utopias. Even more striking is the fact that many of the early socialists' specific policy recommendations – especially those concerning economic management, welfare provision, the redistribution of wealth, and the constitution of property – have now become ingredients of socialism in practice. At the same time some of their most passionate convictions have had less practical impact, including their various conceptions of a social religion, and the emphasis which some of them placed on communitarianism. However, even these theories have always had some support, and evidence suggests that today there is a steadily growing interest in the possibility of a more spiritually-based socialism, and in a socialism which is decentralised rather than state-centred.

The ideas of the early socialists are of great historical interest, but they are also part of the ongoing contemporary debate about how society should be organised. Some of these ideas have been rejected, possibly for ever, while others have gained acceptance, sometimes in modified form. Undoubtedly there are others still which will be accepted and implemented at some stage in the future by men and women whose ancestors in the late twentieth century were quite convinced of their impracticality.

1
Henri Saint-Simon

Life and Work

Claude-Henri de Saint-Simon was born at Berny in Picardy on 17 October 1760.[1] He belonged to a distinguished aristocratic family which claimed to be directly descended from Charlemagne. His father, Balthazar-Henri, was the cousin of Louis, duc de Saint-Simon, author of the well-known memoirs of the court of Louis XIV and the Regency. The family owned a winter residence in Paris, and Claude-Henri was introduced at an early age into Parisian social circles. This enabled him to meet some eminent intellectual figures, including Jean d'Alembert, who stimulated his interest in philosophy and the sciences.

Initially Saint-Simon seemed destined for a military career. He joined the army in 1778, and during 1780-81 served with the forces sent to assist the Americans in their struggle for independence. His experiences in America exerted a profound influence on his intellectual development, as he himself explained:

> . . . I occupied myself much more with political science than with military tactics. The war in itself did not interest me, but its aim interested me greatly, and that interest led me willingly to support its cause. . . .
>
> When I saw peace approaching I was completely overcome with disgust for the military profession. I perceived clearly what career I had to take up, the career towards which my tastes and natural inclinations called me. It was not my vocation to be a soldier; I was destined for a quite different, and I might say quite contrary kind of activity. To study the advance of the human mind in

> order subsequently to work for the improvement of civilisation: that was the aim I set myself.[2]

Already Saint-Simon had a clear idea of what 'the improvement of civilisation' involved, having observed in America what he considered to be its most important manifestations: religious toleration, the absence of social and political privilege, and the acceptance of a social philosophy based on pacifism, industry, and thrift. In sum the regime in America was 'infinitely more liberal and more democratic than the one under which the peoples of Europe lived'.[3]

Returning from America with the French fleet in 1782, Saint-Simon was taken prisoner in an engagement with the English navy. A peace settlement was soon concluded, however, and in September 1783 he was released. He now visited Mexico and presented the Viceroy with a proposal to construct a canal across the Isthmus of Panama, linking the Pacific and Atlantic Oceans. But the plan was rejected, and Saint-Simon returned to France.

Over the next two or three years he found himself virtually unemployed. An exciting opportunity arose in 1787, however. The Spanish Government wanted to build a canal linking Madrid with the Atlantic Ocean, but was unable to go ahead because of lack of money and workers. Saint-Simon offered his services and travelled to Madrid. In collaboration with the project's chief architect, Francisco de Cabarrús, he drew up a plan for obtaining the necessary finance and organising the work-force. Unfortunately, implementation was prevented by the outbreak of the French Revolution, which drew Saint-Simon back to France at the end of 1789.

He soon found himself involved in political affairs in Falvy, near Péronne, where in February 1790 he became President of the municipal assembly. But other tasks offered greater attractions. He wanted 'to organise a great industrial establishment, to found a scientific school of improvement'.[4] In order to acquire funds for this enterprise he decided to invest in the *biens nationaux* (national property) being sold by the Government. In partnership with the comte de Redern, a Prussian diplomat, he acquired a bank loan and launched an investment programme. But Robespierre's 'Reign of Terror' soon threatened to halt his activities. Saint-Simon feared for his own life, and actually took the precaution, in September 1793, of renouncing his title, which he knew would be regarded with suspicion. He had acted too late, however, for in November he was arrested for counter-revolutionary offences. Luckily, the fall of Robespierre on 27 July 1794 ended the Terror and led to his release.

He now renewed his financial activities, and had soon purchased over four million francs' worth of property, the income from which was put to immediate use. He rented a residence in one of the most fashionable quarters of Paris, and hired a train of attendants. An elegant *salon* was established to which the *savants* of Paris were invited. It was a great success but also a great expense, and Saint-Simon's partner, Redern, knew that such luxury could not be maintained. So he declared his intention to dissolve the partnership, the terms to be settled by arbitration. Saint-Simon now had to leave the Hôtel Chabanais, and in 1798 moved to a house near the Ecole Polytechnique, where he intended to study physics and mathematics. The arbitrator's decision was announced in August 1799. Saint-Simon was to be bought out for 150,000 francs. This was less than Redern's share – an *annual* income of 100,000 francs – but the arbitrator recognised that Saint-Simon had been extravagant, and adjusted his award accordingly.

Napoleon Bonaparte's assumption of power on 9 November 1799 resulted in a reorganisation of the Ecole Polytechnique; but this did not affect Saint-Simon's plans, and he continued his studies until 1801. He then transferred to the Ecole de Médecine to follow courses in physiology. In August 1801 he married Sophie de Champgrand, a young writer and musician. Apparently this venture was not motivated by romance but by more mundane considerations: he thought Sophie would be the perfect hostess to help him entertain the scientists of Paris. Not surprisingly the marriage was totally unsuccessful and was dissolved by mutual consent in June 1802.

Saint-Simon now decided to travel abroad. He first visited England, then went to Geneva, where he took the opportunity to publish a booklet in which he set down for the first time his ideas on social reorganisation: *Letters from an Inhabitant of Geneva (Lettres d'un habitant de Genève),* a second edition of which appeared in Paris in 1803. The *Letters* argued that civilisation was threatened by revolution and anarchy, and that the crisis could be overcome only by fundamental social reforms based on the recognition that science and industry (in the sense of all productive activity) were the two great instruments of progress. The first priority was to endow the *savants,* the scientists and artists, with the spiritual power previously exercised by the Catholic clergy. The latter's authority had declined since the Middle Ages because of 'the progress of the human mind', and so could no longer unite men in society. Hence, a totally new religion, in harmony with the level of human enlightenment, was needed. Saint-Simon proposed the creation of a 'Religion of Newton' (so called in recognition of Isaac Newton's role as a founder of modern science), to be organised on both national and international levels with the world's most eminent scientists and artists at its head, exercising their authority independently of temporal power, which would remain in the hands of the property owners.[5]

From Geneva Saint-Simon travelled to Germany and then back to Paris, where he set out to develop further his ideas on social reform. He was convinced that the nineteenth century would witness the development of a science of social organisation, and was himself anxious to contribute something of importance. But he had little money, no job, and his health was deteriorating. Fortunately, in 1806 he received an offer of financial assistance from a friend and former servant – a man called Diard – and this enabled him to continue his studies.

During 1807-8 Saint-Simon had a major work printed: *Introduction to the Scientific Studies of the 19th Century (Introduction aux travaux scientifiques du XIXe siècle),* which presented the view that the task of nineteenth-century science was to construct a new theoretical system incorporating all existing knowledge. The goal must be an all-embracing philosophical synthesis such as Bacon and Descartes had achieved in the seventeenth century, a synthesis which would deal the final death-blow to metaphysics and theology. He also became involved at this time in a renegotiation of his settlement with Redern, inundating the comte with letters proposing reconciliation. In order to rid himself of this nuisance, during 1807-8 Redern agreed to pay an allowance to Saint-Simon, but this arrangement ended in 1811, when Redern became anxious about his own financial situation. This was a crushing blow for Saint-Simon, but he managed somehow to make ends meet while he pursued his investigations. By the end of 1813 he had written two more texts, circulated privately in manuscript form: the *Memoir on the Science of Man (Mémoire sur la science de l'homme)* and *Study on Universal Gravitation (Travail sur la gravitation universelle).* In these works it was argued that the foundations of a science of man and society had been laid by French physiologists and philosophers, and the next step was to unite their theories in one general synthesis – a task requiring the collaboration of Europe's most eminent scientists.

This appeal achieved at least one positive result for Saint-Simon: an offer of secretarial assistance from Augustin Thierry, a brilliant young historian who, following Napoleon's abdication and the inauguration of the first Bourbon Restoration (April 1814), had lost his professorial post at Compiègne. His offer was accepted, and in October 1814 the partnership produced a booklet, *The Reorganisation of European Society (De la Réorganisation de la société européenne),* which outlined a plan for uniting the nations of Europe through parliamentary institutions. This work, which was prompted by the meeting of the Congress of Vienna, created much interest in liberal circles. Its success encouraged Saint-Simon to concentrate on political affairs, and he assumed the role of publicist for the liberal cause. In one article (in *Le Censeur,* volume III) he advocated the formation of an opposition party of owners of national property. He planned a full-length work on the subject, but his attention was diverted to other matters when Napoleon regained power in March 1815.

Napoleon's rule lasted for just one hundred days. Louis XVIII was then given a second opportunity to establish order and stability. It was a formidable task, since the French nation was divided on every major political issue, and in Saint-Simon's view this underlying instability would continue until a 'positive' political philosophy was formulated, a philosophy rooted in the liberal doctrines of such thinkers as Jean-Baptiste Say, Benjamin Constant, Charles Comte, and Charles Dunoyer. He was particularly impressed by their utilitarian economic theories and their advocacy of a more representative system of government favourable to the needs of industry. In 1816 his enthusiasm for liberalism found expression in a scheme for a journal devoted exclusively to 'industrial opinion'. An impressive list of subscribers was drawn up,[6] and the first issue of *Industry (L'Industrie)* appeared in December 1816.

In early 1817 Saint-Simon suffered a setback when Thierry decided to resign his post. He found Saint-Simon's ideas too obscure, and wanted to pursue his own historical studies. Fortunately, Saint-Simon was soon able to enlist the support of another brilliant scholar, Auguste Comte, whose first task was to help prepare volume III of *Industry,* published during September and October 1817. This volume advocated a new 'terrestrial morality' in harmony with positive science and conducive to industrialism. The anti-Catholic implications of this view angered many readers, and some subscribers withdrew their financial support, thereby making it impossible for the journal to continue after volume IV.

Not in the least disheartened, Saint-Simon went ahead with plans for another periodical: *Politics (Le Politique),* which made its appearance in January 1819, and which set out to formulate a political strategy for the 'industrial class'. Saint-Simon, Comte, and the other contributors undertook a scathing attack on the unproductive class of nobles, idle property owners, clergy, magistrates, and military chiefs, and they urged the producers to form an active 'industrial party'. But *Politics* failed to create any impression, and it survived only until May 1819.

Saint-Simon refused, however, to admit defeat, and during the summer he prepared yet another publication: *The Organiser (L'Organisateur).* The work was inaugurated in November with a booklet, *Extracts from the Organiser,* which caused an immediate sensation due to the fact that in an attack on the French State Saint-Simon actually named members of the royal family who, he felt, performed no useful service, and whose loss would be of no consequence. The text aroused the suspicions of the police, who arrested Saint-Simon in January. Soon afterwards the duc de Berry, one of the royal idlers included in Saint-Simon's list, was assassinated by a fanatic as part of a plot to annihilate the Bourbons. This made Saint-Simon's predicament extremely serious, and he was charged with subversion. At his trial he denied being hostile to the Bourbons, explaining that he merely sought to emphasise that the nation's producers would not remain satisfied for much longer with their inferior political status. The members of the jury were not impressed, and found Saint-Simon guilty. On appeal, however, the verdict was reversed.

Saint-Simon immediately resumed work on *The Organiser*, and it proved to be a very successful publication, due chiefly to its originality, which was widely recognised at the time. Most importantly, it provided the first detailed blueprint of the 'industrial society' Saint-Simon envisaged. As one reads through this work, Saint-Simon's dissatisfaction with liberalism becomes increasingly apparent. He was convinced that the liberals would never achieve political success. They were apathetic and had failed to recognise the inadequacies of the parliamentary system. Furthermore, the party contained a conservative element which hindered industrialism's progress. The industrials must dissociate themselves from this alien element and form their own party.

This viewpoint was reiterated in another set of brochures, published in late 1820 and brought together in the first part of *The Industrial System (Du Système industriel)* in February 1821. Their success led to the publication of two more sets during the next eighteen months (*The Industrial System*, parts II and III). All these writings were presented as letters and addresses to various individuals and groups – the King, the industrials,[7] the scientists and artists, the philanthropists, the workers, etc. – in an attempt to convince them of the desirability of establishing the new society. The addresses to the King emphasised that the necessary reforms should preferably be instituted by the monarch, acting as the nation's 'first industrial'. And Saint-Simon's doctrine was now defined as a new, definitive Christianity, a conception anticipating the *New Christianity* of 1825. Henceforth Saint-Simon was to stress the *moral* virtues of industrialism, seen primarily in terms of its capacity to improve the standard of living of the poor – virtues which were seen to correspond to Christian ethics.

The Industrial System aroused widespread interest in liberal circles, but in more practical terms the results disappointed Saint-Simon. He felt that his views were not taken seriously enough,[8] and he began to despair of ever achieving public recognition. Despair gradually turned into severe depression, culminating in attempted suicide on 9 March 1823. He loaded a pistol and fired the bullets at his head in quick succession. Miraculously, the result was not death, but merely a deep wound and the loss of his right eye.

His recovery from this ordeal was remarkably swift. Within a few months he was launching another periodical, *The Industrials' Catechism (Catéchisme des industriels),* assisted by a group of new supporters chief among whom was Olinde Rodrigues, a young Jewish intellectual. In the *Catechism,* published between December 1823 and June 1824, Saint-Simon made complete his break with liberalism, emphasising that industrialism was a quite distinctive doctrine. Comte also made an important contribution to the *Catechism,* in book three, which contained his *System of Positive Politics (Système de politique positive).* Saint-Simon praised this as the best general study of politics ever published, but he also made some criticisms which angered Comte and brought to a head a dispute between the two men which had been developing for some time. During 1824 the dispute became so intense that Comte finally decided to withdraw his support and pursue his own positivist studies.

Rodrigues now became Saint-Simon's chief assistant. By the end of 1824 he had helped to establish the nucleus of a more formal Saint-Simonian organisation, with Léon Halévy, Jean-Baptiste Duvergier, and Dr E.-M. Bailly as the most active supporters. The efforts of the group were united in early 1825, when the first volume of a review, *Literary, Philosophical, and Industrial Opinions (Opinions littéraires, philosophiques et industrielles),* appeared. Another volume was in preparation when, in April, it was decided to publish separately a major work on the religious question by Saint-Simon: *New Christianity (Nouveau Christianisme).* This book was a contribution to the debate on the relationship between Church and State which had been developing since the accession of Charles X to the throne in September 1824, and is notable because of its emphasis on religious sentiment as the most important instrument of social change. A united Christian Church, founded not on the principles of Catholicism or Protestantism but on the original teachings of Christ, is now seen as the necessary means of promoting a just society.

New Christianity was intended to be the first of three texts on the subject of religion. However, Saint-Simon's work was cut short when, soon after the book's publication, he fell ill with gastro-enteritis. For six weeks he was confined to bed in considerable pain. He died on 19 May 1825 and was buried three days later in the Père-Lachaise cemetery in Paris. The funeral was a purely civil occasion. In graveside orations Halévy and Bailly talked of Saint-Simon's achievements. But the orientation of their words was to the future; for the moment of Saint-Simon's death was recognised as the moment of birth of the Saint-Simonian movement. Although no clear strategy had been determined, the young disciples were resolved to fulfil the mission on which their master had embarked.

The Making of a Social Physiology

Saint-Simon always considered his primary aim as a social theorist to be the promotion of the study of man and society to the level of a truly positive science. He was convinced that the degree of certainty achieved in the natural sciences could also be attained in social science if systematic observation of social phenomena were undertaken; and he founded his entire philosophy on this conviction. Regarding himself as the heir of Bacon and Descartes, he attempted from the start to pursue his investigations according to the 'golden rule' of science: that 'man should believe only those things avowed by reason and confirmed by experience'.[9]

Furthermore, in accordance with contemporary scientific opinion in France, Saint-Simon believed that social phenomena had much in common with biological and physiological phenomena, and that the new science must therefore be treated as a branch of the life-sciences, as a 'social physiology'. According to this view human society was seen as an organic entity whose development, like that of any other organic body, was governed by certain natural laws which it was the purpose of scientific inquiry to reveal. From the notion of *organism* it was a short step to that of *organisation.*[10] A healthy society was seen in terms of a well-organised society, a society whose fundamental characteristics were order and stability.

The concept of social organisation came to occupy a central position in French social theory in the years immediately following the Revolution. Because the Revolution offered a clear demonstration of what social *dis*organisation involved, it inevitably encouraged social theorists to turn to the problem of how social reconstruction could be promoted, and how further revolutions and outbreaks of anarchy could be avoided. Saint-Simon was convinced that a positive science of man would reveal the laws of social organisation, that is, a body of rules explaining, on the one hand, the causes of social order, stability, and progress; and, on the other, the causes of revolution and social disintegration. He believed that once these causes had been ascertained with scientific precision, man would be able to promote the construction of the very best form of social organisation. In this sense the realisation of utopia could be regarded as a practical possibility:

> The imagination of poets has placed the golden age in the infancy of the human race, amidst the ignorance and coarseness of ancient times. It would have been much better to consign the iron age there. The golden age of the human race is not behind us; it lies before us, in the perfection of the social order. Our fathers did not see it; our children will arrive there one day; it is up to us to clear the way.[11]

'A series of observations on the course of civilisation'[12] was considered by Saint-Simon to be the necessary starting-point for the development of the new science of social progress. These observations must then be brought together in a general theory of history capable of explaining the fundamental causes of historical change, not only in the past and at the present time, but also in the future; for the causes of future events must already be in existence, and there was no reason why these should not be observed and analysed scientifically.

In stating that it should be possible to forecast the future course of history, Saint-Simon was clearly implying some sort of historical determinism. However, he was not a complete fatalist, for although he was convinced that general historical trends were inevitable, he believed that man could exert some influence over them. Most importantly, man could determine the pace of social change. Thus, if a particular result was shown by scientific investigation to be inevitable, and could also be considered a desirable result, then man could devote his energies to achieving it as quickly and as painlessly as possible.

This belief that a scientific theory could be formulated which would permit man to predict the shape of his historical future was one of Saint-Simon's most important contributions to social thought. It is certainly sufficiently original to justify the view of Saint-Simon as one of the founders of modern historicism.[13] In this respect his importance is matched only by that of his great contemporary, the German idealist philosopher Hegel, with whose works he does not appear to have been familiar. There were thinkers before Saint-Simon who had attempted to develop a scientific analysis of history, notably Montesquieu, Turgot, and Condorcet. But of these only Condorcet, whose influence Saint-Simon readily acknowledged, had suggested that the analysis could be extended to embrace the future.

Saint-Simon's first firm conclusions about what was needed to promote the development of a positive science of man were the result of his studies at the Ecole Polytechnique and the Ecole de Médecine (1798-1802). In his *Letters from an Inhabitant of Geneva* of 1802-3 he acknowledged that physiology was still at an early stage in its progress as a science,[14] but he was optimistic that further steps forward could be taken fairly quickly and without too much difficulty. Such a view was perfectly in keeping with the unbounded confidence in the capacity of science characteristic of the age in which he lived. The natural sciences in general and the life-sciences in particular were making rapid, impressive progress in France by the beginning of the nineteenth century, and Saint-Simon was confident that this progress would soon extend to physiology. Indeed, by 1813 he was convinced that the most basic physiological principles had already been furnished by French scientists. In order to organise the general theory of physiology, it was asserted in the *Memoir on the Science of Man,*[15] little more was needed than to bring together the works of four men: Félix Vicq-d'Azyr (1748-94), author of *Treatise on Anatomy and Physiology (Traité d'anatomie et de physiologie,* 1786); Pierre-Jean-Georges Cabanis (1757-1808), who paid special attention to the relationship between man's physical and moral constitution *(Rapports du physique et du moral de l'homme,* 1802); Marie-François-Xavier Bichat (1771-1802), founder of general anatomy *(Anatomie génerale,* 1801) and embryology; Marie-Jean-Antoine-Nicolas de Caritat, Marquis de Condorcet (1743-94), mathematician and philosopher, author of the *Sketch of an Historical Picture of the Progress of the Human Mind (Esquisse d'un tableau historique des progrès de l'esprit humain,* 1793, published in 1795), which outlined a theory of mankind's unlimited perfectibility. In Saint-Simon's view these four authors had dealt with nearly all important physiological questions, and had based all their reasoning on observation. The contributions of Vicq-d'Azyr and Condorcet he regarded as the most important; the ideas of Bichat and Cabanis were basically 'appendices' to those of Vicq-d'Azyr. There was no doubt in his mind that if only a reorganisation of scientific research could be brought about, the necessary synthesis of physiological knowledge could be achieved in a short period of time. As his two major texts on the science of man, the *Memoir* and the *Study on Universal Gravitation*, make clear, he recognised that he could not possibly fulfil the task alone. But he did consider himself capable of contributing something on the subject of 'the progress of the human mind', and he was willing to offer his services to any physiologist who might wish to employ them.

Saint-Simon's conviction that a theory of social organisation must take as its basis 'a series of observations on the course of civilisation' has already been mentioned. In accordance with this principle he became an enthusiastic student of history and devoted much of his written work to historical analysis. His attempt to study history scientifically has often been dismissed as crude,[16] and there can be little doubt that much of the criticism levelled against him is justified. Nevertheless, the quality of his work does at least represent a definite improvement on that of most earlier thinkers. It must be remembered that before Saint-Simon few serious attempts had been made to apply any kind of scientific method to the study of history. His own efforts do therefore deserve some credit. Moreover, his analysis does in fact contain a body of essential argument which is remarkably perceptive and merits serious attention.

As a student of history his chief purpose was to trace the general course of development of human society since ancient times. His perspective was not that of the specialist concerned with every minor detail, but of the philosopher interested in broad historical trends. Directly inspired by Condorcet's *Sketch of an Historical Picture of the Progress of the Human Mind,* he too aimed to produce an outline history of social evolution which would serve as a point of departure for an analysis of man's present historical situation.

The results of Saint-Simon's investigations are to be found scattered throughout his writings, but principally in his *Introduction to the Scientific Studies of the 19th Century,* the *Memoir on the Science of Man, Industry,* and *The Industrials' Catechism.* The eighth and ninth letters of *The Organiser* also deserve attention in this context, but these are now known to have been the work of Comte. From these texts a clearly defined philosophy of history emerges, the validity of which Saint-Simon believed to be a matter of scientific fact. Its starting-point is the observation that changes in social organisation occur, indeed become necessary, because of the development of human intelligence, of knowledge and beliefs. The failure of historians to examine the relationship between ideas and social organisation was, in Saint-Simon's opinion, a serious mistake. He urged them to look beyond 'secondary or local events', that is, 'political, religious or military facts', and attempt to discover the ideological and doctrinal forces behind them.[17] The development of *moral* ideas deserved particular attention, he argued, since at any period in history the form of organisation of a society was a direct reflection of the prevailing moral code. This code in turn was bound to reflect the state of scientific knowledge. The social order of ancient Greece and Rome was based on one system of moral ideas; that of medieval Europe on another; and the new order which Saint-Simon saw emerging at the beginning of the nineteenth century was being shaped by yet another moral system. Three quite distinctive eras of western civilisation, each based on its own system of morals, were thus identified. They were separated from each other, it was argued, by transitional periods during which one moral system was gradually replaced by another. This process of replacement was made necessary by the advancement of scientific knowledge and the accompanying changes in man's philosophical disposition – changes which eventually became so fundamental that they resulted in the adoption of new moral values.

The values which underpinned the social organisation of ancient Greece and Rome were seen by Saint-Simon to be in harmony with the supernatural, polytheistic beliefs of that age. But with the transition from polytheism to theism, a transition set in motion by Socratic science, a new moral code and with it a new social order were necessitated. This was the major cause of the rise of the theological-feudal system, which reached its zenith under Charlemagne's rule in Europe. In its turn Christian theism was now in decline, being replaced by positivism, which rejected all forms of supernatural belief and relied entirely on the sciences of observation. This explained the gradual collapse of feudalism since the Middle Ages, culminating in the chaos of the French Revolution.

According to Saint-Simon's theory of history, because the social order of feudalism was founded on a theological system of ideas, it could survive only as long as theology remained scientifically valid. In actual fact theology gradually lost its validity as a result of the rise of positive sciences of observation, first of all astronomy, then physics and chemistry, and finally physiology. The inevitable consequence of this was first of all that the Catholic Church, which exercised spiritual power under feudalism, began to lose its authority; and then that the military lords, the holders of temporal power, found their superiority challenged more and more by their subjects. This process of disintegration proceeded most rapidly in France, where it reached its climax in the eighteenth century with the collapse of the *ancien régime,* precipitated by the social criticism of Enlightenment philosophy, in particular the '*antithéologie*' of the Enyclopaedists.[18] The French Revolution represented the final act of this drama. It brought to an end the theological-feudal era, and paved the way for the construction of a new social order appropriate to the level of enlightenment attained by man. However the task of social organisation was not at all easy and could not possibly be accomplished without careful preparation. Before a new system could be inaugurated, it must first of all be conceived, and conceived clearly in all its aspects. The attempts of the revolutionaries in France to establish a new system were totally inadequate, because they were based on vague 'legal-metaphysical' ideas such as the belief in certain fundamental rights of man, which may have been good enough to destroy the *ancien régime* but which could not possibly serve as the basis of a new form of social organisation because they were too negative.

In Saint-Simon's view, therefore, a major crisis threatened France and its European neighbours. It was a crisis which could be overcome, he believed, only through the concerted efforts of scientists and philosophers, with whom the prime responsibility rested for formulating a positive social theory capable of providing man with a new sense of purpose and direction. By 1814 he had resolved to do everything in his power to promote the necessary work, and he made a start in the same year with his booklet *The Reorganisation of European Society*, written with Augustin Thierry. The message of this work was clear and concise: 'The philosophy of the last century was revolutionary; that of the nineteenth century must be organisational.'[19]

The theological-feudal system had collapsed, Saint-Simon argued, because in the light of advanced scientific reasoning the moral code of which that system was a direct expression had become unacceptable to man. The basis of the old moral code was a conception of man's earthly life as nothing more than 'a passage to a future life in which we shall be rewarded or punished by an all-powerful Being, according to whether we have or have not followed the wishes of this Being, as taught to us through the medium of the priests, his direct interpreters'.[20] In accordance with this conception, the teachings of the Catholic Church were acknowledged to be the source of all rights and duties, including political rights and duties. Men were in fact taught to accept a generally repressive system of temporal power, to 'render unto Caesar the things that are Caesar's', and to submit to the law of the strongest. They were also instructed to remain content with their situation on earth, spiritual values being regarded as much more important than material living conditions.

As long as the spiritual authority of the Catholic clergy

was generally recognised, the theological moral code retained its influence over the minds of men. But this authority did in fact begin to collapse in the fifteenth century with the beginnings of the modern scientific revolution, a revolution which persuaded man to reject revelation as a source of knowledge, and to rely instead on reasoning based on observation. On the basis of such reasoning the conviction gradually grew among the laity that neither the spiritual power of the clergy nor the temporal power of the feudal lords could be tolerated. Consequently a process of social upheaval was inaugurated, culminating in the violent Revolution of 1789.

The task facing nineteenth-century Europe, Saint-Simon asserted, was one of social reconstruction. And social reconstruction could not possibly be achieved until a new moral code based on scientific rationality was formulated and accepted as valid by the majority of the people. The 'celestial' morality of theology had been rejected; a new 'terrestrial' morality must be founded – 'terrestrial' because the achievement of happiness on earth must now be man's first priority.

Industrialism and the Rule of Science

Happiness was defined by Saint-Simon in terms of material and moral well-being. Hence for him the fundamental purpose of social organisation was the maximisation of that well-being. 'The greatest happiness of the greatest number' was one way of putting this;[21] and since the greatest number in society were the ignorant and impoverished masses, the improvement of their condition became the essential social aim. In moral terms the validity of this principle was undeniable. It was also defensible in terms of Christian doctrine, since Christ had taught men to treat one another as brothers and give special consideration to the plight of the poor. Having reached this conclusion, Saint-Simon then considered the question of what institutional arrangements were necessary to establish a system of social organisation in accordance with 'terrestrial' morality. More specifically, he was concerned to answer the question: in whose hands should spiritual and temporal power reside? His solution was perfectly straightforward. First, spiritual power must pass into the hands of the most enlightened men, the *savants,* both scientists and artists, since only they could command sufficient respect. Having surpassed theologians in terms of knowledge and understanding, they were the natural intellectual elite of the future. Secondly, temporal power belonged legitimately to the most capable economic administrators, society's most eminent 'industrials',[22] since they alone were qualified to organise the various branches of material production – agriculture, manufacturing, commerce, and banking – so as to fulfil man's material needs. This was what ought to happen, Saint-Simon believed. It was also what he thought was bound to happen eventually, not only in France but throughout Europe, as a consequence of the inevitable progress of the human mind.

The scientific-industrial age of the future would witness a transformation in the nature of social power in both its temporal and spiritual aspects. As far as the temporal power was concerned, Saint-Simon anticipated that with the rise to leadership of the captains of industry, government in the traditional sense of a repressive force, as embodied in the militaristic feudal state, would disappear, to be replaced by a system of administration whose main function would be to supervise productive operations. In the future 'governments will no longer command men; their functions will be limited to ensuring that useful work is not hindered'.[23] Decision-making will be entrusted not to arbitary rulers chosen by patronage, but to 'general directors'[24] selected on the basis of their professional ability, for whom politics will be nothing more than 'the science of production'.[25] This conception of a totally new kind of political system was undoubtedly Saint-Simon's most important and most influential contribution to social theory. He himself regarded it as the focal point of his doctrine.[26]

Saint-Simon did not anticipate that the transition from a governmental to an administrative regime would involve a major upheaval. The Restoration political system of France (a limited parliamentary system, regarded by Saint-Simon as an intermediate, transitional stage between feudalism and industrialism) could, he believed, be transformed quite smoothly once the industrials overcame their political apathy and mounted an alliance with the Bourbon monarchy against the aristocracy. Their immediate aim should be to secure financial reform. Public revenue, instead of being squandered on the army, police, courts, and aristocracy, should be invested in science and industry so as to promote social welfare, develop transport and communications, and provide useful employment for all men.

Saint-Simon believed that the process by which public expenditure was allocated stood in urgent need of reform, and he proposed that control of the national budget should be handed over to those men who knew most about economic affairs, that is, the leading producers: 'It is evident that the most certain way to promote the prosperity of agriculture, commerce, and manufacturing is to give to the farmers, merchants, and manufacturers the task of directing the administration of public affairs, that is of framing the budget. . . .'[27] It is most important to point out that this was just about the only major power Saint-Simon thought necessary to give to industrials. He certainly did not advocate the establishment of a new all-purpose state structure, as some commentators have suggested, thus giving the impression that he was a nineteenth-century 'totalitarian'. While it is true that his social theory does have some *authoritarian* implications (which are discussed in the course of this analysis), the view that he favoured a form of social organisation involving the exercise of a limitless, i.e. *totalitarian*, power over the individual by a coercive elite goes too far. Exponents of this view include F.A. Hayek, who states that Saint-Simon considered freedom of thought to be 'the root-evil of nineteenth-century society', and wanted to establish strong dictatorial government;[28] Peyton V. Lyon, who sees him as an advocate of an organic social system similar to modern communist China and Russia;[29] F.M.H. Markham, who asserts that 'Saint-Simon did not think freedom worth preserving';[30] Giovanni Sartori, who criticises Saint-Simon's belief in the virtues of 'total planning' and the 'abolition of the free market';[31] Leonard Schapiro, who asserts that Saint-Simon 'despised parliamentary democracy and had little use for freedom of speech or thought', and was preoccupied with ends and indifferent to means;[32] H.G. Schenk, who writes that Saint-Simon 'was fully prepared to jettison the ideal of individual liberty';[33] Walter M. Simon, who states that Saint-Simon was a totalitarian 'philosopher-king, extinguishing any right to dissent on the part of the people', who would be 'forced to be free';[34] and J.L. Talmon, for whom Saint-Simon is a 'totalitarian technocrat', intent to achieve 'total integration' in a society.[35] Such views are the result, I would suggest, of a combination of factors: a tendency to confuse the terms 'authoritarian' and 'totalitarian'; a fundamental misinterpretation of Saint-Simon's thought; and also a failure to distinguish carefully enough between his own ideas and those of his disciples, the Saint-Simonians, many of whom were much more authoritarian in outlook than their master. Even for these disciples, however, the designation 'totalitarian' is somewhat inappropriate, since it has obvious connotations of violent repression which cannot be read into the Saint-Simonian literature.[36]

Saint-Simon did in fact believe that the new temporal power should interfere as little as possible in society's affairs, and he constantly reiterated his conviction that industrialism would secure the highest degree of liberty for all members of society.[37] He placed particular emphasis on the fact that the economy should be left as free as possible once the necessary industrial investment had been secured. Workers must be allowed to 'exchange with each other directly and with complete freedom the products of their various labours'.[38] He also predicted that under industrialism public expenditure would actually be cut and taxation thereby reduced as a consequence of efficient administration. The industrials would not need anything like as much money as was presently being squandered, as long as they put what they did have to proper use, and he thus looked forward to a day when the functions and expenses of governments were reduced to a minimum. He was convinced that private enterprise could be relied upon to foster economic development, as long as the right incentives were offered: 'The funds required by useful undertakings, whatever their scale, will be provided by voluntary subscriptions, and the subscribers themselves will supervise the use and administration of their money.'[39]

All those conclusions make it perfectly clear that Saint-Simon considered a large degree of economic liberty to be essential under industrialism. He was never an advocate of absolute *laissez-faire*, but he did maintain that as long as the social framework in which they lived and worked was a just one, all men would be capable of achieving self-development through their own efforts. Only in ensuring that everyone was well educated and provided with useful employment did the government have an overriding responsibility:

> The most direct way to bring about an improvement in the moral and physical well-being of the majority of the population is to give priority in State expenditure to the provision of work for all fit men, so as to assure their physical existence; to disseminate as quickly as possible among the proletarian class the positive knowledge which has been acquired; and finally to ensure that the individuals composing this class have forms of leisure and interests which will develop their intelligence.[40]

This outlook may justifiably be described as essentially socialist in character, although it is not entirely divorced from certain liberal assumptions. The important point to be emphasised is that during the last few years of his life Saint-Simon became increasingly critical of the central element in liberal thought – its negative attitude towards social welfare and its consequent inability to promote a radical improvement in the condition of the working class – and was led to formulate a much more positive alternative in which, I would argue, the socialist tendencies finally predominated.

As far as specific proposals for the reorganisation of political institutions were concerned, Saint-Simon was never entirely consistent. Furthermore, he was always concerned primarily with the situation in France, and so it is not always clear whether he considered his proposals to be of universal application. In *The Organiser* he emphasised the need to transform the French Chamber of Deputies into a new industrial chamber – composed of industrials and elected by industrials. (This implied an extension of the suffrage, perhaps, but certainly not universal suffrage.) This new chamber was given the name 'Chamber of Execution' and was placed side by side with a 'Chamber of Invention' and a 'Chamber of Examination', to be composed respectively of 'inventors' (artists and engineers) and 'examiners' (scientists) who would help the industrials to plan a programme of economic and social development. This was an impressive, but thoroughly unfeasible scheme, and was never repeated by

Saint-Simon. In subsequent years his proposals were more sober. Recognising the obstacles to parliamentary reform, he suggested an alternative strategy: the King should appoint councils of industrials, outside the Parliament, to prepare the nation's budget.

Saint-Simon always stressed that the inauguration of this new industrial structure would not affect the position of the French monarchy as long as the King supported the principles of industrialism. If he failed to do so, however, there was a real danger that the monarchy would eventually be swept away by the inexorable tide of progress. Thus, while Saint-Simon was convinced that the establishment of new temporal institutions appropriate to a scientific-industrial society could be accomplished smoothly, without violent upheaval, he admitted that revolution was a possibility.

The reorganisation of temporal institutions in the scientific-industrial era would have to be accompanied, according to Saint-Simon, by a fundamental restructuring of spiritual power, involving the elevation of positive scientists and artists to the positions of moral and educational leadership formerly occupied by the Catholic clergy. Although he never doubted the inevitability of this transformation, he remained uncertain as to whether the scientists and artists ought to organise themselves as leaders of a new religion – an alternative to Catholicism – or whether they should concentrate on achieving influence in secular institutions. In his *Letters from an Inhabitant of Geneva* and other early works he advocated the first alternative: the Religion of Newton was presented as a new scientific religion to replace Catholicism. This outlook was very much in the tradition of the revolutionary programmes of de-Christianisation. However, once it became clear, under Napoleon, that de-Christianisation was no longer official policy, he suggested that scientists and artists would have to leave the religious question alone and concentrate on increasing their influence in the Academies, Parliament, and other secular institutions.

This position was maintained by Saint-Simon during the Napoleonic Empire and the first few years of the Restoration. Thus, in his first major sketch of the new industrial political system, in *The Organiser*, the scientists and artists were allotted places in new parliamentary chambers – Chambers of Invention and Examination – and were instructed to leave religious questions alone when preparing their plans for a system of public education. However, from about 1820 onwards Saint-Simon gradually reverted to the idea that the new spiritual heads of society should present themselves as religious leaders, but not as *anti*-Christians, rather as *true* Christians whose morality was in perfect accord with the original teachings of Christ.

Precisely how the New Christian spiritual power would function under industrialism is not clear from Saint-Simon's writings. However, some basic principles were outlined in *The Industrial System*:

> I believe that the new spiritual power will be composed at first of all the existing Academies of Science in Europe, and of all persons who deserve to be admitted to these scientific corporations. I believe that once this nucleus is formed, those who compose it will organise themselves. I believe that the direction of education, as well as of public teaching, will be entrusted to this new spiritual power. I believe that the pure morality of the Gospel will serve as the basis of the new public education, and that, for the rest, it will be pushed as far as possible in conformity with positive knowledge, in proportion to the time which children of different levels of wealth will be able to spend at school. Finally, I believe that the new spiritual power will settle a fairly large number of its members throughout all the communes, and that these detached scholars will have as their principal mission to inspire their spiritual charges with a passion for the public good.[41]

In the fourth book of *The Industrials' Catechism* Saint-Simon considered in more detail the question of how the French Academies should be reorganised. He proposed the creation of three new institutions. First, an Academy of Sentiments, consisting of the most distinguished moralists, theologians, lawyers, poets, painters, sculptors, and musicians, who would work together to formulate a code of industrial morality. Secondly, there would be an Academy of Reason, similar in structure to the Academy of Sciences founded by Louis XIV, the main difference being the inclusion of a number of political economists. The task of this body would be to construct 'the best code of interests' for industrial society, to be embodied in the nation's civil laws. Finally, there would be a third institution, a Royal Scientific College, consisting of the most eminent general scientists, to co-ordinate the work of the two Academies and bring their findings together in a national programme of education.

The new spiritual power was intended to be, first and foremost, a source of moral guidance capable of providing the members of industrial society with a clear sense of direction and common purpose. (There are clear authoritarian implications here, but the authority in question is based on respect and confidence, not force.) Eventually, towards the end of his life, Saint-Simon came to realise that if it was to be effective this moral guidance must be channelled through the medium of an organised Church with an appropriate ritual and dogma; and it was for this reason that in 1825 he produced a work dealing specifically with the *New Christianity*.

In addition to the role of moral leadership, another task was allotted to the new spiritual power in industrial society: the training of individuals for employment. This was of crucial significance, since an industrial society was by definition an association of men devoted to useful work in all its forms. The national workshop could not be expected to function properly unless work was allocated to individuals on the basis of their particular skills. And this could not be done until all men were given the opportunity, through education, to develop their abilities to the full. Only in this way, too, could the individual achieve any significant measure of self-realisation.[42]

Saint-Simon also devoted attention in his writings to the question of the relationship between the temporal and spiritual powers. He examined the historical development of this relationship, and observed that in ancient Greece and Rome, while both powers were in the hands of the patrician class, the temporal function assumed the greatest social importance. Subsequently, in the Middle Ages, a formal division between the two powers was established through the influence of Christianity. Spiritual power then achieved predominance, exercising a direct authority over feudalism's temporal rulers. Against this historical background Saint-Simon gave careful consideration to the issue of what relationship between the two powers should be established in industrial society.

As with other aspects of his doctrine, his ideas on this subject changed somewhat between 1802 and 1825. In his earliest writings society's spiritual leaders were accorded supremacy over the temporal rulers, who were reduced to a position of secondary importance.[43] Here Saint-Simon was simply transposing the feudal relationship between the two powers to the post-feudal situation. This theory was maintained during the Empire, but under the new political circumstances of the Restoration, it was eventually rejected in favour of a new conception according to which the temporal-spiritual relationship was reversed, with the industrials being granted predominance over the new priesthood of scientists and artists. This new theory is made perfectly clear in the fourth book of the *The Industrials' Catechism*:

> The scientists render very important services to the industrial class; but they receive from it even more important services; they receive from it their *existence.* It is the industrial class which satisfies their primary needs, as well as their physical tastes of all kinds, and which provides them with all the instruments of use to them in the execution of their work.
>
> The industrial class is the fundamental class, the nourishing class of all society, without which no other could exist. Thus, it has the right to say to the scientists, and with even greater reason to all other non-industrials: We wish to feed you, house you, clothe you, and generally satisfy your physical tastes only on certain conditions.[44]

The same point had earlier been made by Saint-Simon in his preface to Comte's *System of Positive Politics*, where he criticised his 'pupil' for advocating the supremacy of the spiritual rather than the temporal power under industrialism: 'In the system which we have conceived, the industrial capacity is that which should find itself in the first rank; it is that which should judge the value of all other capacities, and make them all work for its greatest advantage.'[45] In stating this principle Saint-Simon believed he was being thoroughly realistic in the face of the undeniable fact that 'the power of the industrials in society has become entirely preponderant.'[46] Where would the scientists and artists be, he asked, if the satisfaction of their basic material needs were not made possible by the efforts of the producers? The answer was obvious: they could not possibly survive; and it was this basic economic fact which made their social subordination inevitable in industrial society. This did not mean that the autonomy of the spiritual power, in the performance of its social function, would be impaired, but merely that the material conditions of its existence must be determined by the temporal rulers.

Industrialism, as Saint-Simon conceived it, was a social system with an international dimension as well as a national one, for the decline of theological-feudal institutions caused by the development of scientific thought and industrialisation was a truly international phenomenon embracing the whole of western Europe. The destinies of the individual nations composing that region had always been closely inter-related, and were bound to become even more so with the improvement of systems of transport and communication which industrialism would promote.

Eventually, Saint-Simon believed, all the western European nations would complete the transition from feudal to industrial society. He saw the adoption of a parliamentary system of government as a half-way stage in this transition, and was encouraged to see, in the early 1820s, that such a system had in fact been established in all of the countries with which he was concerned. To a large extent the nations of western Europe were actually interdependent: the policies of one government invariably had a direct impact on neighbouring states, especially in the military sphere. And it was for this reason that no individual country could proceed to the establishment of the industrial system without a movement in the same direction by all its neighbours. The spread of parliamentary government throughout western Europe was an unmistakable sign that such a common movement was in progress, and at last made it possible for the most enlightened west European nation – France – to embark on the final transition to industrialism, thus setting the example for its politically less developed neighbours.

If industrialism could achieve full development only within the framework of a peace-loving, non-military social system, then clearly it could not make very much progress until some measure of Pan-European co-operation was promoted to provide for the peaceful resolution of international disputes. Such co-operation, Saint-Simon suggested, could best be fostered through a system of international institutions – both temporal and spiritual – through which the countries of western Europe would be able to work together towards the goal of a free association of pacific, industrial communities. Ultimately, perhaps, a formal European federation might be created, such as that envisaged by Saint-Simon and Thierry in *The Reorganisation of European Society*. Until that stage was reached, however, a more loosely-knit arrangement would be acceptable, as loosely-knit it would seem as the Holy Alliance, for which Saint-Simon frequently expressed admiration. Of particular importance in this context, he stressed, was the relationship between England and France. An *entente cordiale* between these two countries, extending perhaps as far as an actual political union, would provide the best starting-point for the creation of a wider European solidarity by making a major continental war virtually impossible.

Although his discussion of international relations was always focused on western Europe, Saint-Simon emphasised that the spread of industrialism was bound eventually to have an impact on the rest of the world. The industrially advanced nations of Europe could, he believed, do a great deal to promote the economic and social progress of the less developed parts of the globe, once their own social reorganisation was completed. It was their historical destiny to extend the boundaries of civilisation to the farthest corners of the earth. In the performance of this task the chiefs of industry and the ministers of the New Christian religion would work together, revealing to the world in both word and deed the social benefits afforded by the industrial system. Always their essential aim would be to eradicate poverty, both material and spiritual:

> The direct aim of my enterprise is to improve as much as possible the condition of the class which has no other means of existence but the labour of its hands. My aim

> is to improve the condition of this class not only in France, but in England, Belgium, Portugal, Spain, Italy, throughout the rest of Europe, and the whole world.[47]

As far as the other branch of modern society, North America, was concerned, Saint-Simon frequently stated that in that part of the world much progress had already been made in the direction of industrialism, so that the United States was well equipped for the role of partner with western Europe in the future programme of social advancement. Relations between the Old World and the New were bound to be friendly and co-operative in the industrial age. On the basis of such a solid association, the ancient dream of perpetual and universal peace could be expected one day to become a reality.

In analysing Saint-Simon's industrial doctrine, some consideration must be given to his conception of the kind of social structure which he saw emerging under industrialism, for in order to support the new arrangement of temporal and spiritual power, that structure would have to be very different from the one prevailing under the feudal system. Saint-Simon analysed social structure in terms of a network of class relationships, using the term 'class' in this context to refer to any distinctive functional, occupation group. He drew a very fundamental distinction between the productive classes – the 'workers' in the broadest sense of that term, including all farmers, manufacturers, merchants, bankers, scientists, artists, etc. – and the idle classes (chiefly the nobility and the clergy), who enjoyed the benefits provided by the workers without themselves contributing to production. In the early years of the Restoration Saint-Simon introduced the term 'industrial' ('*industriel*') to refer to any member of one of the productive classes. From about 1820, however, he modified this usage and applied the term only to members of the 'practical' classes, i.e. in particular the farmers, manufacturers, merchants, and bankers. In other words the scientists and artists were excluded and regarded henceforth as 'non-industrials', although they were still considered to be useful 'theoretical' workers. One further complication is that towards the end of his life Saint-Simon introduced the concept of an intermediate, 'bourgeois' class consisting of those idle lawyers, soldiers, and landowners who came originally from the industrial class and were granted their privileges by the nobility. It was this bourgeois class, he believed, which had gained power in France during the Revolution, and which was attempting to establish a new social system on the basis of its negative 'legal-metaphysical' reasoning.

For Saint-Simon the whole of human history was to be seen as a perpetual struggle between the productive and idle classes. At first, in ancient times, the advantage lay with the idlers, who maintained their supremacy through the institution of slavery. Under the theological-feudal system, however, the producers achieved successive measures of emancipation: the replacement of slavery by serfdom, the enfranchisement of the commons, and finally the establishment of the parliamentary system of government, first of all in England and then, after the French Revolution, in France and other European countries. Strictly speaking, this parliamentary system represented a transitional phase between feudalism and industrialism. It was no more than a partial success for the producers: it gave them a share in political power, but not the whole of political power, because parliaments continued to be dominated by idlers. However, Saint-Simon was convinced that it could only be a matter of time before the producers gained the absolute supremacy they deserved. The spread of enlightenment and the numerical superiority of the productive classes would ensure that.

Saint-Simon fully recognised the division within the productive classes between those men who were employers and managers of labour ('directing industrials') and those who were employees – proletarians – doing the bulk of the physical work ('executive industrials'). However, unlike Marx and Engels, who were to stress the inevitability of conflict between capitalists and proletariat, Saint-Simon believed that these two groups shared a common interest in production, and that consequently there was no reason why relations between them should be anything but friendly and co-operative.[48] At the same time he pointed out that the precise degree of unity would vary from one country to another. It was much stronger in France, he believed, than in England, where the proletariat were likely to take advantage of the first opportunity 'to commence the war of the poor against the rich'.[49] This makes it quite clear that Saint-Simon did not rule out altogether the possibility of a class war. However, he was convinced that such conflict could be avoided, or at least kept to a minimum, if two conditions were fulfilled: society's leaders must provide for the basic moral and physical needs of the whole population; and society must be organised so as to give all men equal opportunities for advancement on the basis of their proven ability.

Saint-Simon believed, then, that the final demise of the unproductive idlers, and the rise to social supremacy of the workers – the practical industrials in the temporal sphere – was an historical inevitability. He also recognised, though, that positive action must be taken to establish the industrial system as smoothly and as rapidly as possible. With this aim in mind he stressed the crucial importance of increasing the parliamentary representation of the country's leading industrials *vis-à-vis* the idlers;[50] and of reforming the laws governing the actual constitution of landed property. It was chiefly on the basis of these laws, he argued, that the privileged social position of the idle property owners rested. Hence, as long as the laws remained unchanged, no real progress was likely to be made towards a truly egalitarian society. In Saint-Simon's view the chief purpose of property law reform should be 'to render it (property) more favourable to production'.[51] A start had been made in France with the sale of *biens nationaux* during the Revolution.[52] But further measures were needed: at least the abolition of entail;[53] and preferably the 'mobilisation' of all landed property, that is, the granting of full entrepreneurial rights to farmers.[54] These measures would surely be sufficient to rid society for ever of all idlers who believed that they had a natural right to live off unearned income.

Saint-Simon's vision of a future society in which all men would be workers is one of his most important contributions to the tradition of socialist thought. This vision has often been interpreted as a theory of the 'classless' society similar to that subsequently developed by Marx and Engels;[55] but such an interpretation is erroneous for the simple reason that Saint-Simon frequently emphasised the inevitability of some class divisions in all societies, including industrial society. The notion of a classless society would have been regarded by Saint-Simon as absurd, since for him the basic meaning of the word 'class' was 'occupational group,' and naturally in industrial society, as in any other society, there would be fundamental group distinctions corresponding to the division of labour: for example, on the broadest level, between industrials, scientists, and artists; and within the industrial class between farmers, manufacturers, merchants, and bankers. Thus industrial society would in no sense be a classless society. It would, however, be a homogeneous society in which all classes would share a common interest in production, and from which all class conflict would thereby be eliminated, or at least reduced to an acceptable minimum.

2
Robert Owen

Life and Work

Robert Owen was born at Newtown, a country village in Montgomeryshire, North Wales, on 14 May 1771. His father, also named Robert Owen, was the local saddler, ironmonger, and postmaster, and in addition looked after the general management of parish affairs. The boy attended the local elementary school from the age of about four or five, and quickly developed a strong passion for reading. He became particularly interested in religious works, and studied the teachings of all the world's major faiths. Confused by the fierce disagreements between them, he soon became convinced 'that there must be something fundamentally wrong in all religions, as they had been taught up to that period'.[1]

After leaving school at the age of nine, he started work as a shop assistant, selling drapery, haberdashery, and groceries. A year later he joined his eldest brother, William, in London, and began to look for a job in a draper's shop. Through one of his father's friends he was given an introduction to James McGuffog, a draper with a business in Stamford, Lincolnshire. This secured the boy an offer of a three-year apprenticeship and accommodation in the McGuffog household. The offer was gratefully accepted.

When his apprenticeship ended in 1784, Owen returned to London, where he found another job as shop assistant, with the drapery house of Flint and Palmer. He did not like the post, though. During the spring rush he was frequently kept busy until two o'clock in the morning, with no proper meal breaks, and such 'hurried work and slavery'[2] became unbearable. At the age of fifteen or sixteen he decided it was time to move on, and he accepted an offer of a job with a wholesale and retail draper, a Mr Satterfield, in Manchester.

New spinning-machines were now being introduced into the Manchester cotton industry, and Owen got to know a great deal about them through Ernest Jones, a mechanic employed by Satterfield. Jones thought there was a lot of money to be made manufacturing these new machines, and asked Owen if he could provide some capital to help establish a business. Owen found the idea attractive, and in 1789, with the help of a loan from his brother in London, he and Jones entered into partnership, employing forty or so men in a newly built workshop. Within a few months, however, Jones had found a new, wealthier partner, and Owen was persuaded to leave the business. He was able to take a certain amount of machinery with him, and this enabled him to open a small workshop of his own, with three employees.

About a year later, in 1791, Owen applied for a job as manager of a large new mill owned by a wealthy cotton manufacturer, Peter Drinkwater. Although he was only nineteen years of age and relatively inexperienced, his qualities impressed Drinkwater, and he soon found himself in charge of some 500 men, women, and children at an annual salary of £300. From the start his relations with the workers were excellent (a fact which he put down to his expert knowledge of human nature), and Drinkwater quickly rewarded him by offering him an increase in salary and a deed of partnership whereby he (Owen) would secure a one-quarter share in the business after two more years as manager. The agreement was signed, but it was never fully implemented, for in late 1794 or early 1795 Owen left Drinkwater following a complicated argument over a merger offer made by Samuel Oldknow, the muslin manufacturer, who insisted that Owen should be excluded from any business deal.

Owen's next venture was to enter into a partnership in a new firm specialising in fine yarns, the Chorlton Twist Company. After supervising the construction of a factory, he became chief manager of the enterprise, in which capacity he found he had to pay regular visits to customers in Glasgow. On one such visit he was introduced to Anne Caroline Dale, the daughter of David Dale, who was one of the most important yarn dealers in Glasgow. The daughter invited him to inspect her father's mills at New Lanark, which had been founded by Dale and Richard Arkwright in 1782. Owen was greatly impressed by the beautiful location of the mills and the New Lanark village, also built by Dale, where most of the workers lived. 'Of all places I have yet seen', he told a colleague, 'I should prefer this in which to try an experiment I have long contemplated and have wished to have an opportunity to put into practice.'[3] The experiment he had in mind was to establish a factory system in which a radical improvement in the condition of the workers would be achieved through new techniques of environmental management. Fortunately for him, it soon became known that Dale wished to retire from business and sell the New Lanark mills, and Owen quickly urged his partners to join him in offering to purchase the establishment. In the summer of 1797 a price of £60,000 was agreed, and the mills became the property of the New Lanark Twist Company. Two years later Owen concluded a no less important agreement, when he married Dale's daughter, Anne Caroline. At first the couple intended to live in Manchester, leaving the control of New Lanark to the two existing managers, but Owen was becoming increasingly dissatisfied with these men, and in January 1800 he established himself as resident managing director.

New Lanark remained under Owen's control for a quarter of a century. During this period he saw himself as much more than a manager in the tradition sense of that term. He was, he believed, responsible for the *government* of the New Lanark community:

> I say "government," – for my intention was not to be a mere manager of cotton mills, as such mills were at this time generally managed; – but to introduce principles in the conduct of the people, which I had successfully commenced with the workpeople in Mr Drinkwater's factory; and to change the conditions of the people, who, I saw, were surrounded by circumstances having an injurious influence upon the character of the entire population of New Lanark. [4]

In 1800 that population consisted of about 1,800 workers,

including between 400 and 500 parish apprentices aged from five to ten years. According to Owen, the majority were 'idle, intemperate, dishonest, devoid of truth, and pretenders to religion, which they supposed would cover and excuse all their shortcomings and immoral proceedings'.[5] That there was much scope for social improvement could hardly be denied.

The methods employed by Owen were numerous and varied, but they all stemmed from the conviction that a man's character is shaped by the environment in which he lives. The main task, therefore, was to construct a better environment, and by way of preparation certain measures were deemed by Owen to be absolutely essential. He started to phase out the employment of pauper apprentices; existing houses and streets were improved, and new building programmes were commenced; modern machinery was brought into the factories; better sanitary arrangements were introduced; and new stores and shops were opened to supply the workers with all the goods they needed at cost price. At first the workers resisted all these innovations, but they soon realised that they were bound to benefit from them. Any remaining doubts about Owen's sincerity were removed in 1806, when for four months he continued to pay his workers full wages even though production had to cease owing to a steep rise in the price of cotton (the consequence of an American embargo on exports to Britain). Confidence in Owen had now reached such heights that he was able, without any opposition, to introduce direct checks on the conduct of individual workers, most notably a system of 'silent monitors' – wooden indicators displaying four colours to denote four grades of character, from bad to excellent, which were suspended in prominent positions near to each employee to show his conduct at work during the previous day. Apparently 'the effects and progress of this simple plan of preventing bad and inferior conduct were far beyond all previous expectation'.[6]

Owen was now becoming increasingly concerned with educational issues, and particularly with the question of how young children should best be educated so as to improve their character. (He was possibly prompted in this respect by his own experience of fatherhood. His eldest son, Robert Dale, was born in 1800, and there followed three more sons and three daughters.) By 1809 he had drawn up plans to construct new school buildings and playgrounds, but the implementation of these plans was opposed by Owen's business partners, most of whom were not convinced of the desirability of his proposed educational reforms. The only solution, he believed, was to buy them out, so he offered them a sum of £84,000, which they accepted. Owen was now joined in a new partnership by four men: John Atkinson (one of the old partners, who had supported Owen), two Glasgow merchants (relatives of Mrs Owen), and one of their business colleagues. This new association proved to be no more successful than the first, however. The four men argued with Owen over financial matters, and refused to approve his reforms, including his educational schemes. He tried to disregard them, and commenced the construction of new school buildings, but then (in 1812) they presented him with formal notice to stop. He immediately resigned as manager, facing the prospect of a dissolution of the partnership and the public auction of the mills. But he was not easily disheartened. He found six trustworthy men who approved his social theories and who were willing to enter a new partnership with him (they included William Allen, the wealthy Quaker and editor of *The Philanthropist*, and the utilitarian philosopher, Jeremy Bentham), and together they succeeded in purchasing the firm at the auction in February 1814 for £114,100 – a high price, but the financial viability of the mills had already been proved: between 1809 and 1813 a net profit of £160,000 had been realised. The new partnership enabled Owen to press on with his educational programme at New Lanark, and on 1 January 1816 his Institution for the Formation of Character was opened.[7]

In 1812 Owen had published for private circulation *A Statement Regarding the New Lanark Establishment*, a pamphlet which outlined the principles underlying his reforms. These principles were expounded at greater length in four *Essays on the Formation of Character* (1812-13), subsequently published together in book form as *A New View of Society*. These writings helped Owen to enlist the support of his six new partners; and the *Essays*, in particular, aroused much interest among political and church leaders, while many of the leading intellectuals of the day – perhaps most notably political economists such as Thomas Malthus, James Mill, David Ricardo, and Francis Place – recognised them as a contribution of major importance. The Prime Minister, Lord Liverpool, granted Owen an interview to discuss his theories, and this afforded him an opportunity to have copies of his *Essays* sent to the sovereigns of various European countries and to the federal and state authorities in America. Believing that the ruling classes could everywhere be persuaded to adopt his 'new view of society' as a basis for their own policies, he was greatly encouraged by this initial response.

In 1815, in order to improve his knowledge of working conditions, Owen undertook a tour of Britain's major factories, and the evidence he gathered (summarised in his *Observations on the Effect of the Manufacturing System*) helped him to draft a legislative proposal providing for the regulation of hours of work and the creation of a factory inspectorate (while stopping all employment of children under the age of ten). This Bill gained some Government support and was introduced in the House of Commons by the elder Sir Robert Peel, but the opposition of manufacturing interests proved sufficiently strong to ensure that the Bill's provisions were severely amended, and the eventual Act of 1819 thus bore little resemblance to the original proposals. (It applied only to cotton mills, where the minimum age for employment was to be nine.) While his Bill was under discussion in Parliament, Owen also took the opportunity to urge the Government to provide useful work for the unemployed, who were growing rapidly in numbers following the conclusion of the war with France in 1815. When in 1816, a committee of statesmen, political economists, and businessmen was set up to investigate the causes of the economic depression, Owen was invited to participate, and this led to his *Report to the Committee of the Association for the Relief of the Manufacturing and Labouring Poor* (March 1817), a most important document which, as G.D.H. Cole puts it, 'marks the turning-point in Owen's career' and 'contains the first expression of his wider positive proposals,' marking 'the transition from Owen the factory reformer and educational pioneer to Owen the ancestor of Socialism and Co-operation'.[8] In the *Report*

Owen explained how modern machinery was gradually superseding human labour and depressing wages, and he called for Government intervention to create new employment opportunities in a network of 'villages of unity and mutual co-operation,' each containing between 500 and 1,500 men, women, and children, and modelled on the New Lanark community, although the intention was to provide mainly agricultural work which would enable the villagers to be self-sufficient in food production. The *Report* was not even discussed by the Government or Parliament, and so Owen decided to put his plan directly to the public. Two open meetings were held in London in August 1817, and it was at the second of these (on 21 August) that Owen chose to make what was undoubtedly the most controversial speech of his entire career, a speech denouncing all existing religions as a barrier to the organisation of society according to rational principles. The speech caused a sensation, and it was not without justice that Owen later came to regard this day as the most important of his public life.[9]

As the second decade of the nineteenth century drew to a close, economic depression gave rise to widespread working-class unrest throughout Britain, and this in turn prompted the Government to take a series of repressive measures, from the suspension of the Habeas Corpus Act in March 1817 to the Peterloo 'massacre' in August 1819. At the time these developments had little direct impact on Owen's thought. In 1818, indeed, he was much more concerned with a European tour which he had decided to undertake. He visited France, Switzerland, Italy, and Germany, and was made welcome in the highest political, scientific, and literary circles. In October 1818 he attended the conference of Great Powers meeting at Aix-la-Chapelle, and in *Two Memorials on Behalf of the Working Classes* he urged the assembled governments to take international action to implement his proposals for social reform. Following his return from the continent he persisted in his efforts to influence the British Government, and the result was the setting up in 1819 of a committee of investigation, chaired by the Duke of Kent, which issued a remarkably favourable report on Owen's ideas, and recommended the founding of an experimental village. The committee sought to raise the necessary funds by public subscription, but it soon became clear that such a plan could not possibly succeed. Only the Government could have saved the project, and this they refused to do.

In the General Elections of 1819 and 1820 Owen stood unsuccessfully as a parliamentary candidate for Lanark Burghs. Also in 1820 he published his *Report to the County of Lanark*, which remains one of his most important works. The *Report* presented a further development of the author's ideas on the foundation of co-operative villages. Much more radical in tone than any of Owen's previous publications, it paved the way for the gradual popularisation of his ideas among the working class during the 1820s and early 1830s. Owen was emerging as an uncompromising critic of private property, the capitalist wage-system, and its associated division of labour, and it was this perspective which now began to attract working-class support. In 1821 the Co-operative and Economical Society was established in London, and the first Owenite newspaper, *The Economist*, was started (it only survived for fifteen months, however). Co-operative organisations sprang up with increasing regularity, and an Owenite movement of a kind could be said to exist by the mid-1820s, although it was extremely fragmented, and Owen himself had very little to do with it. It is indicative of his disinterest that in 1824 he decided that prospects for success were much better in the United States, and when an opportunity arose to purchase some land and property from the Rappite community in Indiana, he did not hesitate to go ahead. In this way the New Harmony village of co-operation came into being, and from 1824 to 1829 it was this experiment in America rather than the development of a movement in Britain which was Owen's chief preoccupation.

The village of New Harmony was situated on the banks of the Wabash River, and in 1824 the site consisted of 20,000 acres of land, including some 2,000 acres under cultivation. About 900 founder members, from various parts of America and also from Europe, were attracted to the community by Owen's initial invitation, and in the first few months Owen and his second son, William, were able to establish a system of internal representative government and an economy based on communal ownership of property and co-operative labour. It was not long, however, before the lack of integration in the community led to serious conflict over questions of organisation, and the consequence was the gradual division of the community into several distinct units, each with its own particular structure and administrative arrangements. Owen was led to the conclusion that no communitarian experiment could hope to succeed without prior moral training of the citizens for life under totally new conditions. He had overlooked this fact, and hence the failure of New Harmony was only to be expected. For all practical purposes the Owenite community came to an end in June 1827, when Owen left for England. He returned to New Harmony for a brief visit a year later, but by then it was clear that the cause was hopeless. Several other attempts were made in America during the 1820s to form communities based on Owenite teachings – in Indiana, Illinois, Ohio, New York, and Tennessee – but Owen himself was not connected with any of them, and none survived for very long. Precisely the same fate befell the one major Owenite community established in Britain during the decade, at Orbiston in Lanarkshire, which lasted from 1825 to 1827.

When Owen arrived back in Britain in 1829, he soon became aware of a growing interest in his theories among the various working-class organisations, most notably the co-operative societies and trade unions, which had emerged since the repeal of the Combination Acts in 1824. At first he did not take these organisations very seriously as a means of advancing towards a new society. Nor was he impressed by the labour exchanges which were being set up to enable workers to buy goods with 'labour notes' (notes representing hours worked) instead of money. Although Owen approved of the principles underlying these organisations (indeed he had advocated many of the same principles himself in his writings), he wished to avoid the kind of social conflict which many elements in the working class seemed to regard as inevitable. And he also doubted the wisdom of linking demands for the extension of economic co-operation with agitation for parliamentary reform, as many workers were doing in 1830. Many of these fears were voiced in the *Outline of the Rational System of Society* (1830) and a new weekly paper, *The Crisis*, which Owen started in 1832, the year of the Reform Act, and which survived until 1834. As the paper's title suggested,

Owen considered British society to be going through a profound crisis, yet he was convinced that the solution to this crisis was to be found in reason (rather than violence) and class collaboration (rather than antagonism). This was the message he wished to convey to the newly organised workers, and for a time it seemed that the workers were willing to follow his leadership, especially after the appearance of *The Crisis* in 1832 and the opening of his National Equitable Labour Exchange in London in the same year.

By the end of 1832 Owen had come round to the view that society *could* be transformed through a system of labour exchanges. Yet, like the communitarian ventures of the 1820s, the new experiments were quickly overtaken by serious problems, and as business declined it became clear that the exchanges in both London and Birmingham (the latter established in 1833) would have to be wound up. This was done in 1834, a year which also saw the end of *The Crisis* and the collapse of Owen's efforts to take over the leadership of the trade union movement. In October 1833 he had succeeded in persuading a national congress meeting in London to establish a Grand National Moral Union of the Productive and Useful Classes which would unite in one federation as many trade unions, co-operative societies, and other workers' associations as possible. The following February this organisation became the Grand National Consolidated Trade Union, and within a few weeks it claimed to have a million members. Just as quickly, however, the G.N.C.T.U. proved impossible to maintain. Conflict with the Government and employers, in many cases leading to strikes and lock-outs (and aggravated by such events as the conviction in March of the 'Tolpuddle Martyrs', six Dorchester labourers sentenced to transportation for administering an illegal union oath), disagreements with other unions, financial problems, and leadership difficulties all contributed to the demise of this bold scheme, and helped to bring the trade union phase of the Owenite movement to an abrupt end.

The death of his wife (in 1831) and two of his daughters (in 1830 and 1832) added considerably to the incredible burden of disappointments which Owen had to bear in the years immediately following his return from America. In the particularly gloomy year of 1834 he reached his sixty-third birthday, and any other man in such a position and at such an age might well have been tempted to retire from active pursuit of the socialist utopia. But Owen survived for another twenty-four years, and for most of this time he remained as vigorous as ever, writing and lecturing a great deal. He also became involved in another major communitarian experiment, at Harmony Hall (Queenwood) in Hampshire, between 1839 and 1845, and in 1840 started a Home Colonisation Society to promote the spread of villages of co-operation. These same years witnessed something of an Owenite revival in America, with four new colonies being founded in 1843: two in Pennsylvania lasted only until the following year, and the other two, in New York and Wisconsin, survived until 1846.

In terms of the development of Owen's thought, the period after 1834 was characterised by the growth of a strongly ethical sectarianism marked by Owen's increasing interest in promoting his teachings as the basis for a social religion, and by a remarkable (and often overlooked) moral radicalism – to be seen, perhaps most notably, in his uncompromising attack on the institution of marriage. Owen's ideas on religion, in particular his rejection of orthodox Christianity, had always caused controversy, and in some ways they had contributed to the conflicts surrounding his involvement with the labour movement between 1829 and 1834. After 1834 Owen gradually moved to a position where he no longer insisted that religion and rationalism were incompatible; rather he advocated a rational religion based on the science of society and a fraternal, and thus truly Christian, charity. Owen provided this new religion with its own bible in his *Book of the New Moral World*, which appeared in seven parts between 1836 and 1844. The message was also disseminated in a periodical, *The New Moral World*, which was issued from 1834 to 1845. Owenite institutes or 'Halls of Science' became the centres for the activities of the new 'Rational Religionists'; 'Social Missionaries' were sent to spread the gospel throughout the country; a book of 'Social Hymns' was published. The word 'socialism' was used increasingly as a summary description of the doctrine.

Between 1844 and 1847 Owen spent most of his time in America, where he undertook extensive lecture tours. In 1848 he was in Paris, encouraged by the revolutionary changes there to attempt to convert the socialist leaders to

Owenism. This remarkable old man even considered standing for election to the House of Commons. In 1849 he reiterated his views in *The Revolution in the Mind and Practice of the Human Race*, and soon afterwards started a series of periodical publications: *Weekly Letters to the Human Race* (1850), *Robert Owen's Journal* (1851-2), *Robert Owen's Rational Quarterly Review and Journal* (1853), *The New Existence of Man upon the Earth* (1854-5), and *Robert Owen's Millenial Gazette* (1856-8). A volume of autobiography accompanied by a selection of documents and writings appeared during 1857-8.

Robert Owen died on 17 November 1858. In his last years he had been converted to the doctrine of spiritualism:

> Having outlived all his old associates, he evokes their spirits at séances, and becomes the willing dupe of mediums, and especially of a certain Mrs Hayden, who had come to England from the United States. Jefferson, Benjamin Franklin, Shakespeare, Shelley, Napoleon, the Duke of Wellington, and the prophet Daniel became his familiars; but the most frequent of all his spiritual visitants was His Royal Highness the Duke of Kent, whose steady support had meant much to Owen in the early days of his crusade.[10]

Owen was convinced that such 'spiritual manifestations,' the reality of which was recorded by numerous witnesses throughout Europe and America, had a clear purpose: to inspire man, and to assist him in the creation of the Millennial State on earth. Convinced that the time was now ripe for the momentous transformation, he actually announced the inauguration of the Millennium on his eighty-fourth birthday, 14 May 1855, at a Convention of Delegates of the Human Race held in St. Martin's Hall, London.

A New View of Society

The first systematic statement of Owen's social theory came in the collection of four essays, *A New View of Society*, originally published in 1812-13. The title of this work is very significant, for it reveals Owen's conviction that he had indeed formulated a new approach to the understanding of society. This approach stems from a single principle:

> Any general character, from the best to the worst, from the most ignorant to the most enlightened, may be given to any community, even to the world at large, by the application of proper means; which means are to a great extent at the command and under the control of those who have influence in the affairs of men.
>
> . . . Every day will make it more and more evident that the character of man is, without a single exception, always formed for him; that it may be, and is chiefly, created by his predecessors; that they give him, or may give him, his ideas and habits, which are the powers that govern and direct his conduct. Man, therefore, never did, nor is it possible he ever can, form his own character.[11]

This view was perhaps not quite so new as Owen suggested. As early as 1819 one commentator, William Hazlitt, argued that Owen's supposedly new principle did not in fact originate with the New Lanark mills, but was

> as old as the royal borough of Lanark, or as the county of Lanark itself . . . as old as the "Political Justice" of Mr Godwin, as the "Oceana" of Harrington, as the "Utopia" of Sir Thomas More, as the "Republic" of Plato . . . as old as society itself.[12]

Francis Place, a friend of Owen, was of the same opinion, and thought that Owen's conviction that he had discovered something entirely new revealed a general ignorance of earlier discussions of the subject.[13] He was probably right, but then Owen never claimed to be a great scholar. His eldest son, Robert Dale, recalled that his father had never really been interested in books:

> He usually glanced over books, without mastering them; often dismissing them with some such curt remark as that "the radical errors shared by all men made books of comparatively little value". Except statistical works, of which his favourite was "Colquhoun's Resources of the

British Empire", I never remember to have seen him occupied in taking notes from any book whatever.[14]

Owen always emphasised, in fact, that his 'new view of society' was the result not so much of great academic research, but rather it arose out of his practical involvement in the workplace. In this respect he must be distinguished from the other utopian socialists under consideration here. Whereas their common inclination was to prepare for practical experimentation and social change by the teaching of fundamental principles and the publication of major theoretical works, Owen considered it essential to have practical confirmation of a theory's validity before that theory was promulgated as the truth. Such confirmation could be found, he argued, only in one's own immediate experience. For this reason one does not find any detailed investigation of history in Owen's writings, as one does in the works of the other utopians. In some respects this is a major weakness, but Owen never doubted that his own involvement with the practical problems of organising co-operative communities was much more useful than any amount of historical research. (It is interesting to note that his efforts to relate theory and practice were greatly admired by Marx and Engels, who believed that Owen's practical experience provided much valuable evidence to support socialist arguments.) One must also bear in mind that interest in the systematic analysis of historical 'laws' was more of a French preoccupation at this time (stemming particularly from Saint-Simon), and was not such a key ingredient in the thought of Owen and his British contemporaries.[15] Owen did have a broad concept of historical development, but it was a very simple one, derived from the conviction that all history up to the present had been characterised by irrationality in social affairs, and that the future would see the gradual replacement of this antiquated system by one based on complete rationality.

Whether or not one believes that the 'new view of society' was entirely original, there can be no doubt that it challenged the prevailing orthodoxy of the age, and it was in this particular sense that Owen was inclined, with some justification, to regard himself as a pioneer. At a time when it was widely believed that idleness, poverty, ignorance, and crime were necessary, unavoidable evils, evils associated with certain naturally inferior groups in society, Owen insisted that these evils were the direct consequence of particular social conditions whose victims were not to be blamed or punished; rather they should be placed in different social conditions conducive to the improvement of their characters. This basic principle, put forward in very simple terms in *A New View of Society,* is the key to almost every element in Owen's thought. It is a principle from which Owen derived his whole approach to the new science of social relations and government, and, in particular, it led him to adopt a strategy for social improvement based on gradualism and co-operation rather than upheaval and conflict.

If all members of society had their characters formed for them by external circumstances, then it was not only the behaviour of the working classes which must be understood in this way, but also the behaviour of the higher classes, the masters who dominated the system of government and economic production. The latter were inclined to regard the working classes as their enemies, and the working classes in turn regarded their masters as enemies; hence both sides might easily be led to the conclusion that conflict was inevitable. Owen, however, urged every individual to understand that *all* his fellow-men were the innocent victims of certain specific social circumstances. This meant that the working classes had a particular responsibility to avoid all attitudes of hatred towards their oppressors. He made this clear in *An Address to the Working Classes* of 1819:

> From infancy you, like others, have been made to despise and to hate those who differ from you in manners, language, and sentiments. You have been filled with all uncharitableness, and in consequence cherish feelings of anger towards your fellow-men who have been placed in opposition to your interests. Those feelings of anger must be withdrawn before any being who has your real interest at heart can place power in your hands. You must be made to know yourselves, by which means alone you can discover what other men are. You will then distinctly perceive that no rational ground for anger exists, even against those who by the errors of the

> present system have been made your greatest oppressors and your most bitter enemies. An endless multiplicity of circumstances, over which you had not the smallest control, place you where you are, and as you are. In the same manner, others of your fellow-men have been formed by circumstances, equally uncontrollable by them, to become your enemies and grievous oppressors.[16]

Owen, in accordance with his view of the historical progress of ideas, liked to refer to his own doctrine as 'the rational system of society'. This doctrine was put forward as a body of certain knowledge based on demonstrable facts, and it was in this sense that its author considered it to be rational. Irrational ideas about man and society, stemming from ignorance, superstition, and prejudice, would have to give way to rationality before social conditions could be improved. Owen's early hostility towards religion reflected his conviction that religion arose out of essentially irrational ideas. According to this view, which Owen maintained for most of his life, religion could be seen as a direct cause of human misery. In the 1830s it was customary for him to group religion together with private property and marriage as the three great evils which stood in the way of social progress. By the 1840s, however, he was willing to regard his own ideas as constituting the basis for a new 'rational religion,' a shift in outlook which was a striking manifestation of the new millenarianism characteristic of Owen's thought in its final phase of development. Some kind of religion, Owen now recognised, was the only effective means of uniting men in a moral crusade to combat unhappiness. But it would have to be a religion based not on mystery and the yearnings of the imagination, but on the highest achievements of man's intellectual capacities.

Owen was almost as fond as Fourier of providing his readers with precisely numbered lists of the major principles or laws governing human behaviour. To take an example, in *The Book of the New Moral World* the basic theory of character formation (which, from one point of view, may be seen as a single principle) was further elaborated by Owen in the form of five 'fundamental facts on which the rational system is founded' and twenty 'fundamental laws of human nature, or first principles of the science of man' (see the first chapter in part one of *The Book of the New Moral World*). Part three of this work listed thirteen 'conditions requisite for human happiness'. In part four we are presented with nine principles underlying the teachings and practice of the rational religion. Part six deals with thirty-one 'universal ideas to enable men to know how to govern aright, and how to be governed rightly', and also lists a code of twenty-five universal laws 'for the government of the human race under the rational system of society'. This attempt by Owen to attain mathematical precision should certainly not be taken too seriously today. In retrospect it seems to be as disastrous as the similar attempt made by Fourier (although the latter was led to even more ludicrous extremes in his theory of the stages of historical development, a feature which is absent from Owen's works). One can identify perfectly understandable reasons why, in an age of enormous enthusiasm for scientific classification, both Owen and Fourier thought that social science must also have its detailed systems of categorisation. But their own efforts were obviously premature, and were not at all definitive. Nor was either thinker consistent: a particular list of principles was readily modified (and might be shortened or lengthened) from work to work, and sometimes from chapter to chapter within the same work.

When examining Owen's ideas, therefore, the student must look behind the form of presentation, with its unnecessarily complicated argument. If one adopts this approach, one is led to some fairly general observations about the way in which Owen applied his 'new view of society', and developed the key principle of character formation. It is very important, especially, to recognise the strongly utilitarian elements in Owen's concept of the good life, and to appreciate how these elements grew out of the materialist philosophy on which Owen based his theories. The social environment, it was argued, shaped the character of every individual person, and in so doing the environment determined the degree of happiness or unhappiness enjoyed by that person. Yet at the same time there could be no doubt that each individual chose the attainment of happiness rather than unhappiness as his basic goal in life. Man's rational capacities and his physical senses both told him that happiness was preferable to misery, and that pleasure was always more desirable than pain. The link between materialism and utilitarianism was thus clear, since the quest for maximum happiness (utility) could only succeed through a reorganisation of material (that is, physical and institutional) conditions. It was the responsibility of government to promote the right kind of reorganisation, as recommended by those trained in the new science of society. In this respect Owen's formulation of utilitarianism was hardly distinguishable from that of Bentham. The opening of the fourth essay in *A New View of Society*, for example, is very reminiscent of Benthamite language:

> The end of government is to make the governed and the governors happy.
>
> That government, then, is the best, which in practice produces the greatest happiness to the greatest number; including those who govern, and those who obey.[17]

As has already been mentioned, Owen eventually came to regard three social institutions – religion, private property, and marriage – as the most significant environmental causes of unhappiness, and all his mature proposals to change the social environment as a means of promoting 'the greatest happiness of the greatest number' involved blueprints for alternative arrangements in these three key areas. In effect Owen, in his later works, was mounting a savage attack on the very foundations of liberal-bourgeois society, not only on the governmental and economic system, but also on the whole framework of values and morals which underpinned that system. In issue number eleven of *The New Moral World* (10 January 1835) he summed up his reasons for rejecting these three institutions:

> *Religion* destroys the *rational faculties* of the human race; *private property* creates poverty in the mass, and engenders all the sordid and meanest vices which now pervade society, and *marriage* generates jealousy, revenge, envy, hatred, deception, anger, violence, and, to complete the catalogue, prostitution and its endless crimes, the greatest evil that could befall the human race.[18]

Owen's rejection of religion and marriage was not in fact a

total rejection; rather he objected to prevailing religious and marital conventions, and wished to see them replaced by new conventions in accordance with the dictates of rational thinking. The religion he despised was that based on superstition and prejudice, and when he looked to the future, he foresaw not the end of all religion, but the emergence of a new, true religion based on truth and sentiments of benevolence. In the introduction to the very first issue of *The New Moral World* (1 November 1834) he described the new society of the future as 'the second coming of Christ', and confidently asserted that the millennium was 'about to commence'.[19] Similarly he was not advocating the complete abolition of the institution of marriage. Owen's own marriage was, by all accounts, a happy one, and so one would hardly expect him to dismiss marriage altogether as an outmoded institution. What he wanted to see was the ending of all control of marriage by the Church, and the recognition that love and affection were the only rational grounds for any marriage. If the ties of love and affection between a man and woman should happen to be broken, then divorce should be permitted, since it was clearly ridiculous to expect two people to remain man and wife in the absence of those feelings. Thus it was the 'priestly marriage' in particular, and not all forms of marriage, which Owen objected to, and which he wished to banish from the New Moral World of the future.

Owen's views on marriage were always part of a much broader critique of the family and its role in existing society. It was his hope that one day the whole notion of the individual, private, self-interested family unit would be dismissed in favour of the concept of a co-operative community of several hundred persons who in many respects would form a single family with one set of interests in common, and in which feelings of love and affection would be so universal that they would unite not simply one man, one woman, and their immediate relations, but all members of the community. Owen's proposal to get rid of private property was also linked to this radical view of the family, since the family's role as a property-holding unit did much to stimulate the sense of individual family interests which he regarded as so inimical to social progress. But perhaps even more importantly, private property was also held to be disastrous because of its economic consequences for the mass of workers in society. The system of private property was considered to be the direct cause of poverty and extreme inequality of wealth, since the competitiveness between private interests which that system involved served only to depress wages, cause unemployment, and deprive human labour of the wealth it had created. If labour was the source of all wealth, as Owen asserted, then the key function in society was the productive function rather than the ownership function; and those who produced wealth should, as far as possible, share directly in the consumption of that wealth. In addition, all men had an equal right to happiness, and this called for the satisfaction of their basic needs through the rational organisation of production and distribution throughout the whole community. The fragmentation of social interests through private property obviously made such a rational organisation impossible.

In criticising the established institutions of religion, marriage, and property, Owen was in effect criticising the whole relationship between church, state, and society as it prevailed in the early nineteenth century. Yet he did not conclude, because of this, that church and state must be overthrown. He hoped instead that those in positions of authority, especially in government, would themselves see the light and accept the doctrines of true social science, thus willingly offering themselves as the chief agents of social transformation. When, in *The New Moral World*, he identified seven possible methods of instituting the new social order, he recommended that the best way was through 'the cordial union of the great powers, or leading governments in Europe and America'.[20] This was in fact the strategy involving the least political upheaval (certainly much less, for instance, than that which would result from direct action by the workers), a criterion of which Owen himself never lost sight, but which lost him quite a lot of popular support after 1834.

The Coming of the New Moral World

> The time approaches, when, in the course of nature, the evil spirit of the world, engendered by ignorance and selfishness, will cease to exist, and when another spirit will arise, emanating from facts and experience, which

> will give a new direction to all the thoughts, feelings, and actions of men, and which will create a new character of wisdom and benevolence for the human race.[21]

All the utopian socialists placed considerable emphasis on the power of education to make men understand how society ought to be organised in order to secure human happiness and well-being. Such an emphasis grew logically out of the utopians' insistence that there must be one, and only one, demonstrably correct method of social organisation, and that this method, once discovered, could be taught to people in precisely the same way as one gave instruction in the principles of physics, chemistry, biology, or any other established science. Of all the thinkers dealt with in this book Owen was certainly the most persistent in his call for educational reform, and in many of his writings education was presented as a panacea for almost every social ill. He remained convinced that 'the best governed state will be that which shall possess the best national system of education'.[22] Nor did he ever doubt that all men would become more co-operative and sociable in their behaviour once they were shown that their own happiness was inextricably linked with the happiness of their fellow men, and that the character of every person was moulded by social conditions. Thus, for Owen, the creation of a new, perfectly moral world was first and foremost an educational task. This was a philosophy which he himself put into practice in a number of educational experiments, in particular at New Lanark in his Institution for the Formation of Character, which was opened on 1 January 1816 and quickly became 'the most famous educational establishment in the world'.[23]

Owen frequently described education as a kind of manufacturing process: 'To educate man is to manufacture a character for him . . . To know how to manufacture the human character, is to know how to remove the chief causes of the miseries of the world.'[24] He thus deliberately presented himself in the image of a social engineer who had discovered a new, operationally perfect method of producing men and women of demonstrably better physical and moral quality. The new system of education would have two essential features: it would be a community responsibility rather than a parental function (and the community in this case would be the locality, town, or village), and the system would be based on the principle of equality in the sense that the same general educational methods would be used for teaching all children irrespective of distinctions in their social backgrounds. Furthermore, on this second point, the emphasis on equality would be strengthened by ensuring that all children in a particular community were educated together as though they all belonged to a single family. (All parents should still have the right of free access to their own children, he stressed, but parents would no longer be directly involved in the process of character-formation.) As far as the content of education was concerned, the central aim must be to acquaint children with

> the outline, and much of the detail, of the whole affairs of society . . . the past history of their fellow-men, the outline of natural history, and what they have to do in the progressive scale of creation, to promote their own happiness, the happiness of their race, and the happiness, as far as practicable, of all that have life upon the earth.
>
> . . . The acquisition of true principles, of real knowledge, of the spirit of charity and love, and of the natural manners thence ensuing, will be a progress of unmixed pleasure, which will lay a solid foundation for health of body and mind, and active happiness throughout a long life of satisfied existence.[25]

Such an educational programme demanded, first and foremost, a new, enlightened teaching profession, and Owen had much to say about the enormous responsibility teachers would have in paving the way for the new moral world. The teachers themselves would have to be instructed in the rational system of society; they 'must be taught the hitherto unknown language of truth without disguise, and how to make it the undeviating habit with all their pupils'.[26]

A perfected system of education was thus considered to be essential in order to ensure that all men and women were of sound and charitable character. A second basic requirement had to be fulfilled, however, if the evils of the old type of society were to be eradicated, and this was the provision of permanent, useful employment for all fit persons. Such security of employment would not only make each individual worker happier by allowing him always to exercise his skills, but, even more significantly, it would eliminate poverty by creating an abundance of wealth and hence the material resources with which the basic needs of all persons – and not just those of the rich – could be satisfied. Owen saw that the spread of mechanisation through the application of new productive techniques was in some ways a threat to human labour, for the simple reason that the productivity of a machine was incredibly high when compared with that of the individual worker. In March 1817, in his *Report to the Committee of the Association for the Relief of the Manufacturing and Labouring Poor*, he tackled the question of how one could hope to increase the employment of human labour at a time when the advantages of mechanisation seemed to be so great. He began the *Report* by stating that in his view the chief cause of the economic depression which prevailed in Britain at that time was the depreciation of human labour resulting from the mechanisation of manufacturing. The recent war in Europe had stimulated full employment of labour in response to a huge increase in demand for manufactured goods, but with the onset of peace the demand for goods had fallen:

> The war demand for the productions of labour having ceased, markets could no longer be found for them; and the revenues of the world were inadequate to purchase that which a power so enormous in its effects did produce: a diminished demand consequently followed. When, therefore, it became necessary to contract the sources of supply, it soon proved that mechanical power was much cheaper than human labour; the former, in consequence, was continued at work, while the latter was superseded; and human labour may now be obtained at a price far less than is absolutely necessary for the subsistence of the individual in ordinary comfort.[27]

Owen went on to argue that 'the working classes have now no adequate means of contending with mechanical power', and that there were only three possible outcomes to this situation: the process of mechanisation could be reversed; or the process could be allowed to continue, thus leading to mass starvation; or, thirdly, a deliberate effort could be made to find new work for the poor and the unemployed, 'to whose labour mechanism must be rendered subservient'.[28] The first alternative was unrealistic; the second could not possibly be tolerated. It was thus the third strategy which Owen put forward as the only justifiable response to the problem of unemployment.

The *Report* outlined what Owen considered to be a thoroughly realistic proposal for providing the poor with useful work. It called for the establishment of small villages of between 500 and 1,500 persons (Owen seemed to favour a population of about 1,200). In terms of its facilities and buildings each village would be self-contained and self-sufficient. All necessary living accommodation, schoolrooms, kitchens, medical centres, workshops, and recreational areas would be provided within the confines of a simple rectangle, and a suitable area of land – between 1,000 and 1,500 acres – would surround the whole community. All adult males in the village would have work to do for the benefit of the community, whether that work be in agriculture, manufacturing, or in some other (presumably service) occupation. The responsibility for looking after children, doing housework, making clothes, and cultivating gardens would be given to the women in the community; and they would also be allowed to work in suitable manufacturing jobs, although not for more than four or five hours per day. They would take turns in working in the public kitchens, mess-rooms, and dormitories, and, when properly instructed, they might also be allowed to teach in the schools. All children above the age of three would attend school, the older ones being given a certain amount of work to do in gardening and manufacturing so that they might learn appropriate skills.

Owen did not insist upon any one particular method of establishing his proposed villages. He was willing to encourage the efforts of individual philanthropists, but also foresaw the possibility that his plan might be put into operation by the Government (either centrally or through local authorities). The area of land which each village needed could be purchased or rented. The inhabitants of each village, he argued, might reasonably be expected to repay the capital advanced on their behalf through a modest annual rental. No sensible method of creating the new system should be ruled out:

> Some may prefer one mode, some another; and it would be advantageous certainly to have the experience of the greatest variety of particular modes, in order that the plan which such diversified practice should prove to be the best might afterwards be generally adopted. It may therefore be put into execution by any parties according to their own localities and views.[29]

Three years after the publication of Owen's first major scheme for achieving full employment of human labour, a more detailed and more radical proposal was included in his famous *Report to the County of Lanark* (dated 1 May 1820). Although the language of this new *Report* still gave the impression that the author was dealing with the technicalities of poor relief, what was actually being suggested was that society must be completely reorganised on a new, rational basis according to the principle of unity and mutual co-operation. The system was to be rooted, as before, in a network of village communities. This time Owen recommended a population for each village of between 300 and 2,000, but preferably within the medium range 800-1,200. A population of 1,200 would require a land area of between 600 and 1,800 acres. The greater the importance attached to agriculture, the larger the land area would have to be. Spade husbandry would replace the plough as the chief instrument of agricultural cultivation, and this would not only lead to an increase in agricultural production (because the spade's loosening of the subsoil improved the water supply to crops), but would also create more employment opportunities for farm workers. Owen went further, and argued that the general introduction of spade husbandry was the single most effective way of assisting the unemployed. It was the one 'certain source of future permanent occupation for them', and it alone could be relied upon to supply the labouring poor 'with permanent beneficial employment for many centuries to come'.[30] Thus it can be seen that although Owen did not wish to halt the spread of mechanisation, he believed that it could be controlled, and that in agriculture the individual labourer with a spade did not have to be superseded. The process of mechanisation in manufacturing was perfectly compatible, therefore, with a substantial increase in the number of labourers employed in agriculture.

The continuing importance of agricultural employment was a central theme in the *Report to the County of Lanark*, and Owen felt justified in describing his proposed communities as 'agricultural villages' and 'associations of the cultivators of the soil'.[31] It is essential to bear this fact in mind when examining the development of Owen's thought at this time. The *Report* has generally been regarded as an expression of a new form of co-operative socialism which Owen was now pioneering, yet that co-operative socialism, it must be recognised, was motivated as much by an awareness of the significance of agricultural work as by an emphasis on the kind of modern manufacturing techniques Owen himself had been dealing with in the factories under his management. Furthermore, the small size of the proposed villages placed obvious limitations on the scale of manufacturing production, and it seems evident that Owen did not welcome the idea of huge factories employing vast numbers of workers. Indeed, it is interesting to note that a village population of 1,200 would actually have been smaller than the population of Owen's own New Lanark establishment; and it follows that a manufacturing unit of the size of New Lanark could not easily be accommodated within Owen's communitarian scheme of 1820. With this point in mind, it is surely significant, as J.F.C. Harrison has observed, that 'no attempt was made to integrate factory production on the scale of New Lanark into any Owenite community'.[32]

The issues of (a) community size and (b) the relative importance of agriculture and manufacturing also have direct bearing on Owen's theory of property. In his *Report to the County of Lanark* he took the first tentative steps in his move to dispense with private property by stressing the desirability of establishing a form of common ownership within his proposed villages. But even this suggestion was not made very explicit, and was merely hinted at in a passing comment on communitarian experiments abroad:

> But a very erroneous opinion will be formed of the proposed arrangements and the social advantages which

> they will exhibit, if it should be imagined from what has been said that they will in any respect resemble any of the present agricultural villages of Europe, or the associated communities in America, except in so far as the latter may be founded *on the principle of united labour, expenditure, and property, and equal privileges.*[33]

Owen in fact qualified this principle by allowing, once again, for a number of different methods of setting up the villages, and he obviously recognised that some methods were more likely than others to lead to the high degree of voluntary co-operation necessary if private property was to be abolished:

> The peculiar mode of governing these establishments will depend on the parties who form them.
>
> Those founded by landowners and capitalists, public companies, parishes, or counties will be under the direction of the individuals whom these powers may appoint to superintend them, and will, of course, be subject to the rules and regulations laid down by their founders.
>
> Those formed by the middle and working classes, upon a complete reciprocity of interests, should be governed by themselves, upon principles that will *prevent* divisions, opposition of interests, jealousies, or any of the common and vulgar passions which a contention for power is certain to generate.[34]

In other words legal ownership of property in a village community could assume a variety of forms, although of the alternatives Owen favoured communal ownership and that 'complete reciprocity of interests' which he hoped to stimulate among co-operative groups drawn, as he put it, from the middle and working classes. Yet Owen knew from his own experience that the role of the individual landowner or capitalist could be decisive, and on this point it is instructive to note that nine of the Owenite communities which were actually established 'were financed by a single person . . . or by a small group of proprietors'.[35]

Because Owen wished to see communal ownership of property organised on a small scale, and in villages where land rather than capital could well be the most important category of property, his views must be carefully distinguished from those of Cabet and Weitling, who were more interested in achieving a large-scale communist society, preferably a nation-wide system, and one in which new manufacturing techniques of mass production would be highly developed. The contrast between the two approaches is so fundamental that it reveals quite clearly the danger of grouping all communist theories together under one heading; and it serves to remind one, in particular, that the principle of communal ownership of property could involve either a centralised structure of power or one based on considerable decentralisation.

Owen intended his villages of unity and mutual co-operation to develop a collective provision of welfare benefits which, like the new property system, would combat the old evils of individualism and competition. 'What are the best arrangements,' he asked, 'under which these men and their families can be well and economically *lodged, fed, clothed, trained, educated, employed, and governed*?'[36] In answering this question, Owen further developed the ideas already set out in his earlier report of 1817 concerning collective community responsibility and the importance of having a good physical design for the new villages. The virtues of establishing a simple parallelogram arrangement were stressed, and there was a remarkable emphasis on matters of detail in physical planning, such as the need to do away with all courts, alleys, lanes, and streets, which were seen to be 'injurious to health, and destructive to almost all the natural comforts of human life'.[37] With the good health of the population always in mind as a chief priority, Owen described how apartments could always be kept well-ventilated and how, through a system of central heating, constant interior temperatures could be maintained. There would be no private kitchens, since they would be superseded by public facilities. And he even had something to say about the best type of clothing to be worn by the inhabitants:

> In the present case he recommends that the male children of the new villages should be clothed in a dress somewhat resembling the Roman and Highland garb, in order that the limbs may be free from ligatures, and the air may circulate over every part of the body, and that they may be trained to become strong, active, well-limbed, and healthy.

> And the females should have a well-chosen dress to secure similar important advantages.[38]

When Owen came to deal with the question of how consumer goods should be distributed, the spirit of collective responsibility once again intervened. He predicted that the new villages would produce so much, far in excess of what individuals would actually desire to consume, that 'each may be freely permitted to receive from the general store of the community whatever they may require'.[39] The surplus produce would be used mainly for exchange between different villages, the 'trading' to be based on a new paper currency taking labour time as its unit. Monetary values in the traditional sense would thus cease to exist, and with their demise one of the major sources of inequality and corruption would be eradicated.

After 1820 Owen did not depart in any fundamental ways from his basic plan for villages of unity and co-operation put forward in the *Report to the County of Lanark*. It is true that he was disillusioned by the failure of his experiment at New Harmony, Indiana (1824-9), but this certainly did not weaken his resolve to persist in his campaign for further experimentation. Indeed, his outlook became even more radical, and his opposition to religion, private property, and marriage became even more steadfast from the early 1830s onwards. In his later writings he tended to describe his proposed communities as home colonies or townships rather than villages, but this was merely a change of terminology. His original scheme for small communities was still defended in the same passionate terms, although he did raise the maximum population of each community to 2,500 (in *A Development of the Principles and Plans on Which To Establish Self-supporting Home Colonies*, 1841) and then to 3,000 (in *The Revolution in the Mind and Practice of the Human Race*, 1849). His own preference, however, seemed to be for a population of about 2,000. As the millenarian character of his work became more pronounced, the communitarian cause was presented increasingly as a kind of religious crusade. The ultimate vision was one of a network of co-operative townships covering the entire globe:

> As these Townships increase in number, unions of them, federatively united, shall be formed, in circles of ten, hundreds, thousands, &c.; until they shall extend all over Europe, and afterwards to all other parts of the world, uniting all in one great republic, with one interest.[40]

Whenever he discussed the political organisation of his proposed communities, Owen always expressed a keen interest in securing a high degree of democracy; yet at the same time he disliked certain features of the traditional liberal view of representative government. In particular, he hated the divisive role of political parties and elections, and saw no virtue in the idea of representation of large numbers of people by a much smaller group in government and parliament, given that it was almost impossible to determine how representative these institutions were at any particular point in time. His solution to this problem was what amounted to a form of direct democracy which would dispense with parties and elections, and which would involve *all* members of the community above a certain age of maturity in a general council, committee, or assembly responsible for all major decisions. In the *Report to the County of Lanark* he recommended that all associations formed by the middle and working classes acting in co-operation should govern themselves by a committee consisting of those members between the ages of, say, thirty-five and forty-five. Nearly thirty years later, in *The Revolution in the Mind and Practice of the Human Race*, he advocated a similar arrangement. All domestic affairs would be dealt with by a general council consisting of those members of the community between the ages of thirty and forty; and this council would sub-divide into a number of specialised committees responsible for particular departmental matters. For external affairs there would be a second council consisting of the more senior persons, those aged between forty and sixty. For Owen one of the great advantages of such a scheme was that every member of the community would have a share in the exercise of political power at some stage in his or her life, but for a strictly limited period of time (ten years in the case of the domestic affairs council), thus emphasising the close mutual responsibility of the rulers and the ruled. Owen regarded this as 'a real democratic government',[41] but held that it was also sufficiently 'parental' to guarantee sensible regulation of the community's affairs. 'It has the democratic perfection of numbers, and the parental perfection of unity and decision of action.'[42]

As well as being democratic, the system also had the advantage that it involved no cumbersome bureaucracy. This was not only because of the provision for direct citizen involvement and small-scale organisation, but also because, according to Owen, some of the old machinery of government and administration would no longer be necessary, since social affairs would be run much more economically and there would be no social evils for governments to deal with. In particular, crime and unemployment would be eradicated, thus making possible the abolition of courts of law, prisons, and institutions of poor relief.

Owen did have certain reservations to make about the viability of this type of direct democracy. He was always especially worried about the dangers of giving people power without the necessary education and training, and in most of his later writings on this subject he suggested that the reform of the educational system must *precede* the institution of full democracy. During the period of transition, it seems, Owen was willing to see community affairs placed in the hands of an elected leader. 'The *Elective Paternal System* is alone calculated to carry out any new and complicated system successfully in the transition-state.'[43] Owen's view of the future structure of political power was thus in one respect extremely democratic, yet, on the other hand, this democratic approach was not offered as an immediately practicable method of government. Nevertheless, it is surely noteworthy that he proved himself more willing than almost any other early socialist to recommend a combination of the principle of popular participation in decision-making with that of local self-government.

3
Charles Fourier

Life and Work

François-Marie-Charles Fourier was born just eleven months after Owen, on 7 April 1772 at Besançon. He was the son of a successful cloth merchant, but strangely enough at a very early age he seems to have developed a positive dislike of commerce. Apparently on one occasion – when he was just seven years old – his parents punished him for telling customers that they were not being given a fair deal by his father; and this prompted a conviction in his mind that business must be based on falsehood and injustice. This view was reinforced as he grew up and got to know more about the workings of the commercial system, and it eventually emerged as one of the central themes of his mature social theory.

In 1781, following his father's death, he inherited 80,000 francs. His mother wanted him to continue in his father's business, but this was the last thing that appealed to him. He preferred to concentrate on his studies at the local school, where he was already developing a strong interest in the arts and sciences. By the late 1780s his great ambition was to become a military engineer, but he soon discovered that this profession was reserved for the sons of the nobility. Disappointed, he reluctantly agreed to take the advice of his mother and uncle, and in 1789 he made his way to Lyons to serve his commercial apprenticeship.

He returned to Besançon in early 1793. In the intervening four years he had worked hard and travelled extensively, visiting the major cities of France, including Paris, and also parts of Germany and the Low Countries. He was fascinated by the cultural and social diversity of the places he saw, and also began to develop an interest in architecture. After a short break he was back in Lyons, buying cotton, rice, sugar, coffee, and other colonial produce. But Lyons now became the centre of a rising against the ruling Convention, and in the upheaval that followed Fourier lost all his property and narrowly escaped death at the hands of the Government's forces, who captured Lyons in October 1793. After a brief prison sentence he was obliged to enter the army, but on grounds of bad health he was released from duties after less than two years.

1797 found Fourier in Paris, on a mission to persuade the Government to reorganise its armed forces. But this first serious venture in the realm of social affairs met with no success, and he was soon working once again as a commercial traveller. It was an occupation which filled him with dismay, for commerce seemed to be based firmly on principles of deception and corruption. Good food was kept off the market during a time of famine in order to increase scarcity and thereby inflate prices. The price of apples in Paris was incredibly high compared to their cheapness in the country. Were these really the characteristics of a civilised society? Fourier now began gradually to develop a vision of an alternative social order. A number of journal articles appeared between 1801 and 1804. Then, in 1808, his first major work, the *Theory of the Four Movements and the General Destinies (Théorie des quatre mouvements et des destinées générales)*, was finished. Its chief purpose was to announce to the world what its author considered to be a great scientific discovery, namely, the laws of a new social science. According to Fourier, the universe consisted of four spheres of activity or movement – the social, animal, organic, and material spheres – each of which was governed by precise mathematical laws which were open to scientific investigation. So far, however, scientists had made discoveries only in the material sphere. Fourier was now offering to complete the picture, although he emphasised that this first work was no more than an introduction to the subject, one which would be followed in due course by a more extended and detailed treatment. However, this did not prevent Fourier from committing himself to an incredibly precise account of social evolution according to which history was divided into four major 'phases' and thirty-two more specific 'periods': Phase one (seven periods, total duration 5,000 years) took man from his original terrestrial paradise, through an age of violent misery, to the beginnings of civilisation (the present) and growing human co-operation. Phases two and three (eighteen periods, duration 70,000 years) would be marked by various gradations of true harmony. And phase four (seven periods, duration 5,000 years) would witness a deterioration of the human condition (phase one in reverse) culminating, after stage thirty-two, in the physical extinction of the planet earth.

When his mother died in 1812, Fourier inherited a share in the family estate and a life pension of 900 francs per annum, which helped to support him in the continuation of his studies. The political instability which bedevilled France as the Napoleonic Empire drew to a close prompted many thinkers to offer proposals for peace and stability. Saint-Simon, as was seen in chapter 1, was convinced that only he knew what steps had to be taken by the leaders of Europe's nations. Fourier, for his part, believed that the time had now come for man to turn his back on the civilised order, but, as he put it in 1818 in an introductory note added to a copy of his book, the French had decided to remain in civilisation, and the cost was 'a loss of 1,500,000 heads in battle, humiliations, and spoilations of every nature'.[1] Before 1816, in fact, Fourier's works did not really attract a single serious admirer. However, in that year a Monsieur Just Muiron wrote to Fourier, who was now residing in Belley, to express his support for the author's theories and to ask if there was anything he could do to help. A correspondence between the two men began, and in 1818 Muiron was able to stay with Fourier for some months, during which time it was agreed that Muiron and certain friends would finance the publication of the next series of writings, to be printed at Besançon. In the spring of 1821 Fourier went there to make the necessary arrangements, and in 1822 a two-volume *Treatise on Domestic-Agricultural Association (Traité de l'association domestique-agricole)* appeared. This work could have been much longer (Fourier had originally intended to issue eight volumes), but the author considered many of his theories, especially those on sexual relations, to be too unorthodox and too advanced for the public, and so he preferred to leave them in manuscript. The *Treatise* explained how mankind could begin to establish conditions of social harmony in small-scale communities (Phalanxes) organised according to the scientific principles of human association which Fourier claimed to have discovered. A fairly detailed account was given of how a trial Phalanx should be founded, and, it was argued, the plan could be put into operation at once if only a wealthy patron could be found. Over the next two years Fourier devoted much time and money to the quest for such a person. He sent copies of the *Treatise* to politicians, scientists, artists, businessmen, journalists – to men of influence in almost every conceivable profession. (Two copies were sent to Robert Owen with a letter proposing the creation of a company for an experiment in association. In reply, Owen's secretary thanked Fourier for sending the work, which Owen apparently thought admirable, and informed him that Owen was going ahead with his own communitarian schemes. For a time it seems that Fourier even considered joining Owen in Scotland.) Much to Fourier's dismay, these efforts met with almost no serious response. At first he thought that the length of the work made it unattractive to readers, but a shorter summary published in 1823 met with exactly the same negative reaction.

His funds exhausted, Fourier now decided (in March 1825) to move to Lyons, where he found employment as a cashier in a commercial establishment. The following January, however, found him back in Paris, the only place in France (indeed perhaps in the world) which he considered to be suitable for the propagation of his ideas. During 1826-7 he was employed in a modest clerical post as a book-keeper, but he then gave this up in order to complete a further abridgement of his theories, which appeared in 1829 as *The New Industrial and Societary World (Le Nouveau Monde industriel et sociétaire)*. Convinced that no further progress could be made until the editors of the major Parisian journals were persuaded to review his work, Fourier spent a great deal of time attempting to make contacts and convince journalists of the value of his enterprise. Some critics did begin to take notice of his writings, but their comments were generally disparaging and sometimes abusive. Not only the content of his books, but also his novel literary style (described as 'grotesque' by the *Revue française*[2]) were condemned as worthless. Only in one periodical, the *Mercure de France du XIXe siècle*, did a favourable review appear. It recognised *The New Industrial and Societary World* as a work of poetry, eloquence, and genius, and even found its wilder excesses of imagination acceptable:

> Even when the author may appear to us lost in imaginary space, we have doubts of our own reason quite as much as of his: we call to mind that Columbus was treated as a visionary, Galileo condemned as a heretic, and yet America did exist, the earth did turn round the sun.[3]

The *Mercure* also published an article supporting Fourier and written by Victor Considérant, a sub-lieutenant of engineers at the Metz military school (and graduate of the Ecole Polytechnique). Considérant, later to emerge as one of Fourier's leading disciples, now began to organise conferences to promote the master's teachings, and in this way a small but enthusiastic Fourierist circle gradually emerged.

The year 1829 also saw Fourier attempting to establish links with the Saint-Simonians. He rejected their movement's collectivist tendencies and religious pretensions (which he regarded as a form of theocracy), but he seems to have entertained the hope that they would be receptive to his own arguments on association. While there is some evidence that the Saint-Simonians 'borrowed' various ideas from Fourier, such as his notion of attractive industry and his concept of the emancipation of women, and while there can be no doubt that certain individual supporters of Saint-Simonism were converted to Fourierism (Jules Lechevalier and Abel Transon, for example), the Saint-Simonian leaders in general showed no interest in modifying the essential tenets of their doctrine. In any case, as an organised movement Saint-Simonism was soon forced by the intervention of the Government to put a halt to its activities. (Some of the individuals who subsequently became Fourierists clearly did so because of the ban on Saint-Simonism.) Having tried unsuccessfully to get both Robert Owen and the Saint-Simonians to adopt his teachings, Fourier published a scathing attack on both schools in 1831: *Pitfalls and Charlatanism of the Sects of Saint-Simon and Owen (Pièges et charlatanisme des sectes Saint-Simon et Owen).*

In 1832 a great step forward was achieved by the Fourierist circle: the start of a weekly journal known as the *Réforme industrielle*, which was to last for eighteen months. Initial plans were also made at this time for the founding of a trial Phalanx at Condé-sur-Vesgre, on land bordering the forest of Rambouillet. However, although the land was acquired for the Fourierists by a member of the Chamber of Deputies, Monsieur Baudet-Dulary, the funds required in order to commence the experiment were not forthcoming. Public lectures helped to spread the word, and Fourier himself was persuaded to give a number during the winter of 1833-4. Fourier then devoted himself to the preparation of what was to be his last book, *False Industry (La Fausse Industrie)*, which was published in two volumes in 1835 and 1836. In this work he made a final appeal for a patron to assist in the setting up of a Phalanx. He reiterated the theoretical justification of his proposals, responded to his critics, and declared that even a modest experiment, such as one involving a group of children (preferably young enough to be uncorrupted by civilisation) would soon lead to the desired results.

Fourier's health had been gradually getting worse since 1831, a year in which he complained of 'this new disease called cholerine, grippe, cramp, etc.'.[4] The decline became more rapid following the winter of 1836-7, and from the autumn of 1837 he was confined to bed. The previous year Victor Considérant had started a new journal, *The Phalanx (La Phalange)*, but Fourier was not well enough to take much interest in it. He died on 10 October 1837, hopeful to the end that the first Phalanx would soon be set up, revealing to the world the truth of the theories which so many people had either mocked or, perhaps even more unjustifiably, ignored. There were many attempts to create Fourierist Phalanxes after the master's death, especially in America during the 1840s, when Fourierism dominated that country's socialist movement. This was due in particular to the hard work of Albert Brisbane, who had met Fourier in 1833 and had decided at once to export the doctrine of association to America, and also Horace Greeley, converted to Fourierism by Brisbane in 1842. There are records of at least forty

American Phalanxes in the 1840s, but none of them achieved the startling success for which Fourier had hoped, and they were all of short duration.

A Philosophy of Human Passions

Of all the utopian socialists Fourier is the most difficult to write about for the simple reason that his ideas were expounded in a bewilderingly disorganised and often incoherent way. He was never too concerned with literary conventions, and even such mundane considerations as pagination, punctuation, continuity of argument, and spelling were often overlooked in his enthusiasm for originality. He used what could justifiably be described as a new kind of language, not so much a language of intellectual communication in the traditional sense – rather a language of emotional suggestion and stimulation.[5] In order to facilitate the study of Fourier's thought some attempt must be made to set out his ideas in an orderly and systematic fashion; yet he was usually disorderly and unsystematic in his working methods. There is indeed more than a touch of eccentricity about all his writings which, although at times endearing, frequently proves annoying and easily frustrates scholarly efforts to understand what he had to say.

However, of one thing at least we may be certain: if there is a key to Fourier's thought, and thereby to his complex personality as well, it is undoubtedly to be found in his philosophy of human desires or 'passions', as he preferred to call them. These passions were seen to be the motivating forces underlying all human behaviour, and Fourier identified a total of twelve such passions, divided into three categories. The first category consisted of the five sensual passions: taste, touch, sight, hearing, and smell. Secondly, there were four affective passions, four 'simple appetites of the soul' urging men towards group relationships: friendship, love, paternity or family, and corporation or ambition. In the third category were three distributive or mechanising passions – the passion for intrigue ('cabalist'), the passion for change and contrast ('alternating' or 'butterfly'), the passion for that kind of enjoyment produced through the simultaneous attainment of physical and spiritual pleasure ('composite') – whose essential function was to co-ordinate the various sensual and affective passions already listed. In addition Fourier listed a thirteenth, collective, passion: 'harmonism' or 'unityism', the inclination to relate one's own happiness to that of all other men. This inclination was formed through the combined action of the affective and distributive passions; or put another way, it could be seen as the trunk of 'the tree of passion', from which all the other individual passions stemmed like branches.[6]

Fourier was convinced that human happiness was always the result of a particular passion or group of passions being satisfied, and that, conversely, unhappiness arose when a passionate urge remained unfulfilled. The key problem, therefore, was to organise social affairs so that passions were not frustrated or repressed. At first sight this view might seem to conjure up a picture of a society in which each individual is selfishly seeking personal satisfaction without a care for anyone else. Such a way of life might indeed be the consequence if man were a purely selfish creature. But Fourier, as we have seen, believed man to be governed also by four affective passions which involved him in a perpetual quest for positive relations with others. Sensuality was never entirely absent from these relations (for example, friendship and love could often be expected to have a sexual aspect), but it was not the dominant factor. The appetites of the soul were just as important as those of the body; each had a role to play in human happiness, and the demands of both must be co-ordinated (this was the function of the three distributive or mechanising passions). Man's inherent sociability was strengthened, according to Fourier, by the mysterious harmony passion (number thirteen), a passion which could also be described as a kind of moral altruism, for it urged man to give consideration to the happiness of others.

It can thus be seen that Fourier had a fairly optimistic view of human nature in the sense that he attributed to man a variety of instinctive passions which, once harnessed in the right way, would lead to general happiness. Society, in other words, must be moulded to fit in with human nature. (This is very different from Owen's conviction that human nature was moulded by the social environment.) In order to clarify this point Fourier introduced the notion of attraction, or rather he extended the use of this term from the material world, where forces of attraction had been identified by Newton as the underlying mechanism which maintained the universe in a state of equilibrium or harmony, to the social world, where, he argued, the same basic principle of attraction, once understood and applied by man, would lead to social harmony. This view, which is very similar to Saint-Simon's belief that it would be possible to understand society in terms of the Newtonian concept of universal gravitation (see, for example, Saint-Simon's *Study on Universal Gravitation* of 1813), was normally presented by Fourier as a God-given principle which had remained unknown until he (Fourier) had discovered it at the end of the eighteenth century.

The passions were considered by Fourier to be stimulants of human action and behaviour through the natural force of attraction. True morality was accordingly seen as a kind of gravitational pull, compelling man to do certain things and develop patterns of behaviour in compliance with God's grand design. In existing society, however, man was often prevented from following these natural impluses by social conventions which set out to impose an alternative, artificial morality in the name of 'civilisation'. For Fourier the repression and suffocation of passions was one of the foremost characteristics of nineteenth-century society, and he saw this as the cause of a whole range of social, economic, political, psychological, and sexual problems. By way of illustration he pointed to the efforts made by philosophers to convince man that it was immoral to seek satisfaction of the five sensual passions – taste, touch, sight, hearing, smell:

> Have they not been declaiming for the past two thousand years about the need to moderate and change the five sensual appetites? Have they not been trying to persuade us that the diamond is a worthless stone, that gold is a base metal, that sugar and spice are abject and contemptible products, that thatched huts and plain, unvarnished nature are preferable to the palaces of kings? So it is that the moralists wish to extinguish the sensual passions . . .[7]

And, Fourier went on, philosophers also despised the four affective passions – friendship, love, paternity (family), corporation (ambition):

> How often they have vociferated against ambition. According to them one should only desire mediocre

> and unremunerative positions; if a job provides an income of a hundred thousand livres, you should only accept ten thousand to satisfy morality. The moralists are even more ridiculous in their opinions about love; they wish love to be ruled by constancy and fidelity, which are so incompatible with the designs of nature and so wearisome to both sexes that no creature remains constant when he enjoys complete liberty.[8]

As for the three distributive passions (and the vital thirteenth passion, harmonism), philosophers seemed to be completely ignorant of their existence.

In Fourier's writings this theory of human passions served as the basis for a critical analysis of the vices of so-called civilised society, vices which included, most importantly, widespread poverty, disease, ignorance, economic exploitation and oppression, appalling working conditions, the subjection and degradation of women, marital conflict, and sexual anxiety. These evils arose, according to Fourier, because the totality of human passions could never be satisfied in civilisation. More specifically, because the existence of the three distributive passions (serving to co-ordinate all the other passions) and the supremely important harmony passion was not even recognised, civilisation was in fact founded on an ignorance of some crucial human needs, and therefore this particular type of social order could not possibly secure true and universal happiness.

This analysis of civilisation's shortcomings is in some ways very similar to that of Jean-Jacques Rousseau (1712-78). Both he and Fourier believed that man's natural propensities were stifled by modern social conditions, and both envisaged the possibility of man regaining his natural identity through a process of social transformation. One commentator, Mark Poster, sees a very close link between the ideas of the two men, and suggests that 'Fourier's utopian thought may be viewed as a detailed program designed to realise Rousseau's wistful dreams'.[9] Frank E. Manuel makes a similar point: 'The spirit of Jean-Jacques, the enemy of the *philosophes*, hovers over every line that Fourier ever wrote'.[10] Yet in his discussions of civilisation's vices Fourier was, if anything, much more uncompromising than Rousseau had been; for whereas Rousseau accepted that man had lost his original liberty, in the sense of complete self-direction, for ever and must seek a new kind of freedom through devotion to the 'general will' of society, Fourier insisted that man *could* achieve total self-direction and liberation of all his passions. In order to achieve this goal, however, the foundations of civilisation's economic and political system must be reconstructed, and this demanded the demolition of that body of values and beliefs which supported the system, namely, liberalism. From Fourier's point of view this was an inappropriate designation for a doctrine which he believed to be a major obstacle to the achievement of true liberty. Yet he realised that many people were seduced by its promise of progress, and he accordingly regarded it as particularly important to reveal liberalism's inadequacies and failings before attempting to recruit support for his own alternative vision of a free society.

Economic liberalism was condemned by Fourier on a number of grounds. He could see in the system only a chaotic anarchy which formed the basis for mechanisms of production, consumption, distribution, and circulation (or exchange) which were in the interests of only a small minority in society – the unproductive or 'parasitic' classes.[11] The system of production involved the virtual enslavement of large numbers of workers, including women and children, who toiled for long hours, often in appalling conditions, for extremely low wages. At the same time many people could find no work at all, and thus had to suffer the terrible consequences of unnecessary unemployment. The division of labour was also illogical and inefficient. It was often based on the family unit ('the most inefficient and most wasteful of groups: the family system often requires one hundred workers to do a job which might be done by a single individual under societary management'[12]), and usually allotted tasks with no particular reference to workers' physical and mental capacities:

> In our societies the healthiest men may often be seen performing tasks fit for four-year-old girls. In the streets of our large cities you can see strong men busy shelling peas, peeling vegetables, and cutting paper to make candy wrappers. . . .
>
> Is it not also common in all our cities to see strong young men of twenty who spend their days armed with

> napkins and carrying about cups of coffee and glasses of lemonade? . . .
>
> This strange division of labour is characteristic of all work in the incoherent order. Should a man of twenty spend his time crouched in an office and scrivening?[13]

As far as consumption was concerned, Fourier was struck by the fact that under economic liberalism the workers who actually produced society's wealth received such low wages that they could never afford to purchase very much themselves. In effect, therefore, the most important consumers were the unproductive and affluent minority, the financiers, businessmen, and property owners. The producers were condemned to 'spend the best years of their lives trying to earn enough so as not to die of starvation in old age', and in the end they were confronted by the inescapable fact that 'an excess of work brings them to the same poverty as does excessive idleness'.[14]

Turning to the distribution process, Fourier emphasised that it was rooted in the principle of competition, and this inevitably meant that workers' wages, no matter how low they were to start with, would be reduced even further as enterprises sought to cut their costs. (Here we see an anticipation of Marx's theory of the increasing impoverishment of workers under industrial capitalism.)

The fourth pillar of economic liberalism was commerce, that system of circulation or exchange dominated by merchants. Fourier's own experience of commercial life led him to regard merchants as the most despicable of all unproductive groups, and he spared them no criticism. Commerce could be defined, he suggested, as 'a mode of exchange in which the seller has the right to defraud with inpunity and to determine by himself without arbitration the profit which he ought to receive'.[15] For merchants liberalism meant that they could do whatever they wanted with their commodities, irrespective of any consumer interests:

> They have the right to take their goods out of circulation, to hide them, and even to burn them as was done more than once by the Dutch East India Company which publicly burned supplies of cinnamon in order to raise its price. What it did with cinnamon it would have

> done with wheat, had it not feared the anger of the common people; it would have burned a part of its wheat, or allowed it to rot, in order to sell the rest at four times its value. Well! Every day on the docks can you not see people throwing into the sea supplies of grain that a merchant has allowed to rot while waiting for a rise in prices. I have myself presided as a clerk over these foul operations, and one day I jettisoned twenty thousand quintals of rice which could have been sold before it rotted for a fair profit, had the owner been less greedy for gain.[16]

When Fourier came to put forward his criticisms of political liberalism, he did so mainly in terms of the failure of liberal constitutionalism to eradicate any of the major economic evils associated with modern civilisation. One could grant people a whole series of legally protected rights and freedoms in the political sphere, he argued, but for the vast majority of men this would not make the slightest bit of difference to their standard of living or their economic situation. Furthermore, no liberal constitution ever attempted to protect the right of all men to work or their right to enjoy a pleasurable existence. Fraternity, also, although it was generally upheld as an important political goal, was conspicuous by its absence from existing society. 'How', Fourier asked, 'could there be any fraternity between sybarites steeped in refinements and our coarse, hungry peasants who are covered with rags and often with vermin and who carry contagious diseases like typhus, mange, plica and other such fruits of civilised poverty?'[17] Fourier had no time, either, for such liberal principles as ministerial responsibility, the separation of powers, or balanced government. Concepts like this were 'devoid of sense'.[18] They were supposed to limit the powers of the political authorities, but in reality they did no such thing. Supposedly responsible governments were able to pursue their own self-interest, and the good of the vast majority of people in society was invariably overlooked.

Political liberalism was thus considered by Fourier to be a system of authoritarian rule by the strongest, who made the laws to their own advantage. Underlying this system was the concept of the supremacy of the male sex. Women were everywhere regarded as inferior beings, and suffered all kinds of oppression and degradation in work, education, sexual relations, the family, and government and administration. This oppression was sanctioned by the legal system (the laws were of course made by men) and also by the teachings of the Christian Church. So important did Fourier consider the situation of women to be as an indicator of the quality of life in society that he put forward the following proposition as a general law of social development:

> *Social progress and changes of period are brought about by virtue of the progress of women towards liberty, and social retrogression occurs as a result of a diminution in the liberty of women.*
>
> Other events influence these political changes; but there is no cause which produces social progress or decline as rapidly as a change in the condition of women. I have already said that the simple adoption of closed harems would speedily turn us into Barbarians, and the mere opening of the harems would enable the Barbarians to advance to Civilisation. In summary, *the extension of the privileges of women is the fundamental cause of all social progress.*[19]

Working-class women, Fourier argued, suffered the worst oppression, since their only means of subsistence was marriage or prostitution, and in fact there was not much to choose between the two, since for most women marriage meant nothing more than a kind of conjugal slavery – both sexual and economic. In Fourier's view, neither men nor women gained much satisfaction from the traditional family structure and the institution of permanent, monogomous marriage, since both sexes had natural inclinations towards polygamy and unrestrained amorous relationships. It followed that the vast majority of men and women would also seek extra-marital sexual pleasure, usually in secret. Adultery, however, was only one of sixteen marital misfortunes identified by Fourier. He also listed: the chance of unhappiness ('Is there any game of chance more frightful than an exclusive and indissoluble tie on which you stake a lifetime's happiness or unhappiness?'); disparity of tastes and personalities; complications (i.e. 'incidents which quickly dispel the charm of married life'); expense; vigilance (the husband must keep an eye on the running of the household); montony; discord in education; finding jobs for sons and dowries for daughters; the departure of children; disappointing in-laws; incorrect or misleading information ('about events transpiring before or during marriage, about one's wife or her parents'); sterility ('Children come in torrents to people who are unable to feed them, but rich families seem particularly subject to sterility'); false paternity; widowhood; orphanhood.[20] Thus Fourier, who remained a bachelor all his life, condemned the 'unnatural' family system on which modern bourgeois society was based. Convinced of the futility of trying to achieve social transformation from above through governmental action (this distinguishes Fourier from Saint-Simon and Owen, both of whom frequently appealed directly to governments to introduce their measures), he insisted that the only realistic strategy was to lay the foundations for a new world at the level of inter-personal and small-group relationships.

Liberation through Love

Like Owen, Fourier believed that the way to transform society was to found numerous small associations. Fourier called these associations 'Phalanxes', and recommended that they should each have a population of between 1,500 and 1,800. The Phalanx would be housed in a communal building, the Phalanstery or Palace of Harmony, which would be a kind of miniature town incorporating all the necessary residential blocks, workshops, assembly halls, recreational facilities, and so on, with a network of street-galleries providing rapid communication between the various areas. In communities of this modest size, inhabiting a single edifice (based on the same kind of rectangular shape recommended by Owen), it should be possible to create a new kind of family spirit, rooted in the harmony of the passions. Fourier condemned the numerous communitarian experiments of his day which rejected the family as the key unit of association, and which tried to replace it by a larger, more comprehensive social bond. Owenism came in for the most severe criticism in this respect, and the failure of Owenite schemes was explained by Fourier in terms of this elementary error of social science.

In 1822, in his *Treatise on Domestic-Agricultural Association* (a work now known by the title of its second edition: *Theory of Universal Unity*), Fourier gave a detailed account of how a trial Phalanx might be established. He began by pointing to the advantage of having a wealthy patron such as a monarch, an aristocrat or businessman, or a powerful company. Under these circumstances a site should be chosen with an area of at least one square league or some six million square *toises* (the *toise* was equivalent to about two yards). Economic necessity demanded that the site should have a good stream of water, a forest, and the land should be hilly and suitable for a full range of crops. Then, Fourier continued:

> The 1,500 or 1,600 people brought together will be in a state of graduated inequality as to wealth, age, personality, and theoretical and practical knowledge. The group should be as varied as possible; for the greater the variety in the passions and faculties of the members, the easier it will be to harmonise them in a limited amount of time....
>
> At the very outset an evaluation should be made of the capital deposited as shares in the enterprise: land, material, flocks, tools, etc. This matter is one of the first to be dealt with; and ... all these deposits of material will be represented by transferable shares in the association....
>
> A great difficulty to be overcome in the trial Phalanx will be the formation of transcendent or collective bonds among the series before the end of the warm season. Before winter comes a passionate union must be established between the members; they must be made to feel a sense of collective and individual devotion to the Phalanx; and above all a perfect harmony must be established concerning the division of profits among the three elements: *Capital, Labour* and *Talent*....
>
> Let us discuss the composition of the trial Phalanx. At least seven-eighths of its members should be people involved in farming or industry. The remainder will consist of capitalists, savants and artists....The Phalanx

> would be poorly graduated and difficult to balance if, among its capitalists, there were several worth 100,000 francs and several worth 50,000 francs without any of intermediate wealth. In such circumstances, one should try to find men with fortunes of 60, 70, 80 and 90,000 francs. The most precisely graduated Phalanx yields the highest degree of social harmony and the greatest profits.[21]

The 'alternative society' represented by the Phalanx would have two particularly important characteristics: it would be geared towards satisfying productive work, and it would be loving or 'amorous' ('*amoureux*') in the sense that interpersonal relations would be characterised by strong emotional ties and positive feelings of care and sympathy. Members of the Phalanx would love work, and they would love each other. In both respects the primary goal of the association should be to apply the principle of attraction. In the case of work it was a matter of organising human labour in accordance with the system of 'industrial attraction', and this system was seen by Fourier to have the following essential requirements: The traditional wage-system would be abolished, and every worker would receive a dividend (out of the Phalanx's annual profits) reflecting his contribution in terms of capital, labour or talent.[22] At the same time everyone would be guaranteed useful employment and a 'social minimum', that is, a basic income sufficient for present and future needs. Work sessions would be varied about eight times each day 'because a man cannot remain enthusiastic about his job for more than an hour and a half or two when he is performing an agricultural or manufacturing task', and work would be done by 'groups of friends who have gathered together spontaneously and who are stimulated and intrigued by active rivalries'.[23] Everyone would work in clean and pleasant surroundings, and through an extensive division of labour all persons would be given jobs to do in accordance with their abilities and qualifications. No distinction would be made in this respect between men, women and children. Every fit person, male or female, young or old, would be able to find something useful and fulfilling to do. The development of everyone's industrial talents would be one of the chief goals of the Phalanx's educational system, and in this way, Fourier believed, one would be able to ensure that all workers had a chance to choose tasks in accordance with their physical and mental capacities.

In order for work to be completely fulfilling, Fourier maintained, it must satisfy man's basic passionate drives, and this meant, in particular, that the demands of the three supremely important distributive or mechanising passions must be met. The cabalist passion stimulated man's taste for intrigue, and in the work situation it was therefore vitally important to to have competitive, although still friendly, rivalries or 'discords', possibly arising out of the desire to win prizes or earn the praise of other members of the Phalanx. The alternating or butterfly passion led man to seek change and contrast, and this made it necessary to give every worker a variety of tasks to perform rather than one particular job which would soon become boring and tedious. (New methods of industrial training were devised by Fourier which, he believed, would endow every child in the Phalanx with some thirty or so vocational interests.) The composite passion, that 'state of inebriation and rapture which is produced by the simultaneous gratification of the soul and the body',[24] would find satisfaction in the Phalanx through the emergence of a spirit of fellowship and common identity (gratifying the soul) as workers were brought together in a shared enthusiasm for a particular task or tasks, and through a developing pride in perfect workmanship and special excellence (gratifying the senses). On the basis of this concept of human labour Fourier went on to argue that a passionate attraction towards a particular productive activity would unite a number of workers in a 'passionate industrial series', each series promoting a common enthusiasm among its members for its own special occupation, thus creating the foundations for a real social solidarity and sense of association in the Phalanx. A series should consist of at least twenty-one persons, and every series should be sub-divided into groups (at least three per series), each group representing one special variety of the general passion motivating the series. A series of flower-growers, for example, might be sub-divided into a range of groups, each cultivating one particular variety of flower. In that case the general passion for growing flowers could be said to consist of several subtle nuances: the passion for growing tulips, the passion for growing daffodils, and so on. Friendly rivalries and contrasts of taste within each group and between the groups composing a series would do no harm, but would, on the contrary, produce a neatly graduated social order as aesthetically delightful as a spectrum of colours or the notes of a musical scale. The butterfly passion would be perfectly satisfied.

True association in the Phalanx would come about through the meshing together of at least fifty passionate industrial series. Every member of the Phalanx would move from group to group and from series to series every hour or two, undertaking a variety of occupational tasks so as to avoid monotony and maintain enthusiasm. Fourier estimated that such a system could operate at its simplest level with 400 people, but a 'compound association' demanded at least 400 series and a population of between 1,500 and 1,600. In a trial Phalanx the following criteria should be taken into account when deciding what industrial series ought to be organised:

> 1. The care of animals is preferable to work with plants and vegetables because it will keep the series permanently occupied during the winter's idleness.
> 2. Work with plants and vegetables is preferable to work in manufactures because it has more intrinsic attraction.
> 3. Kitchen work should be stressed because it is permanent, with no periods of seasonal idleness. It serves to initiate workers in industrial attraction. Since it is linked both to production and consumption, it is the kind of work best suited to maintain the cabalistic spirit.
> 4. In factory work attraction is more important than profit-making. The policy of the founders of the Phalanx should be to create a fine balance among the passions and not to speculate on profits poorly related to the societary system. Profits are a hoax when they distract us from our goal, which is the speedy activation of the mechanism of industrial attraction.[25]

It can be seen, then, that Fourier wished to keep manufacturing industry in a subordinate position within the Phalanx's economic system. Convinced that such work could never be very attractive, he insisted that it should on no account take up more than a quarter of a man's labour-time. In any case, much less would be needed for manufacturing in the Phalanx for the simple reason that the quality and durability of manufactured goods would be greatly improved, and hence products such as clothing and furniture would last for a very long time, perhaps for ever, and would not need to be replaced as frequently as in the civilised order.

Fourier certainly did not believe that one could eliminate unattractive work completely. He frequently referred to the problem of drudgery in the Phalanx, and acknowledged that certain basically repugnant tasks would still have to be performed even under conditions of perfect harmony. However, he was confident that he had found ways of overcoming these difficulties. Drudgery tended to arise when a job had to be done by one individual working in isolation: for example, driving a coach, delivering the mail, sentry duty. In the Phalanx there would be a special series of 'Drudges', persons who would be given extra financial incentives and social privileges (such as very good food) to undertake such tasks, and whose activities would be the occasion for regular social festivities. In addition children between the ages of four and fifteen and a half could be relied upon to take care of the most repulsive jobs in the Phalanx – such as cleaning sewers, tending dung heaps, supervising slaughter-houses, hunting reptiles, maintaining roads – because at that age most boys and some girls 'love to wallow in the mire and play with dirty things. They are unruly, peevish, scurrilous and overbearing, and they will brave any storm or peril simply for the pleasure of wreaking havoc'.[26] Fourier thus envisaged several 'Little Hordes' of children getting a great deal of pleasure out of these occupations which most adults would regard as thoroughly loathsome.

Fourier also recognised that certain manual jobs might fail to attract some members of the Phalanx not so much because of the nature of the work involved, but because traditionally manual work was associated with the lower classes, with men and women whose manners and behaviour were regarded with distaste by the wealthier, better educated, and more refined groups in society. One of the main educational priorities, therefore, must be to eliminate the 'coarseness' of the common people, and to cultivate in all persons good manners and common standards of speech and civility. This could best be achieved by providing all children with the same communal education, and by eliminating any significant parental involvement in the upbringing of children. If these conditions were met, then everyone would feel free to choose work solely on the basis of its inherent industrial attraction.

In the Phalanx labour would be one of two vital sources of human joy and fulfilment. The other important source would be love, in both its physical and sentimental-emotional senses. In Fourier's view, no person deprived of love could be happy. Everyone had certain basic amorous needs, and these must be met: 'Without love life would lose its charm. When love has gone man can only vegetate and seek distractions or illusions to hide the emptiness of his soul.'[27] Fourier accordingly felt impelled to write a great deal on the subject of man's sexual and sentimental needs, and how society should be organised so as to allow for their fullest possible satisfaction. Most of his thoughts on these matters were recorded in manuscript form in notebooks which he either did not wish to publish, or which he knew could not be published in his lifetime because of their frequently explicit reference to sexual activities. However, a collection of these manuscripts, *The New Amorous World*, was finally published (in French) in 1967, thus making it much easier for students to analyse this previously neglected aspect of Fourier's grand utopian design.[28]

Man's natural inclination, Fourier observed, was to enter into amorous relationships with a wide variety of partners. Yet according to the prevailing notion of civilised marriage, man should remain monogamous. In fact this meant that most husbands and wives simply pretended to remain faithful to each other while actually taking every opportunity to enjoy extra-marital affairs. Unmarried persons, according to the code of civilised morality, should not enjoy the pleasures of love at all, yet in reality such persons rarely refused amorous fulfilment if it were available. In the Phalanx polygamy would be recognised as a perfectly acceptable and healthy practice for all adults, male or female – healthy from the point of view of the individual, who would gain pleasure from it, and also from the point of view of the community as a whole, which would quickly develop strong ties among its members as they became physically and emotionally linked together. In this way a process of increasing inter-personal harmonisation would take place. Every adult would possess the right to have several lovers, and it was perfectly in order that some of these liaisons should be prompted by purely sexual desire (whether of an orthodox or more unusual kind). Recognising that 'the sexual needs of men and women can become just as urgent as their need for food',[29] Fourier argued that all adults were entitled to a 'sexual minimum', a certain basic level of physical satisfaction, just as they were all entitled to the 'social minimum' income. A Court of Love would ensure that there were regular opportunities for all members of the Phalanx to engage in amorous activities, which would include orgies for the release of sexual tension. An additional incentive would be provided by the Phalanx's residential arrangements: everyone capable of enjoying amorous relations (which in fact meant almost all persons except for the very young and the very old) would live on the same floor of the Phalanstery. Children would be housed in separate quarters, and so would not disturb the adults in their quest for love. Many amorous ties would thus be formed in a more or less spontaneous manner, and for those men and women whose basic needs were still not satisfied special groups of attractive partners would make their services available. The members of these groups would be performing what for them was a very enjoyable and quite voluntary function. One could always rely on human nature to provide an adequate number of such persons in every Phalanx.

The initial aim must be to guarantee to all adults the gratification of their basic sexual appetites and hence the elimination of their anxieties and frustrations. Only then, in Fourier's view, would it be possible for the more noble and sentimental dimension of human love to play its true role. In civilisation physical desire was often confused with sentiment. Thus marriage was commonly presented as a noble relationship, yet the real motivation behind it was predominantly sexual. Such ambiguities could not arise in the Phalanx: everyone would be sexually satisfied, and so truly sentimental ties would be more distinctive and would be valued for what they could offer as a complement to sensuality.

These radical ideas on the liberation of amorous instinct

are clearly central to Fourier's image of a future society based on the principles of harmony. Yet, it must be emphasised again, the vast majority of people interested in Fourier's doctrine in the early nineteenth century were unaware of these ideas, and even those Fourierist movements which sought to give practical expression to the doctrine had to do so in ignorance of the master's detailed teachings on the nature of love and its social requirements. Strictly speaking, therefore, all Fourierist movements at this time were bound to be inadequate and unsuccessful. There is surely some irony here, for Fourier, who always liked to be precise in his practical recommendations, was able to publish only very general and vague pronouncements on the one issue which concerned him more than any other. The architect of utopia was convinced that he had designed the perfect community, but knew that he could never reveal the most impressive parts of the plan. In one respect this was perhaps fortunate; for it is doubtful whether Fourier's most startling views on amorous liberation would have been acceptable to more than a small minority of those followers who were inspired by the other elements of his thought, such as his ideas on the transformation of work and the economic system. Fourier himself believed that his new morality of love must be introduced very gradually, and that it might take several years of re-education to prepare people for such an immense change. (In addition, Fourier pointed to more mundane considerations: there was the suggestion, for example, that venereal diseases would have to be eradicated before the principle of freedom of amorous relations could be put into practice.) Indeed, it might be the case that the founder members of the Phalanx would never be very receptive to these ideas, and that only with the next generation of persons – that is, those born in the Phalanx and hence with no direct experience of civilisation's way of life – would it be possible to make an effective start.

If liberated work and love were destined to become the twin pillars of harmony, what impact, we must now ask, would this have on the structure and distribution of power in society? This crucially important political question was frequently neglected by Fourier (such neglect is not uncommon in utopian thought), and only occasionally did he deal with it explicitly. The issue lends itself to discussion in two stages: the first concerns the internal political arrangements of each Phalanx; the second relates to political relationships between Phalanxes, and the consequent use of the Phalanx as an instrument of national and international government.

The internal political arrangements of each Phalanx would be characterised by what Fourier regarded as a perfectly justifiable and functionally necessary hierarchy of authority. To begin with, a newly established Phalanx would have to be organised and administered according to the laws of passionate attraction. Certain individuals would have to be given responsibility for performing this task, and the best thing to do at the outset would be to establish a regency or council composed of those shareholders in the community (male or female) 'who had made the greatest contribution in terms of capital and industrial or scientific knowledge'.[30] A small minority of people, singled out by their wealth and expertise, would thus be vitally important in promoting the initial development of the Phalanx, and in supervising the foundation of the industrial series and the establishment of the right conditions for communal life and love. The regency would be responsible for issuing shares in the Phalanx (backed by its holdings of land, buildings, flocks, and other assets) to all persons who had made some initial investment or had contributed goods or materials. The regency would also administer the guaranteed minimum income scheme and distribute the Phalanx's annual profits.[31] Such arrangements, it must be emphasised, would not eliminate all distinctions of wealth, since there would still be those who owned more property than others (Fourier always considered equal ownership in the sense of communism to be totally unacceptable), and some people would earn more than others because they contributed more to the community in terms of capital, labour, or knowledge. In every Phalanx, therefore, there would inevitably be a certain amount of inequality. This would be acceptable, Fourier believed, for a number of reasons. Since everyone would be guaranteed a minimum standard of living (provided at the community's expense), there would no longer be any absolute poverty; in allocating the Phalanx's annual profits, the greatest share (five-twelfths) would go to reward manual labour; and because everyone would have something tangible to gain from the Phalanx's economic success through the profit-sharing scheme, relationships between different social ranks would be characterised by a new spirit of co-operation:

> In Harmony individual interests are combined and everyone is an associate, if only in the sense that he receives a share in the portion of the Phalanx's income which is allotted to labour. Everyone wants to see the whole community prosper because everyone's interests are harmed when the territory suffers the slightest damage. The mere fact that the members of the Phalanx are partners, and not wage-earners, gives them a personal interest in each other's welfare.[32]

The organisation of work would be supervised by a supreme industrial council, the Areopagus, consisting of one senior member from each industrial series. The Areopagus would be an advisory body, issuing recommendations but exercising no coercive power:

> Its opinions and decisions are subordinated to the wishes of attraction, and each series remains free to make decisions concerning its own industrial interests. Thus the Areopagus cannot order that the mowing or harvesting be done; it can only declare that a certain time is propitious according to the available meteorological or agronomic data; thereupon each series acts according to its wishes. But its wishes can scarcely differ from those of the Areopagus whose opinion is held in high esteem.[33]

In order to facilitate the co-ordination of the work intentions of the various series in the Phalanx (without co-ordination confusion would obviously result, made worse by the fact that each member of the Phalanx was encouraged to make frequent moves from one job to another) an Exchange would be established, holding general meetings each evening at which everyone in the Phalanx would assemble to make arrangements for the following day's work (and indeed for amorous and gastronomic activities as well). The leaders of all the series and their constituent groups, who would be leaders by virtue of their personal qualities and industrial talents, would take the initiative in proposing work schedules to their colleagues, who would then approve or reject these proposals by majority vote. Conflicts between series and between groups (for example, two series or groups with overlapping membership might wish to meet the following day at the same time) would necessitate careful negotiation, but in the end, Fourier believed, a detailed plan of work would be agreed. Harmonians, once they got used to this unusual method of taking decisions, should be able to conclude all the necessary business within half an hour.

The point has already been made that Fourier did not expect his views on love and sexuality to be applied in their entirety in the earliest stages of the Phalanx's existence. At first, therefore, the Exchange might well be the only institution in the Phalanx concerned with the organisation and planning of personal relationships. However, *The New Amorous World* presents us with a remarkably vivid picture of how these relationships could be much more systematically ordered in a well established community whose ties with civilisation have been broken, and whose members are therefore more likely to accept a totally new set of rules governing their amorous activities. The rules would in fact be fairly complicated, and the need to ensure adherence to them would demand the establishment of appropriate institutions of government and administration. These institutions would not be coercive, but they would embody such a high degree of social authority that one would not expect many people to disregard them. Once again hierarchy would be the dominant characteristic. A Court of Love would be responsible for bringing members of the Phalanx together according to their particular desires, inclinations, and personal characteristics in a wide range of assemblies, festivals, and orgies. The Court would have its own skilled priesthood (divided into various grades: matrons, fairies, fakirs, genies, confessors, and so on), and its dignitaries would supervise the setting up of a number of amorous groups or corporations. Young men and women between the ages of fifteen and a half and twenty, for example, would be divided into two major corporations: the Vestalate (two-thirds of the members would be female) would consist of persons wishing to remain chaste until the age of eighteen or nineteen; the Damselate (two-thirds of the members would be male) would be willing to lose their virginity at an earlier age, but would do so in accordance with a rule of fidelity to their lovers. (This rule could apparently be relaxed: Fourier, believing that no normal couple could remain faithful for a period of four or five years, did not want anyone to be expelled from the Damselate until he or she had committed either seven infidelities or three infidelities plus one inconstancy.) For adults over the age of twenty there would be a further set of carefully defined groups catering for every conceivable taste and idiosyncrasy.

In the fully developed Phalanx the amorous institutions recommended by Fourier (and described by him with such obvious delight) would become the focus of attention for a kind of spiritual regeneration, a deeply emotional fervour which could be seen in some respects as a social religion. Such a view was never put forward in any coherent fashion by Fourier himself, and therefore certain reservations must be made when using the idea of a social religion in this context; but the writings which deal with the rule of love in a truly harmonious society, in particular *The New Amorous World*, frequently give the impression that Fourier foresaw the eventual emergence of the passion of love as a new religious bond. For example, the Court of Love, as was mentioned above, would be organised very much along the lines of a priesthood, and many of its activities would be ritualistic and geared towards the stimulation of feelings of fellowship and communal well-being. Certain officers of the Court of Love, the confessors, would be particularly important in the arrangement of amorous relationships, since it would be their responsibility to collect intimate declarations (confessions) from individuals concerning their past experiences and present needs; and on the basis of this information a complicated match-making process would take place, with new relationships being organised by the confessors in a thoroughly scientific fashion, using algebraic formulae and complicated systems for classifying personality types. Just as this notion of confession has fairly clear religious connotations, so also does Fourier's suggestion that in every community an 'angelic group' will be the object of public adoration. This couple, a man and a woman of extraordinary physical beauty, will stimulate the desires and passions of all other adults in the Phalanx; and in a spirit of amorous philanthropy they will bestow their sexual favours on twenty or thirty selected individuals, while the couple themselves will postpone their own physical consummation until after they have satisfied everyone else (Fourier estimates that this will take two or three months). Such a perfect union of one man and one woman, Fourier argued, would surely inspire feelings of religious veneration in their partners, and the favours bestowed by the couple would be 'a balm of saintliness, a token of amorous concord, of religious unity and of the absorption of human jealousies in the spirit of God'.[34]

On the subject of Fourier's views on religion and its social function the point must be made that although he frequently acknowledged God to be the creator of all that exists, and the moving spirit behind the laws of harmony in the world, he never expressed much interest in the idea of God being worshipped directly within some kind of orthodox theistic religion. Occasionally he recommended that the members of a Phalanx should gather together to sing hymns or bow down to God in a demonstration of collective humility, but this was as far as he went in his support of traditional rites. He was generally unsympathetic towards Christianity (although he became more accommodating towards the end of his life), and nowhere in his writings do we encounter the view which appealed to Saint-Simon, Cabet, and Weitling, that a new, reformed Christianity could be established as the spiritual basis of future society. This is not really surprising, since it is difficult to see how Fourier's views on sex could ever be reconciled with Christian morality. Strangely enough, in the late 1820s and 1830s it was the Saint-Simonians rather than the Fourierists who were regarded as the advocates *par excellence* of sexual permissiveness. In fact Fourier's ideas were much bolder and, in moral terms, much more revolutionary. Since his major writings on this subject were not published, however, the public were bound to remain ignorant of these matters.

The typical Phalanx, as we have seen, would be a community of 1,500 to 1,800 persons. It follows that for an entire nation such as France to be organised in accordance with the requirements of harmony, thousands of Phalanxes would have to be established. Fourier was confident that this would happen. Indeed he went even further, insisting that one day the entire population of the globe would be incorporated in a network of some 600,000 Phalanxes. In view of the problems which Fourier encountered in attempting to set up even a single trial Phalanx, it is difficult to regard his plans for world transformation as anything more than an exercise in pure fantasy or science fiction. This does not mean to say, however, that his ideas on the gradual spread of Phalanxes and the consequent relations between Phalanxes were entirely useless. On the contrary, he had some very reasonable and practical things to say on these subjects, things which must be very carefully distinguished from the much more imaginative speculation which he was inclined to introduce into his writings. Fourier certainly recognised that in the short- and medium-term the extension of the Phalanx system would be a slow process. Only in the far distant future could one hope to achieve the transformation of the entire globe and the establishment of universal harmony. Fourier was here thinking of a period which might conceivably be as long as 70,000 years, his estimate of the duration of mankind's harmonic phase.[35]

In the meantime more urgent problems would have to be faced. The movement towards social harmony was bound to be very gradual. It would probably begin with a single trial Phalanx, and this would present immediate difficulties concerning the Phalanx's relations with the outside world. The 'social vipers' of civilisation must not be allowed to destroy this first experiment in harmonious living, and hence the Phalanx would be compelled 'to withdraw itself from all passionate or spiritual relations with its neighbours'.[36] The creation of more Phalanxes in the same part of the country as the first would alter the situation, since this would make it possible for a number of communities to establish direct links with one another, and to enter into schemes of mutual assistance. Provincial and regional administration could be set up to co-ordinate such schemes. In the sphere of economic production large-scale operations, either in agriculture or manufacturing, would almost certainly emerge only after the establishment of a combined network of several Phalanxes. (Fourier's own preference, of course, was for agriculture.) Such a network would also be necessary for the purpose of direct trade between Phalanxes (trade, that is, without the involvement of parasitic merchants). One could not expect all Phalanxes to be self-sufficient, although the initial trial communities might have to be so as to avoid contamination through contact with the civilised order.

Once a substantial number of Phalanxes had been founded over a fairly large geographical area, perhaps over the territory of an entire nation, it would be possible to organise huge industrial armies consisting of up to half a million volunteers (male and female) who would undertake great engineering projects and technological campaigns. Whereas civilisation assembled armies of destruction, harmony would abolish these and utilise in their place legions of construction and productivity. Warriors armed with weapons of war would be replaced by industrial athletes equipped with tools and scientific knowledge. The organisation of these new armies was the one significant function which Fourier seemed willing to reserve for national administrations. Eventually, as conditions of harmony came to be established in more and more countries, it ought to be possible to form even larger, international armies (of several million members) which would co-operate in even more dramatic industrial projects:

> For instance, the combined order will undertake the conquest of the great Sahara desert. It will be attacked at various points by ten or twenty million workers if necessary. Men will transport earth, cultivate the soil and plant trees everywhere. Finally they will succeed in rendering the land moist and the sand firm; the desert will give way to fertile soil. Navigable canals will be made in areas where we are now unable to dig irrigation ditches, and great ships will sail not only across isthmuses like those of Suez and Panama, but even in the interior of continents, as from the Caspian Sea to the seas of Azov and Aral and the Persian Gulf. Ships will sail from Quebec to the five great lakes, and from the sea to all the great lakes whose length equals a quarter of their distance from the sea.
>
> In every empire the diverse legions of men and women will be divided into several armies, and these armies will join with those of neighbouring empires. In the combined order no task will be undertaken by a single army; at

> least three will work together at the same time in order to create rivalry and emulation. If the sandy wastes of Gascony are to be covered with earth, the job will be done by three armies: one French, one Spanish and one English. In return France will send armies to Spain and England to help with their tasks. Thus all the empires of the globe will be mixed.[37]

It can thus be seen that although Fourier always wished to retain the small-scale Phalanx as the basic unit of social organisation in the age of harmony, he nevertheless expected a great deal of economic interchange and co-operation to take place between these units. Such interchange and co-operation would also have to characterise love relationships, since amorous desires could never be confined within the walls of a single Phalanstery. In each Phalanx the Court of Love would usually be willing to give a warm welcome to visitors from other Phalanxes and indeed other nations. The confessors would be available to assist these visitors in their quest for suitable partners. Occasionally, however, those wandering from place to place in search of love might find themselves engaged in a kind of amorous warfare as a Phalanx decided to defend itself against the 'adventurers'. This warfare would not be violent, but would be purely strategic and positional (as in chess). However, prisoners could be taken, and in order to gain their freedom they would have to meet certain negotiated demands involving, for example, the surrender of precious stones and the granting of sexual favours. The industrial armies, too, would help to forge amorous links between members of different Phalanxes, for in all their campaigns there would be regular breaks for sessions of love (an excellent way of attracting recruits, Fourier thought). The troops would always be accompanied on their missions by groups of desirable men and women, from the virginal Vestalate to the sexually expert Bacchants and Bacchantes, who between them would be able to provide every kind of physical and emotional satisfaction.

In discussing future governmental arrangements Fourier had very little to say about the fate of monarchies, parliaments, judiciaries, bureaucracies, and the other institutions normally associated with bourgeois politics. Whereas Saint-Simon devoted an enormous amount of attention to this question, and was always concerned with such immediate, practical issues as parliamentary reform and the establishment of constitutional monarchy, Fourier preferred to concentrate on what he considered to be more important matters. This makes much of his political argument extremely unsatisfactory, since he never really tackled the very basic question of how Phalanxes could spread and survive in the face of, say, a hostile monarchy or parliament, or opposition political parties. His descriptions of how Phalanxes would operate allowed no clear role for any conventional political institutions, and, as was mentioned earlier, central government would have very little to do apart from organising industrial armies. One inevitably wonders, therefore, whether Fourier seriously believed that normally powerful institutions would willingly agree to be relegated to an almost insignificant position. As far as France was concerned, it does seem that Fourier accepted the continuation of the monarchy as inevitable, and he argued that an intelligent monarch might well decide to take the initiative in promoting the first trial Phalanx. Just as Saint-Simon, after the demise of Napoleon, hoped that the French King would become the nation's first industrial, so Fourier invited the King to offer his services as the first Harmonian. Neither appeal was heeded.

4
The Saint-Simonians

The Disciples and Their Work

As was made clear in chapter 1, during his lifetime Saint-Simon never achieved the public recognition for which he was hoping. It was not until the second quarter of the century that his ideas began to exert any significant measure of influence, and this was due largely to the efforts of those disciples who immediately after their master's death resolved to devote themselves to the cause of social reconstruction which he had pioneered. At first these disciples did not constitute a properly organised group; they were merely a collection of young intellectuals – many of them had been students at the Ecole Polytechnique – who shared a common social philosophy rooted in the same enthusiasm for science, industry, and the arts which had inspired Saint-Simon. They came together to found a new journal which Saint-Simon had been planning shortly before be died: *The Producer (Le Producteur),* the first issue of which appeared at the beginning of October 1825 and included contributions by Antoine Cerclet (the general editor), Saint-Amand Bazard, Auguste Comte[1], Barthélemy-Prosper Enfantin, Olinde Rodrigues, and Pierre-Isidore Rouen. *The Producer* suffered a setback in November 1826 when it had to be suspended because of lack of funds; but before long the financial difficulties were overcome, and through the medium of public lectures and published writings a systematic exposition of Saint-Simon's doctrine was undertaken. The guiding forces behind this exposition were Bazard and Enfantin, whose forceful personalities now began to exert a decisive influence over the disciples' activities. Bazard, born in 1791, became an active revolutionary conspirator following the Bourbon Restoration of 1815. He helped to found the French Carbonari, and in 1822 took part in the Belfort plot. Enfantin, the illegitimate son of a Paris banker, was born in 1796. He began to train as an engineer at the Ecole Polytechnique, but chose to leave to help defend Paris against the allies in 1814. He subsequently travelled throughout Europe, visiting Germany, the Netherlands, and Russia, before returning to Paris, where he began to participate in the activities of secret societies. During 1828 and 1829, mainly due to the talents of these two men, the teachings of the disciples – who now regarded themselves as a Saint-Simonian 'School' – aroused widespread interest, and their ideas began to reach a large audience for the first time, not only in France, but also in neighbouring countries. A weekly publication, *The Organiser (L'Organisateur),* founded in July 1829 by Laurent de l'Ardèche, devoted itself exclusively to the propagation of the doctrine and succeeded in attracting many new supporters to the movement.

In the course of their exposition the Saint-Simonians introduced many of their own views, with the result that the doctrine that finally emerged was significantly different from that of their master. It is this fact, above all, which entitles the disciples to separate treatment in this present analysis. Their contribution to modern thought was very distinctive – certainly more so than that made by the disciples of Owen and Fourier – and can in no way be regarded simply as an elaboration of Saint-Simon's doctrine, even though they themselves often declared that to be the case. Especially important was their critique of the existing economic system, and in particular the institution of private property. This critique was much more radical than that contained in the writings of Saint-Simon, and is justifiably regarded as extremely collectivist in character. The chief architects of this new system were undoubtedly Bazard and Enfantin.

The disciples also introduced into their exposition, very tentatively at first, a theory of female emancipation which was not present in Saint-Simon's works. This modification was largely due to the influence of Enfantin. It was also mainly due to his efforts that at the end of 1829 the School was formally transformed into a 'Church', with himself and Bazard as 'Supreme Fathers' of the Saint-Simonian 'Family' (by election). This change was made, it was stated, in recognition of the religious character of Saint-Simon's teachings. A number of disciples and associates did not approve and left the group. Among them was Auguste Comte, whose links with the Saint-Simonians had always been tenuous, and who now proceeded to found a rival 'positivist' school in Paris, the main purpose of which was to promote the development of a science of society or 'sociology', to use the term later invented by Comte. In subsequent years he went to great lengths to dissociate himself from the doctrine of Saint-Simon and his followers; but the fact remains that his positivist theories owed a great deal to the influence of Saint-Simon's ideas on the possibility of constructing a 'positive science of man' or 'social physiology'.[2]

The loss of support resulting from the formation of the new Church at the end of 1829 did not seriously hinder the success of Saint-Simonism, and by July 1830, when revolution broke out in France, it had established itself as one of the country's most important social and political movements. In a number of respects the July Revolution represented the fulfilment of Saint-Simonian prophecies. During the last ten years of his life Saint-Simon had issued numerous warnings to the Bourbons, declaring that unless the monarchy dissociated itself from the feudal aristocracy and embraced the principles of industrialism, its downfall was inevitable. When the downfall of the Bourbons came in July 1830, the Saint-Simonian doctrine was inevitably taken much more seriously than ever before. Inspired by success, the Church mounted a major effort to spread the Saint-Simonian gospel through educational 'missions' sent from Paris to various parts of France and neighbouring countries, including Belgium, Germany, and England, where they received a considerable amount of support from two of their most fervent admirers, John Stuart Mill and Thomas Carlyle. Progress was made in another direction, too, with the conversion to Saint-Simonism of Pierre Leroux, editor of *Le Globe*, one of the most important Paris newspapers, which Leroux helped to found in 1824. In November 1830 the paper announced its support for Saint-Simonism, and the following August it formally adopted the sub-title 'Journal of the Saint-Simonian Religion'. It is also interesting to note that in the issue of 2 February 1832 the word *'socialisme'* was used, in an article by H. Joncières, to describe the new system of social organisation advocated by the Saint-Simonians.[3]

These propaganda efforts soon produced remarkable results. By mid-1831 some 40,000 persons had joined the sect.[4] Among them were many of France's most eminent intellectuals, including such important theorists as Cabet, Reynaud, Buchez, Pecqueur, Blanqui, and Louis Blanc. The doctrine was also very popular among the literary and artistic community, whose members were greatly impressed by the Saint-Simonian conception of the artist's role in society. Such major writers as Maxime du Camp, Renouvier, Renan, Sainte-Beuve, Lamennais, Georges Sand, and Béranger, and the composers Berlioz, Liszt, and Félicien David were attracted to the new religion. And Saint-Simonism was also the main inspiration behind the Young German school of literature which flourished during the early 1830s (with Heinrich Heine as one of its most active members), and which soon succeeded in arousing widespread enthusiasm for the Saint-Simonian doctrine among German radicals.

So rapidly did the Church's influence spread that in February 1832 one of the chief Saint-Simonians, Charles Duveyrier, felt assured enough to predict that 'within the next few years the whole of France will be Saint-Simonian'.[5] Since 1830, in fact, the Saint-Simonian leadership, under the supervision of Bazard and Enfantin, had been confidently drawing up a detailed strategy for the last stage in their rise to power, which they had no doubt could be accomplished quickly and without violence. Louis Blanc, who was for a time associated with the movement, has left an evocative picture of this stage of Saint-Simonian development:

> They proceeded to plan the establishment of great workshops and manufactories; they admitted adherents from among the proletary classes; the children of a number of these were adopted into the society with solemn forms. The capital and the provinces were next ambitiously partitioned out among them, and St. Simonianism framed its own map of France; the two supreme fathers

> assumed the title of popes, an appelation which was at once a daring plagiarism and a betrayal of the proud ambition at work within; in short, the question was no longer the collecting together of a select body of choice men to form a respectable synagogue, but how to constitute a powerful force, of the progressive numbers of which the *Globe*, every morning, published the emphatic and imposing census. This new turn and tendency of things gave birth to illusions of an almost incredible description. The chiefs ventured to direct their eyes towards the Tuileries: Louis Philippe was summoned by letter, to give place to Messieurs Bazard and Enfantin. St. Simonianism, which was at first but a school, then a family, now started as a government, and a government destined to supersede the authority of catholicism.[6]

Such assurance was soon to be shaken; for just as the Saint-Simonian movement appeared to be going from strength to strength, its very existence was seriously threatened by a dispute which arose among its members concerning the status of women and the whole question of relations between the sexes. By the end of 1831 Enfantin was making an overt attempt to steer the movement towards advocacy of a much freer form of relations than was sanctioned by orthodox Christian doctrine. It was a move which achieved little besides the loss of a considerable amount of support, both within the Church's hierarchy and among the general public. Many leading members, including Bazard, Rodrigues, and Leroux, withdrew from the movement and proceeded to mount an attack on Enfantin and his followers. (Bazard died prematurely in 1832, and the anti-Enfantin group thus lost its most gifted spokesman.) After such a serious split within its ranks, the Church totally lost its sense of direction. Enfantin, now the sole Supreme Father of the Family, attempted to restore its vitality, but he faced severe opposition from the Government of Louis Philippe, which was now becoming extremely suspicious of the sect's philosophy and frightened of its potential influence, probably because of the workers' revolt in Lyons in 1831, in which some of the Saint-Simonians were known to have been involved. So the Government first of all initiated a prosecution against its leaders (in April 1832), and then declared it to be an illegal association (August 1832). After a trial at the Assize Court, Enfantin, Duveyrier, and Michel Chevalier (formerly co-editor of *Le Globe*) were each sentenced to a year's imprisonment for offences against public order and morality. The Saint-Simonian religion thus found itself reduced to impotence. Its dissolution on 15 December 1832 by the Supreme Father, shortly before he was taken to prison, was a mere formality. A few members, led by Emile Barrault, attempted to maintain the sect's religious vigour with a journey to Constantinople in search of the 'Woman Messiah'. But even they soon became disillusioned, and their faith in a mystical regeneration of mankind quickly disintegrated.

The French Government was now confident that the spread of Saint-Simonism would quickly abate, and in one sense this hope was fulfilled, for the most important phase of Saint-Simonian theorising had indeed now come to an end. But the ideas associated with Saint-Simonism continued to exert a strong influence throughout France after 1832. The first collected edition of Saint-Simon's writings, prepared by Olinde Rodrigues and published in 1832,[7] received widespread attention; and it did at least enable the public to study the original social doctrine of Saint-Simon, freed from the more controversial theories introduced by Enfantin. The Government could at least find some cause for satisfaction in this, since Rodrigues' book made it quite clear that Saint-Simon had never sanctioned the new moral code advocated by Enfantin and his followers.

The appeal of Saint-Simonism broadened during the 1830s and 1840s with the emergence of doctrines of socialism and communism as the basis for organised workers' movements in Paris. Numerous thinkers assimilated Saint-Simonian ideas in the French capital at this time, including, most importantly, Proudhon, Weitling, Marx, and Engels. At the same time, however, many prominent ex-Saint-Simonians were coming to regard the new workers' socialist and communist movements as too revolutionary, and they declared their intention to work for peaceful change within the existing social framework. One such man was Enfantin, who, together with a group of loyal supporters, entered new careers in industry in order to help promote the creation of large-scale enterprises such as Saint-Simon had advocated in his writings on industrialism. They regarded the construction of railways and the organisation of credit facilities to be especially important, and devoted themselves to these tasks with an almost maniacal enthusiasm. (Ironically enough, they thus contributed to the rapid expansion of that capitalist system against which many of their former colleagues were now fighting.) They were guided in their work by an ambitious plan for industrial development outlined by Michel Chevalier in *Le Globe* during February 1832 under the title *Exposition of the Mediterranean System (Exposition du système de la Méditerranée)*. This plan proposed nothing less than the creation of a 'universal association' of the peoples of Europe and the Orient through a comprehensive network of railways, rivers, and canals, the finance for which would be provided by new industrial banks. These ideas, which were subsequently elaborated by Chevalier in numerous writings and also in his lectures at the Collège de France (where he was made Professor of Political Economy in 1840), inspired many of his colleagues, and in particular Emile and Isaac Pereire, who soon emerged as two of Europe's most able bankers and entrepreneurs. During the 1830s and '40s, together with associates such as Henri Fournel, Léon and Edmond Talabot, and Enfantin, they pioneered the construction of railways in France and other countries, including Switzerland, Austria, Hungary, Spain, Italy, and Russia. Later, under the Second Empire of Napoleon III (1852-70), himself an enthusiastic admirer of Saint-Simon, they founded the Crédit Mobilier bank – capitalised at sixty million francs – which did much to foster economic expansion and industrialisation in France, and which in subsequent years served as a model for new commercial banks in the majority of continental countries.

The Second Empire also witnessed the realisation of another major Saint-Simonian enterprise: the Suez Canal, advocated by Chevalier in 1832 as an essential part of the Mediterranean system. The first positive steps towards the realisation of the project were taken in 1846 when Enfantin founded a study group for the Suez canal project (*Société d'études pour le canal de Suez*); and it was the preparatory work done by this society which made it possible for de Lesseps to embark on the actual construction of the canal in 1854.

Finally, the Anglo-French free trade treaty of 1869 also deserves to be included in the list of major Saint-Simonian achievements, since its chief architect on the French side was Chevalier, who had been a passionate advocate of free trade since his association with the original Saint-Simonian movement forty years earlier.

By the end of the Second Empire most of the original group of disciples, including Enfantin, were dead, and the last remnants of the movement they had founded were rapidly withering away. By any standards its achievements had been impressive. In the space of fifty years it had provided an impetus for the development of philosophical and sociological positivism, socialist thought in all its varieties, the ideology of industrialism, and secular religious thinking – in short, as Durkheim was later to write, for 'all the great intellectual currents produced during the nineteenth century'.[8]

Beyond Positivism

'Let no one seek to master Saint-Simonian literature. The Saint-Simonians were a numerous company of men, and of young men at that, who talked and preached incessantly, and who seem to have printed all that they said. Anyone who allows himself to be sucked into this whirlpool will never emerge again.'[9] Alexander Gray is perhaps guilty of some exaggeration in this statement, but his point about the size of the Saint-Simonian literature is true enough. It is indeed a daunting task to have to present a concise summary of the disciples' thought. Furthermore, their ideas were constantly developing; new elements were regularly added, and principles once expounded with great passion were dispensed with as circumstances altered. And if that does not cause enough complications, it must also be recognised that within the Saint-Simonian movement a wide range of individual opinions were voiced which in some ways make it impossible to speak of a single, integrated theory.

The Saint-Simonians made their own most systematic attempt to present a coherent body of ideas in their *Exposition of the Doctrine of Saint-Simon (Doctrine de Saint-Simon. Exposition),* a series of public lectures extending over two years (1828-9 and 1829-30) and under the overall supervision of Bazard, although the content of each lecture was always prepared beforehand on a collective basis. The title is misleading, for it implies that the aim was merely to summarise the thought of Saint-Simon, whereas in actual fact entirely new lines of argument were developed. Particularly important was the disciples' rejection of positive science as a fruitful method of social analysis. As was made clear in the second section of chapter 1, Saint-Simon sought to establish a new science of society firmly rooted in the systematic observation of social phenomena. In this sense he could be described as a positivist. The disciples, however, believed that positivism had already had its day. Its great achievement had been to disprove all theories based on essentially supernatural or metaphysical principles by showing that such theories had no empirical basis. Positivism could not in itself offer any alternative social theories, though, since the empirical observation of phenomena merely furnished a number of facts without any clear or necessary relationship between them. Such a relationship between facts (a crucial ingredient in the formulation of a social theory) could be established only through the intuitive understanding of genius:

> The common opinion is that the human mind, when observing a large number of facts, passes successively from one to another and proceeds thus uninterruptedly from particular facts to the general fact, to the law which links them. That would be to say that the conception, the discovery of this law, would be the consequence, the logical result of the last observed fact. There has been no example of such a course in the history of human discoveries. Certainly the facts surrounding us constitute the circumstances exterior to man which inspire an idea of co-ordination. But between this idea and the occasional fact that has taken place, there is no immediate contact. Rather there exists a gap that cannot be overcome by any method, and which genius alone can span.[10]

It was thus the task of the genius to produce a theoretical conception linking a range of empirically observed social facts, a conception which the observer – the scientist – could then seek to verify through an examination of society's historical development. The great achievement of Saint-Simon, so his disciples argued, had been to apply his own genius to the problem of explaining the nature and causes of social change. In this respect Saint-Simon was seen as 'an eminently sympathetic man, a poet before being a scientist'.[11]

In their emphasis on the role of genius the Saint-Simonians were articulating a concept that was provoking widespread debate in literary, political, and even medical circles at this time, especially in France. The man of genius – previously denied a clearly defined role in social and political affairs – was beginning to lay claim to a position of intellectual supremacy, supported in this claim by numerous poets, authors, and scientists. (The growing enthusiasm for phrenology in the early nineteenth century – that is, the study of the conformation of the skull, and the attempt to explain genius by reference to the skull's physiological characteristics – bears witness to the widespread belief that the causes of genius could be identified by medical investigation.) It is with some justification that Theodore Zeldin regards the French utopians as responsible for the introduction of the idea of genius into politics,[12] and there can be no doubt that the influence of the Saint-Simonians was particularly important in this respect.

In identifying what they considered to be the limitations of positivism, the Saint-Simonians were in effect mounting an attack on the ideas of Comte and his followers. Comte – 'the student of Saint-Simon', as the disciples called him – was at first associated with the Saint-Simonian movement, but decided to depart when it became clear that the religious aspects of the doctrine were assuming more and more importance. What the disciples found totally unacceptable in Comte's teachings was the view that 'there is no religious future for mankind', a claim based on the argument that since all known sciences had passed through three developmental stages (the theological, the metaphysical, and, finally, the positive stage), 'it should be the same with the science of social phenomena', and that accordingly 'the social future would be entirely extricated from theology'.[13] According to the Saint-Simonians, this attempt by Comte to formulate a scientific law governing the evolution of human knowledge – the law of the three states or stages, as it became known – could not be derived from the writings of the master, Henri Saint-Simon, since he had stated quite clearly, most notably in his *New Christianity*, that mankind *did* have a religious future, a statement which Comte was apparently quite happy to disregard. But even more importantly, the Saint-Simonians claimed that the inadequacies of Comte's conception of history were highlighted by their own, alternative theory, one which was demonstrably true, and which could be seen to be faithful to the ideas of Saint-Simon himself.

The foundation of the Saint-Simonian theory was a distinction between 'organic' and 'critical' phases in the historical development of the western, civilised world. The past could be divided into

> organic epochs in each of which a social order is developed, incomplete since it is not yet universal, provisional since it is not yet peaceful; and into critical epochs in which the former order is criticised, attacked, and destroyed; epochs which extend up to the moment when a new principle of order is revealed to the world.[14]

Here we see repeated Saint-Simon's contrast between, on the one hand, ages of social organisation in which there is a generally accepted code of morals, ideas, and beliefs; and, on the other hand, ages of social disorganisation in which there is a critical rejection of the prevailing code, and a consequent loss of social unity and order. In organic epochs, it is emphasised by the disciples, there is always a dominant religion embodying the shared world-view which has gained acceptance. In critical epochs, however, religious authority is lost, and a philosophy of doubt and uncertainty rules until a new religion emerges to put an end to the chaos, and to lead man into the next organic epoch. In organic epochs social relations are characterised by association, that is, a union established for a certain, clearly defined purpose. Western history reveals the gradual extension of the sphere of association from the family to the city, to the nation, and then to an international union (through the Catholic Church). In critical epochs, by contrast, antagonism replaces association as the primary characteristic of social relations. Such antagonism may involve conflict between the members of a family, between different families, between social classes, between cities, or between nations. In past history the seeds of antagonism have been present in all forms of association. This is why the Saint-Simonians insist that every organic epoch so far has been provisional. Similarly, previous forms of association must be regarded as incomplete because they have all been partial rather than universal, although the widening of the sphere of association is undoubtedly moving towards eventual universality and the end of antagonism.

The application of this theory led the Saint-Simonians to identify four major epochs of history, two of them organic and two of them critical. In so doing they followed Saint-Simon's own analysis quite closely,[15] although they added many of their own observations and new points of interpretation. The first organic epoch was marked by the ascendancy of Greek and Roman polytheism. The first critical epoch, involving the rejection of polytheism, began with the early Greek philosophers and lasted until the preaching of the Christian Gospels. The second organic epoch saw the triumph of Catholicism and the rise of feudal society; and this was followed by a second critical and increasingly irreligious epoch, inaugurated by Luther, and already three centuries old by the early 1800s. This most recent period of upheaval and disorder was destined to pave the way into a new organic epoch, the third and (for the Saint-Simonians) the final stage of organisation, in which, contrary to Comte's predictions, a new religion would arise to restore social stability.[16] The first two organic epochs could be seen as two stages in the progress of association and the decline of antagonism. In the first stage cities (which in an even earlier period had been created out of the union of a number of families) were united to form nations ('nation' in this context meant an area of common rule). During the Middle Ages, in the second stage, a Catholic confederation based on common belief provided a framework for international unity. It followed that a universal union, embracing the entire globe, could be expected to emerge as the next stage in the progress of association. Antagonism, in the form of war, had dominated the two critical epochs, but the nature of war had been completely transformed. At first it had been a method of achieving nothing more than violent destruction; but it then became linked to the acquisition of territory, and later to the winning of commercial advantages and the gaining of wealth. The purpose of war thus became synonymous with the goals of economic activity – industry. In future peaceful industrial techniques would become so efficient and so productive that war itself would no longer be necessary to achieve economic goals. Furthermore, as the sphere of association widened, a process actually stimulated by the experience of antagonism, society became more integrated and its constituent parts more interdependent, thus making war increasingly difficult. In a truly universal association, precisely because it would be a single, perfectly integrated unit, war would actually be impossible.

For the Saint-Simonians the declining historical importance of war was only one particular manifestation of a more general shift in the role of physical force in social relations which took place as the boundaries of association were extended. The exercise of force by certain individuals or groups over others – the exploitation of man by man – had been a permanent feature of every known society; but it had become steadily less significant as societies had grown in size and geared themselves increasingly towards the exercise of power over the natural world through industry – the exploitation of nature by man. When the disciples referred to the exploitation of man by man, they had in mind, in particular, a perpetual struggle between social classes which, they argued, had always characterised civilisation's development since ancient times. In its earliest phase this class struggle was institutionalised through slavery, a system which involved the exploitation of man's whole being – material, intellectual, and moral:

> The slave is placed outside mankind; he belongs to his master like the land, the cattle, and the stock. The slave is property the same as they; he has no recognised right, not even that of living. The master can dispose of his days, can mutilate him at will, and can use him for whatever function he decides. The slave is not only condemned to misery and physical suffering, but also to intellectual

> and moral brutalisation. He has no name, no family, no property, and no religious existence. In short, he can never lay claim to the acquisition of any of the benefits that have been denied him, or even come nearer to them.[17]

At first, then, the relationship of master to slave was one of complete control and domination. In the course of time slaves won certain rights, and occasionally an individual slave might have the opportunity to gain his freedom. In the Roman republics the class of plebeians was exploited by the patrician class, but the plebeian was undoubtedly better off than the slave, and in fact achieved his emancipation before the latter. It was the rise of Christianity, with its concept of a single brotherhood of all mankind, which set in motion the events leading to the downfall of classical civilisation, and the ending of both slavery and plebeianism.

The exploitation of man by man continued under the feudal system in the distinction between masters and serfs, but the nature of this exploitation was now becoming less severe as a result of the impact of Christianity. The serf enjoyed some very important privileges, and in the realm of spiritual affairs he was actually treated as the equal of his master:

> The serf was no longer the direct property of the master as the slave had been. He was bound only to the sod, and could not be separated from it. He received a part of the fruits of his labour; he had a family; his existence was protected by civil law and, even better, by religious law. The moral life of the slave had nothing in common with that of his master. Lord and serf had the same God, the same belief, and received the same religious instruction. The same spiritual assistance was given them by the ministers of the altars. The soul of the serf was no less precious in the eyes of the Church than that of the baron. It was even more so, for according to the Gospels the poor were the chosen of God. And finally, the serf's family was hallowed like the lord's.[18]

The antagonism between master and serf gradually declined as the serf gained successive liberties, and came to an end completely with the serf's full emancipation from the soil. The exploitation of man by man now assumed the form of domination of the proletarian wage earner by a new class of masters: the propertied employers. This domination was not as severe as that involved in slavery or serfdom, but it was still a matter of fundamental inequality in social relations:

> In such a state of affairs, the worker appears as the direct descendent of the slave and the serf. His person is free; he is no longer bound to the soil; but that is all he has gained. And in this state of legal emancipation he can exist only under the conditions imposed upon him by a class small in numbers, namely the class of those men who have been invested through legislation, the daughter of conquest, with the monopoly of riches, which is to say, with the capacity to dispose at their will, even in idleness, of the instruments of work.[19]

In this new form of social domination the managers of industry played an important role, but one which was also ambiguous, since although they assisted in the exploitation of the workers, they were themselves subject to a certain degree of exploitation by the property owners. This concept of an intermediate managerial class is not to be found at all in the writings of Saint-Simon, but was given considerable emphasis by the disciples.

The Saint-Simonians regarded the laws governing the inheritance of property as the chief obstacle to any further weakening of the forces of antagonism in nineteenth-century society. In fact they shared Saint-Simon's view, that the constitution of property was the foundation of all social orders, and no new social order could be established without an appropriate change in the constitution of property. They disagreed with Saint-Simon, however, when it came to recommending specific changes in property law, for they concluded that *all* forms of hereditary succession in rights of property ownership were unacceptable, since inheritance perpetuated the capacity to exploit one's fellow man. Such exploitation would not end until the whole concept of inheritance of property was eradicated, and the best utilisation of property was determined for the whole of society by modern methods of economic analysis.

The possibility of putting an end to antagonism in human affairs was thus recognised, and the alternative – peaceful, universal association – was offered as the guiding principle for future social development. Industry, although it was based in the early nineteenth century on antagonism, actually contained within it the seeds of a future movement towards association, for it made it possible for man to shift the focus of his physical power in the direction of the exploitation of the natural world. New techniques of industrial production provided man with a thoroughly efficient means of improving the material conditions of life, a means, furthermore, which was bound to lead to a steady growth in benefits as the level of human co-operation for the specific purpose of exploiting nature increased. The benefits could be maximised only through maximum social co-operation.

Towards Universal Association

The Saint-Simonians were never interested in setting up small associations or isolated experimental communities. Their mission, they argued, was to serve the whole of humanity and achieve the transformation of all nations, forming them into a single society or family of which they were merely the constituent parts. They therefore mocked the Owenites and other movements which set out to establish a new way of life for a few hundred people in 'an unknown valley in Scotland' or 'a wild river-bank in America'.[20] In their view such a localised, piecemeal approach could justifiably be condemned as utopian (in the sense of being thoroughly unrealistic). The goal must be nothing less than 'universal association'.[21] Paris, regarded as the centre of civilisation, was considered to be the perfect base from which to mount numerous missions to the major cities of France, to other European countries, and, later, to the other continents of the world. Saint-Simon himself had not been interested in communitarianism, and his disciples never doubted the validity of his view that the chief priority must be to promote a change in the organisation of French society as a whole. This was the indispensable first step towards the gradual transformation of Europe and the world, a process to be based on French leadership and the example France would provide in the third and final organic epoch.

The form of social organisation recommended by the Saint-Simonians – and the one which they considered to be an inevitable consequence of historical development – was one based on the three key characteristics of unity, order, and hierarchy. The need for unity and order, they asserted, was demonstrated by man's experience in previous organic and critical periods of history. Organic periods, in which a development of association in social relations occurred, were phases characterised by progress and harmony. This was due directly to the unity of belief and orderliness of social organisation which dominated those epochs. In the critical ages, by contrast, unity and order disappeared, and the result was social upheaval, violence, and antagonism. It followed that a future change from antagonism to association, from an essentially critical age to a new organic phase, would demand the restoration of unity and order. It also demanded the third of the three key characteristics listed above: hierarchy. This is a crucial concept, and is quite distinctively Saint-Simonian. It is not to be found in the works of any of the other utopian socialists (including Saint-Simon), and its meaning must be grasped if one is to fully understand the disciples' view of the role of authority in society. Furthermore, the emphasis on hierarchy raises some obviously important questions concerning the Saint-Simonians' whole approach to the subject of equality. In particular, it would seem reasonable to ask how, if at all, the notions of hierarchy and equality may be reconciled, given that the Saint-Simonians are here being studied as socialists (and socialism, after all, is normally held to involve some degree of egalitarianism).

When they were dealing with the issue of hierarchy in future society, the Saint-Simonians often introduced the formulation, 'ranking according to ability, reward according to work'. This was the so-called 'law of peaceful labour', as Abel Transon called it in one of his sermons.[22] The *Globe* newspaper adopted a similar wording as its motto in January 1831: 'from each according to his ability, to each ability according to its work'. In order to understand the origins of this principle, it has to be realised that according to Saint-Simonian theory, the unity and order of each organic epoch arose primarily out of the success of a hierarchical system of social relations, a system involving the leadership and co-ordination of society by specific groups able to command general respect and obedience. In such periods 'it may be observed from every point on the social circumference how all minds and deeds are directed sympathetically toward a centre of affection'.[23] This sympathy was motivated primarily by religious sentiment: by Greek and Roman polytheism in the first organic epoch, by Catholicism in the second, and the third organic epoch would witness the triumph of the Saint-Simonian religion. In each of the first two organic epochs the necessary religious sentiment was stimulated by the teachings of a priesthood organised hierarchically within itself, and standing in a hierarchical relationship to the rest of society. Future society would also require a priesthood, a priesthood expounding Saint-Simonian teachings just as their predecessors had taught the principles of polytheism and Catholicism. The first implication of the idea of ranking in terms of ability, therefore, was that a spiritual hierarchy must be established in society on the basis of the ability of persons to perform the function of the priesthood and to exercise religious authority. The Catholic Church already offered an example of how such a system of ranking might operate, but in the second organic epoch the significance of Catholicism's meritocratic hierarchy was weakened because it was not accompanied by a similar arrangement in politics. Temporal power under feudalism was in fact based on hereditary privilege instead of any technical capacity, and as long as the Church recognised the distinction between temporal and spiritual power, this political supremacy of the privileged was thereby given religious sanction. In future society ability would also determine the hierarchy of temporal power. This would be possible because it would be generally recognised that temporal functions were clearly directed towards specific technical goals, and that some people were therefore better qualified than others to exercise those functions:

> If the earth were today the appanage of the industrialist on the basis of personal ability, as it was that of the warrior by hereditary right, one would understand how a peaceful society could adopt a principle in use in a military society, because, as in the case of feudalism, there would exist a union of men having a common goal:

> in short, there would be a society. And the counts and barons of industry, organised hierarchically according to merit, would be the natural judges of the material interests of that society, as the lords in the Middle Ages were the natural judges of the military society.[24]

Like Saint-Simon, the disciples considered 'the material interests of society' to involve the question of how best to organise the production and distribution of goods and services. If universal association called for 'the combination of human forces into a peaceful direction',[25] then the direction was clearly not going to be military but industrial, and hence matters of industrial progress were central to the organisation of future society, although it was always emphasised that industry must be in the service not only of mankind's physical needs, but also of its moral and intellectual requirements. From one point of view it might be thought that this principle necessitated the future superiority of the spiritual power in society over the temporal power, since the leading theoreticians of the Saint-Simonian doctrine would be the only people in a position to co-ordinate programmes for moral, physical, and intellectual improvement. However, the disciples were convinced that in future the separation between spiritual and temporal power, a phenomenon introduced originally by the rise of Christianity, would disappear, giving way to the complete integration of the two spheres. Such a view was not derived from the thought of Saint-Simon, but was a conclusion reached by the disciples on the basis of their own analysis of history. One of the most persistent themes developed in their lectures and writings during 1830-32 was that concerning the need for a new unity of religion and politics. Without this integration it would be impossible to achieve unity, order, and hierarchy throughout society. In its material aspects future society must operate within an overall religious conception. At the same time spiritual functions must be concerned directly with the earthly, material well-being of all people, and not with salvation in any other-worldly sense. Thus, to distinguish religion from politics, spiritual from material interests, was a mistake. This was one of the major errors of Catholicism, and the disastrous consequences which the error had brought about under feudalism provided clear evidence of the need to unite religion and politics in the future age of universal association.

Within the new, integrated, thoroughly hierarchical structure of authority which the Saint-Simonians sought to establish, it would obviously be necessary to have rules for ranking the different tasks involved in the regulation of social affairs. At the summit of this hierarchy would be a priesthood of general or social thinkers who would determine the major goals to be pursued by society, organise education and the arts, and supervise the more detailed work of the priests of science and the priests of industry, making sure, in particular, that science and industry operated under the guidance of an overall social plan. The priests of science and the priests of industry would be responsible for the central control and co-ordination of work in their respective fields. The chief priority, once again, would be to stimulate a sense of unity and common purpose among all scientists and all workers in industry, in whatever branch of science or industry people were employed. Each of the three sections of the priesthood as envisaged by the Saint-Simonians was seen to correspond to one of the three basic elements in human nature. The general priests were representative of man's moral-emotional capacity – the capacity to feel; the priests of science dealt with matters pertaining to the rational capacity – the capacity to know; and the priests of industry were concerned with practical effort – the capacity to act. Each of these three sections, if it was to function properly, required its own supreme leader, the most important of the three being the supreme general priest, the Father of the entire Saint-Simonian society – a man such as Enfantin or Bazard, one whose incomparable genius, charisma, and sensibility would earn him the greatest possible respect and admiration. Genius, in fact, was to be the source of all authority in the hierarchy of priests: 'Religion alone gives the solution to the great problem of the origin of power . . . The genius reveals himself; he does not come from the ballot box.'[26] The supreme general priest's qualities would be recognised by the people, and there would be no need for any kind of election. Once chosen, this 'living symbol' of authority would see to it that the other positions in the priesthood were filled by the most capable individuals.

It was always intended by the Saint-Simonians that the whole of society should be ranked hierarchically according to ability, with every single individual placed in an appropriate functional position depending on his particular talents. One word frequently used to denote this system of ranking was '*classement*', and the image presented here was clearly that of a society in which many distinct 'classes' would exist, and, indeed, would be encouraged in order to fulfil the criterion of meritocracy. Thus, like Saint-Simon before them, the disciples did not envisage the ending of class divisions; but rather they foresaw the creation of a homogeneous society in which the notion of classification would be generally acceptable because it was based on indisputable ability. In the realm of economic activity, the ranking system would be especially important, since in the previous critical epoch unjustifiable economic distinctions, maintained primarily by outmoded laws governing inheritance, had led to an oppressive class system based not on ability but on aristocratic privileges derived from the ownership of property. The Saint-Simonians did not object to the principle of private ownership of the means of production, but insisted that rights of ownership should never pass from one person to another through inheritance. Those rights must be determined by the leaders of society purely on the basis of the capacity of persons to put property to productive use, and thereby to contribute to society's economic development. A cornerstone of the Saint-Simonian doctrine, therefore, was a rejection of the whole notion of inheritance, and its replacement by a more scientific method of allocating property rights.

In most of their accounts of future social organisation, the Saint-Simonians gave the chief responsibility for overall economic planning to a network of central banking institutions, headed by a supreme state bank which would delegate certain planning functions to a secondary group of banks, each one concerned with a particular geographical area or a specific branch of production. The heart of the system would be

> a central bank representing the government in the material order. This bank would be the depository of all the riches, of the total fund of production, and of all

> the instruments of work; in brief, of that which today comprises the entire mass of individual properties.
>
> On this central bank would depend banks of the second order which would be merely extensions of the first, by means of which the central bank would keep in touch with the principal localities to know their needs and productive power. The second order would command within the territorial area of their jurisdiction increasingly specialised banks which embrace a less extensive field, the weaker branches of the tree of industry.
>
> All needs would converge in the superior banks; from them all endeavours would emanate. The general bank would grant credit to the localities, which is to say, transfer instruments of work to them only after having balanced and combined the various operations. And these credits would then be divided among the workers by the special banks, representing the different branches of industry.[27]

These industrial development banks, then, would be public rather than private institutions, and they would be under the direct control of the governmental hierarchy. They would determine the distribution of the means of production, and would be the sole source of financial credit in society, making it available to those undertakings which could be relied upon to put it to good, productive use. The banks would not charge high interest rates on these transactions. Indeed, the long-term aim was to abolish interest payments altogether, since there was no good reason why a producer should be deprived of a proportion of the wealth he had created. Furthermore, interest rates were really a legacy of a market system in which producers were forced to compete with one another for a limited amount of credit. Under these conditions the interest rate was a market price which a producer in need of funds had to pay. But in future, with the replacement of economic competition by central organisation and planning, interest rates would become redundant. A borrower in receipt of credit from a bank might still have to pay something in order to guarantee his solvency, but this could be regarded as an insurance premium rather than interest in the traditional sense.

Although the Saint-Simonians did not propose the abolition of private ownership of the means of production, they did intend to transform the role and social responsibilities of the owner in some fundamental ways. The initial right to ownership would be fixed by the directors of the banking system, as has been seen; but this would not entitle the owner to dispose of all the revenue from his enterprise. The revenue would remain at the disposal of the banks, while the owner would receive an appropriate salary for his entrepreneurial services. So in fact the owner might more reasonably be regarded as a manager, since he would always be accountable to the banks for the running of the enterprise, and would not, as owner, have any right to profit from the resulting business revenue. Nor, of course, would he be able to decide who should take over his duties after his death. This decision, too, would be reserved for the banking authorities. Thus, in future society private *ownership* of the means of production would not mean absolute private *control* of production, and for this reason one could say that the Saint-Simonians were advocating an extensive socialisation of production through the new agencies of centralised planning and co-ordination.

'To each ability according to its work' was the second part of the Saint-Simonian principle of social hierarchy. This implied, in particular, that each skill in society would be allotted an appropriate remuneration through a wage or salary which was fixed as part of the general economic plan. Unequal skills deserved unequal rewards, and in this respect one can say that the Saint-Simonians were condoning a certain amount of consumer inequality in the new order: 'It is evident that since the capacity of individuals reveals great *inequalities*, the *equal* division of wealth among them would be essentially contrary to the principle that requires each man to be rewarded according to work.'[28] Exactly how great income differentials would be was never made clear. However, Isaac Pereire, who had more to say on this subject than any of the other Saint-Simonians, stressed that the aim was *not* to arrive at a perfectly proportionate relationship between service and reward; rather it must be recognised that in future the best workers 'will always give more to their inferiors than they will receive from them'.[29] This was regarded by Pereire as an essential method of assisting those persons at the bottom of the industrial hierarchy, of encouraging them to develop their talents, and of stimulating a healthy respect for their superiors. And respect, it should be added, was always considered by the Saint-Simonians to be an important element in the reward given by society to those who contributed most to production.

The concept of reward according to work was further complicated by the fact that the Saint-Simonians wished to ensure that the most basic needs of all members of society were fulfilled. This led them to argue the case for state provision of essential goods and services to all workers irrespective of precise differences in their functions and levels of productivity. To a certain extent, therefore, they were willing to endorse the egalitarian principle of reward according to needs (a principle which was later to become central to the thought of Marx and Engels, who at the same time were happy to retain the first part of the original Saint-Simonian formula: 'from each according to his ability'). Following Saint-Simon, the disciples emphasised the importance of caring for 'the most numerous and poorest class', and meeting the welfare requirements of this class was regarded as so fundamental an ingredient of progress that in all the Saint-Simonian schemes provision was made for extensive state assistance to the poor. Everyone would be provided with adequate food, clothing, and housing, as well as the necessary educational, health, and recreational facilities. Society would evolve as one single, united family, and naturally the paternal state could be relied upon to look after the interests of its children.

In the future industrial society envisaged by the Saint-Simonians the economy would be subject to such comprehensive planning that money would gradually become redundant as a medium of exchange. The long-term aim was to do away with buying or selling in the orthodox sense. The means of production, in any case, would be distributed directly by the state, and the state would also provide essential goods and services, and would allocate a range of rewards for work done by different groups in society. Eventually payment of all wages or salaries would be made in the form of ration coupons, entitling the holders to specific quantities of goods to be provided by local merchants. In this way a perfect balance between production and consumption would always be maintained.

The foregoing account has dealt largely with the issue of material well-being in a society organised on the basis of the Saint-Simonian doctrine. It must not be forgotten, however, that the disciples placed equal emphasis on spiritual and emotional well-being. Indeed, because they presented their movement as a church, and issued their doctrine as a set of religious teachings, the question of spiritual and emotional fulfilment was always of great importance. In certain respects the key to this question was a conception of love and its role in cementing social relationships and promoting happiness which was very similar to Fourier's notion of amorous liberation. The Saint-Simonians, too, wished to see the liberation of sentiments of love as a method of integrating society and of fostering a sense of belonging to one social family with one interest in common (although, of course, they did not restrict the family unit to the scale of a Fourierist Phalanx). Enfantin and his supporters actually proclaimed the need to secure the 'rehabilitation of the flesh' (a phrase with undeniable Fourierist connotations), and thus gave recognition to the importance of physical/sexual desires. Like Fourier, they believed that these desires were perfectly natural, and that they should be satisfied, not frustrated. The Christian view of the sanctity of an exclusive, marital relationship between one man and one woman was certainly rejected by Enfantin, but he was never able to gain very much support for this approach. Even the more moderate proposal to sanction divorce encountered considerable hostility within the movement, although it was eventually approved.

The Saint-Simonians were generally agreed on the need to transform the role of the family in modern society. The traditional family group, they argued, must be superseded as a focus of love and affection if a broader and more universal association of people was to be achieved. Economically, the family was bound to become less important, in future, since all inheritance of property would be abolished, and man's basic economic and social needs would be fulfilled not by the family, but by the state. Social unity would develop as the family's hold on the individual's economic interests and emotions weakened, finally to be replaced by a bond of universal love for the whole of humanity and its progress. This change in the role of the family would also help to liberate women from the kind of oppression to which they had hitherto been subjected. Mainly due to the influence of Enfantin, the issue of women's liberation became a chief preoccupation of the Saint-Simonian movement in its last phase (1831-32). While the issue was often discussed quite soberly, as one particular example of the need to put an end to all exploitation of human beings, at other times discussion merged into quite fantastic images of woman as a future symbol of peace and love, and even the prospect of a 'Woman Messiah' was seriously entertained by Enfantin and a small circle of devoted followers.

The Saint-Simonians always placed a great deal of emphasis on the power of education to stimulate the individual's sense of attachment to the community, and that 'love of humanity' which, they asserted, must one day replace egoism, individualism, and self-interest as the moral basis of social organisation. In this context they were perfectly willing to apply techniques of instruction already used successfully in the Catholic Church, and this partly explains their own tendency to present their teachings in the form of 'sermons', and to regard themselves as 'preachers'. Most men, they argued, were receptive to teachings offered in the form of authoritative dogma as long as those doing the teaching were respected and could inspire the layman's confidence. While they knew that education in a modern society must be linked in some way to the requirements of specialised training for work, they warned of the danger of neglecting moral education, by which they meant 'the initiation of individuals into society, the inculcation into individuals of sympathy and love for all, the union of all wills in one sole will, and the direction of all efforts toward one common goal, the goal of society'.[30]

This conception of authoritative moral education brings one back to a point made earlier concerning the Saint-Simonians' intention to eventually unite politics and religion so that future society would in some respects resemble a theocracy (this latter term was not favoured by the disciples themselves, but it would seem appropriate in view of their attitude towards the role of religion in organic epochs). As Georg G. Iggers has put it, in future, according to the Saint-Simonian conception, the power of the state would rest 'less on its priestly ruling class than on the individual's awareness of his religious duty to obey the political authorities'.[31] On different occasions the Saint-Simonians chose to depict future society as a church, a family, or even – particularly in the writings of Isaac Pereire – as an army (pacific rather than warlike, of course). In each case the dominant characteristic was that of discipline, a discipline, however, which was always seen to be based on voluntary consent from below rather than physical coercion from above. Hence, while it cannot be doubted that the Saint-Simonians were architects of a distinctly authoritarian form of early socialism, it would be going too far to see them as precursors of twentieth-century totalitarianism with its emphasis on ruthless, violent repression through the unlimited extension of police control over the civilian population.[32]

The criticism of Saint-Simonism as an excessively authoritarian doctrine is not at all new, but was already well established by 1832, when the organised movement came to an end. In 1865, looking back on their earlier fortunes, some of the original members of that movement acknowledged the fact that

> of all the objections encountered by Saint-Simonism when it first emerged, the most general and most serious was that which issued from the bosom of liberalism against the excessive role given to the principle of authority in the new doctrine.[33]

Surprisingly, the Saint-Simonians seemed to overlook the fact that it was not only liberals but also many socialists who objected to the authoritarianism of their system. Despite the vehemence of this opposition, and even though their movement did not survive beyond 1832, the Saint-Simonians had a remarkable intellectual influence on the development of modern socialism, an influence exceeded only by that of Marxism in the nineteenth century. However, this was not because of the Catholic-religious element in their thought, which was usually rejected, but because of the accuracy of much of their economic analysis of the emerging industrial society, and because they succeeded so brilliantly in situating industrialism within a general view of the development of man's capacities. In doing so they inevitably built upon the theories of Saint-Simon, but having taken these as their starting-point, they struck out in bold new directions which not even their perceptive master could have foreseen.

5
Etienne Cabet

Life and Work

Etienne Cabet was born at Dijon on New Year's Day 1788. His father, Claude, was a master cooper who hoped that his four sons – Etienne was the youngest – would also become craftsmen. But Etienne's eyesight was weak and prevented him from taking up such work. Besides, he made rapid progress at school, and was obviously well suited for a professional career. When he was just fifteen, his headmaster gave him responsibility for teaching mathematics, astronomy, and drawing to a class of sixty pupils.

During the French Revolution Dijon was an important centre for Jacobin activities, and this may have influenced the young Cabet. There is certainly evidence of an early tendency towards political radicalism – probably encouraged by his headmaster – and a rationalist reaction against the Christian religion. He even had a childhood introduction to communist ideas through a reading of Fénelon's *Télémaque*, a book which apparently impressed him a great deal.[1]

Cabet's first choice of career was medicine, but the length and expense of the necessary training deterred him, and he decided that the legal profession offered better prospects. After gaining his degree in 1812, he soon discovered that his position as a lawyer could not be divorced from his political principles. The Restoration of the Bourbon Monarchy in 1814 offended his by now deep-rooted sense of democracy, and it seemed to him to be a thoroughly retrograde development. He supported Napoleon during the Hundred Days, and even after the defeat at Waterloo he demonstrated his loyalties by defending a number of former Bonapartist administrators in the prosecutions which the Bourbons brought against them. Increasingly popular in liberal circles, increasingly out of favour with the Government, he himself was singled out for prosecution in the wake of the duc de Berry's assassination in February 1820. At about the same time as Saint-Simon was being accused of subversion, Cabet was faced with a doubtful charge of professional malpractice. Found guilty, he was suspended from the bar for one year.

This experience pushed Cabet even further in the direction of conspiratorial opposition to the Bourbons, and he moved to Paris and joined the French Carbonari organisation which Bazard, the future Saint-Simonian leader, had helped to found. His own ideas on the strategy of revolution were gradually being formulated, and they were set out systematically for the first time in a manuscript tract of 1828, *Exposition of a Necessary Revolution in the Government of France (Exposé d'une révolution nécessaire dans le gouvernement de France).* Here Cabet argued in favour of a popular republic, but he added the qualification that France needed a constitutional monarchy to ensure stability, and he urged the people to support Louis Philippe, duc d'Orléans. When, in 1830, a revolution did occur which resulted in Louis Philippe gaining power, Cabet could afford to be well satisfied. The new regime even granted him an official appointment as chief judicial administrator for Corsica.

Cabet hoped that the July Monarchy would pursue liberal reforms and do something to improve the condition of the poor. He was quickly disillusioned, however, and in 1831 he offered himself as an opposition candidate for a Chamber of Deputies seat in Dijon, his native city. He won the election and immediately started to organise support for a new, unified republican movement. In the Chamber he made little impact,[2] but outside he won increasing recognition, especially after the publication, in 1832, of his first major work, dealing with the failures of the July Monarchy: *The Revolution of 1830 (La Révolution de 1830).* In 1833 he became Secretary-General of the Free Association for the Education of the People *(Association libre pour l'éducation du peuple),* a voluntary organisation which provided free education for the poor workers of Paris. He edited its newspaper, *Le Fondateur,* and, also in 1833, he began publication of a new paper, *Le Populaire,* which quickly became 'the most widely circulated republican sheet of the era'.[3]

Both the Association and *Le Populaire* were now being carefully watched by the Government. Cabet's increasingly radical outlook, his growing interest in neo-Jacobin doctrines (as expressed, for example, by the important Society for the Rights of Man – *Société des droits de l'homme*), his willingness to advocate revolution (by force if necessary), his attempts to instruct the workers in political affairs – all this was making the Government extremely uneasy. Just as the activities of the Saint-Simonians proved too provocative for the Government to tolerate in 1832, so, two years later, Cabet's opposition was seen as a serious threat to public order. A swift prosecution was brought, and Cabet, found guilty, chose a five-year period of exile as an alternative to two years in prison and a four-year suspension of his civil rights. He travelled first of all to Brussels, but the Belgian Government expelled him, and so he decided, as his second choice, to go to England.

In terms of Cabet's intellectual development the years of exile in England (1834-9) were to prove vitally important, for it was during this period that the radical republicanism he had come to embrace in France was renounced in favour of an uncompromising communism. His historical studies in the British Museum convinced him that the bourgeoisie's present political supremacy was rooted in their ownership of private property, and that consequently any attempt to transform the condition of the mass of propertyless workers in society demanded the establishment of a system of collective ownership. While he was in England Cabet also encountered other exiled French radicals, many of whom were communists, as well as Robert Owen and his followers. These personal contacts undoubtedly contributed to his conversion to communism. It is also worth noting that during 1835-6 he read Thomas More's *Utopia*, a book for which he soon developed a profound admiration. It was not long before he was at work on his own description of an imaginary utopia, *Journey to Icaria (Voyage en Icarie),* which was completed in 1838 but not published until 1840, after his four-volume *Popular*

History of the French Revolution, from 1789 to 1830 (Histoire populaire de la Révolution française, de 1789 à 1830, 1839-40).

Cabet returned to France in 1839, and immediately set about making plans for the organisation of an Icarian movement, that is, a movement whose strategy was to be rooted in the principles of pacific communism elaborated in *Journey to Icaria*. As has already been pointed out in the introduction, Cabet was remarkably successful in this enterprise, and in fact created, in a relatively short period of time, the largest and the most conspicuously working-class of all utopian socialist movements, claiming between 100,000 and 200,000 adherents in the mid-1840s.[4] At a time when French communism, particularly in its neo-Babouvist guise, was generally understood to imply violent revolution, Icarianism introduced a new emphasis on legality and pacific change. Instead of leading an underground secret society, Cabet organised his movement quite openly from the Paris headquarters of a revitalised *Le Populaire* newspaper, which appeared for the first time in March 1841. He placed increasing emphasis during the 1840s on communism as a new Christian doctrine, and this was the subject of his one major theoretical work of this decade, *The True Christianity According to Jesus Christ* (*Le Vrai Christianisme suivant Jésus-Christ,* 1846). Such a suggestion was hardly original, yet it did much to reinforce the image of Icarianism as a perfectly respectable movement.

During the 1840s, then, Icarianism went from strength to strength as it gradually spread its appeal and attracted more and more supporters. At the same time, however, Cabet became increasingly doubtful of the chances of actually establishing a communist regime in France through legal and pacific means. The ruling bourgeoisie resisted all offers of co-operation with the proletariat, and indeed encouraged governmental persecution of socialists and communists. As economic conditions worsened, particularly during the winter of 1846-7, working-class demands for revolution threatened the unity of the Icarian movement, and Cabet's strategy of peaceful, non-violent change was subject to widespread criticism. It was in these circumstances that Cabet took the bold decision to leave France and lead a group of between 10,000 and 20,000 followers to America in an attempt to proceed immediately to the foundation of the first Icarian society. This decision, announced in the pages of *Le Populaire* in May 1847, was in some respects a reversal of Cabet's earlier pronouncements attacking the whole idea of experimental communities, but he took care to distinguish his scheme for a new nation of communists from the much more modest, small-scale efforts of the Owenites and Fourierists. He also defended his decision in religious terms, referring to the teachings of Christ: 'If thou art persecuted in one city, get thee thence to another'.[5]

There can be no doubt that the emigration decision lost Cabet a large number of previously faithful supporters, and although there were also some new recruits (including, ironically, several Fourierists), the net result was a definite decline in the standing of Icarianism as a working-class movement in France. Nevertheless Cabet went ahead with the scheme, and in the summer of 1847 he contacted Robert Owen to seek his advice concerning possible locations for Icaria in the United States. As a result a large area of virgin land by the Red River in Texas was found to be available, and preparations began at once for the emigration of a small advance party. On 3 February 1848 sixty-nine Icarian pioneers boarded the *Rome* at Le Havre and set sail for New Orleans. Cabet remained behind, convinced that it would not be long before he too could make his way to Texas. In fact he found himself delayed in Paris, for on 22 February a major revolutionary upheaval got under way in the French capital. Two days later the Second French Republic was formally proclaimed.

The events of 22 to 24 February presented Cabet with a profound dilemma. He disapproved of violent revolution, yet he realised that the establishment of democratic republicanism must be welcomed as a first step towards a radical transformation of French society. The day after the proclamation of the Second Republic, therefore, he issued a communist manifesto in a special edition of *Le Populaire*. The manifesto urged Icarians to support the Republic's provisional Government, and it listed a number of important communist demands, 'especially the guarantee of all the rights and of all the interests of the workers, the formal recognition of the right to live by working . . . the organisation of work, and the assurance of well-being by work'.[6] There was no suggestion that private property should be abolished. Nor was there any mention of the emigration to America. Cabet now thought that it would be necessary to begin by endorsing a more moderate programme of socialist reforms. The fact remained, however, that Cabet's ultimate aim was the creation of a communist society, and for those moderate republicans and conservatives who opposed him this could only mean violence and repression. They pointed with horror to the close association which was developing between Cabet and Auguste Blanqui, the conspiratorial leader, and also emphasised Cabet's suggestion that ordinary workers should be armed and admitted to the ranks of the National Guard. The opposition forces did not hesitate to make use of such excellent ammunition, and during March and April, as preparations were being made for elections to the National Assembly on 23 April, a full-scale anti-communist campaign was mounted. The campaign was successful, and it resulted in a substantial electoral defeat for the radical and socialist groups.

The experience of this defeat and of the abortive workers' rising which followed in June 1848 impelled Cabet once again to consider the question of Icarianism in America. The advance party had arrived in New Orleans on 27 March to the sound of an artillery salute, welcoming them as glorious representatives of the new French Republic. They had been told by Cabet that it should take them another fourteen days to complete the journey from New Orleans to the site chosen for Icaria. In fact the journey was so hazardous and the site was so remote that they did not arrive there until 2 June. They were immediately disappointed. They had hoped to acquire one million acres, but the land regulations (of which they were apparently unaware) limited the distribution to 320 acres per married man and 160 acres for each bachelor. Furthermore, the plots of land were not even adjacent to one another, which clearly made the task of establishing an integrated community extremely difficult. They persevered for over two months, but by mid-August the strangeness of their new environment and way of life had finally proved too much for them. There had already been seven deaths from fever, one person had been killed by lightning, and four others had deserted. A retreat from Icaria was accordingly approved, and preparations were under way when a second advance party arrived at the community. Between August and December seven more groups of Icarians left France for Texas, most of them unaware of the problems the first pioneers had encountered. Cabet himself left France on 3 December, arrived in New York on the last day of 1848, and proceeded to New Orleans. Convinced that he could be of much more use to his disillusioned followers in America than the remnants of his movement in France, he arranged a general assembly of the Icarians to decide on their future. Those who wished to withdraw were given money to help them on their way. But a majority, some 280 in all, decided to press on to a new location. On 1 March they left New Orleans for Nauvoo, Illinois, a town on the Mississippi which had recently been abandoned by the Mormons.

This time the establishment of an Icarian Community (this was to be its official name) was accomplished without too much difficulty. The urgent tasks of housing everyone and organising work, education, and recreation were given first priority; then serious attention was given to political matters. In February 1851 the Illinois State Legislature approved an Act legally incorporating the Community as a company with a capital stock of 100,000 dollars divided into shares of 100 dollars each. No individual was allowed to own more than one share, however, and thus the principle of equality was safeguarded. The company was to have six Directors (elected annually), one of whom would be President. A constitution for the Community, originally adopted in February 1850, was revised in accordance with the Act of Incorporation in May 1851. The constitution stipulated that the executive power (the President and the other five Directors) should be subordinate to the legislature (a General Assembly composed of all male members of the Community over the age of nineteen years; women would have a consultative role only).[7] In fact the executive quickly emerged as the preponderant force in shaping the Community's affairs, and within the executive the influence of Cabet himself, elected President each year between 1850 and 1855, steadily increased, a development which angered many Icarians, and which eventually led to Cabet's downfall.

To be perfectly accurate, Cabet's increasing domination was interrupted by a period of fourteen months' absence from the Community (May 1851 to July 1852). His departure was prompted by a prosecution brought against him in Paris by the French Government, who claimed that his colonisation scheme was nothing more than a deliberate attempt to defraud people of their money under the false pretext of leading them to a new home in Texas. This charge, which was undoubtedly supported by some of those disillusioned Icarians who had returned to France after the disastrous first attempt to create a community in 1848, had no real foundation, but nevertheless Cabet was found guilty by a Paris court (even though he was not present to defend himself), and sentenced to two years in prison and deprived of his political rights. On 19 July 1851 Cabet was at last able to make a personal appearance before the Court of Appeal, and after producing indisputable evidence that he had genuinely acquired land in Texas for the purpose of establishing a colony, he was acquitted. He now took the opportunity to revive his links with the French socialist movement by attempting to found a new paper under the joint direction of Louis Blanc, Pierre Leroux, and himself. This idea never came to anything, although during October and November Cabet did succeed in starting *Le Républicain populaire et social*, a successor to the *Le Populaire*. He was compelled to cease publication, however, following Louis-Napoleon's coup d'état of 2 December. In January the new regime arrested him on charges of political agitation, and after a few days in prison he was transported to London. He became very interested in the possibility of starting an Icarian community in England, but felt that he must return to Nauvoo as soon as possible. He arrived back there on 23 July.

Cabet immediately resumed his position as leader of the Icarian Community, but it soon became clear that opposition to his authoritarian style of control was becoming more and more vigorous. What the opposition objected to, in particular, was the way in which Cabet sought to regulate many aspects of life in the Community through detailed rules which Icarians were expected to obey. By the end of 1853 a list of forty-eight conditions was in in force governing membership of the Community. Every Icarian was required to have a good knowledge of relevant Icarian texts, to completely adopt the Icarian way of life and accept its basic communistic principles; to love order, organisation and discipline; to abstain from smoking tobacco and drinking strong alcohol; to agree to marry; to become a True Christian; to allow the Community to control the education of children; and so on. By December 1855 Cabet realised that the issue of his authority was causing such serious divisions within the Community that he had no alternative but to present the Icarians with an ultimatum: the Community must choose between him and his opponents. No compromise was possible. He decided that the best way to resolve the crisis one way or the other was to introduce a series of constitutional amendments in the General Assembly which, if approved, would greatly strengthen the position of the Presidency. It was proposed, for example, that the President should be elected for four-year terms instead of annually, and that he alone should be responsible for the overall management of the Community and the execution of its laws. This strategy was unnecessarily bold, and it had the effect of uniting all opposition groups as never before. Cabet now had second thoughts on the possibility of compromise. First of all he modified his constitutional proposals; then he suggested that it would be best if further discussion of the question were postponed for twelve months in order to allow the Community to calm down and take stock of the situation. On 5 February 1856 Cabet was once again elected to the Presidency.

Many Icarians, however, remained dissatisfied with life in the Community, and a substantial number were rapidly coming to the conclusion that they ought to leave. On 17 February fifty-seven men, women, and children departed. Cabet, convinced that the whole future of Icarian communism was in doubt, put forward a new solution: the Community should split up into two sections, one remaining at Nauvoo, the other moving to Adams County in south-west Iowa, where work had begun in 1853 for a new colonial site, and where several Icarians were already living. This proposal failed to gain sufficient support, though, and the opposition pursued an alternative course. They succeeded in getting a commission appointed to examine Cabet's management of the Community's finances, and in May this led to the closing of the Icarian Offices in Paris on the grounds that their accounts were not in order. The opposition now refused to have anything to do with Cabet and his supporters, and the two groups were in effect physically segregated from one another for much of the time. The situation became intolerable, and on 12 August Cabet led his band of followers to a new residence just outside the Community – 'Little Icaria' as it soon became known. Two months later they made their way to Saint Louis. Cabet had been there for just a few days when, on 7 November, he suffered a severe brain haemorrhage. He died at five o'clock the following morning.

The Icarians who remained at Saint Louis, numbering 165 by the beginning of 1857, attempted to establish a new colony, but their three residences were half a mile apart from each other, and their places of work were also quite separate. A real sense of community was almost impossible to achieve in such circumstances. In May 1858, therefore, the Icarians moved to a new site at Cheltenham, some six miles from the centre of Saint Louis; but it was not long before new disagreements arose over constitutional matters, and this led, in March 1859, to the departure of forty-four dissidents, that is, over a quarter of the Cheltenham colony's population. The Icarians who were left had to face mounting problems under the impact of the widespread economic and political chaos caused by the American Civil War. By the beginning of 1864 only about twenty people remained, and by March they too had decided to leave.

Following the schism of August 1856 the Icarian Community at Nauvoo (total population: 219 persons at 1 January 1857) took stock of its situation, and the decision was taken to move to the new site which had been prepared in Iowa. By the end of 1860 the transfer of Icaria to Corning, Adams County had been completed. The new Icarian Community withstood the difficulties of the 1860s, although its population declined to double figures (it was a mere thirty-three in August 1866, but went up again to over seventy by 1871). Only in the 1870s did any serious problems arise, when a youthful opposition group ('Young Icaria') put forward what it considered to be a truly libertarian alternative to the established Icarian system, a kind of third way between centrally organised communism and anarchism.[8] Once again confrontation resulted in a division of the Community into two parts: in 1879 the Old and the Young Icarians were each allocated a share of the Corning colony's landholding, and they were permitted to organise themselves quite independently of each other and according to whatever constitutional principles they chose to adopt. Young Icaria survived until 1886, when it became clear that it was no longer viable economically or politically. A decision to move to a better location in California, eighteen miles from San Franciso, offered some hope, and a charter for this new Icaria Speranza Commune was signed in 1883, but the plan did not get very far. In the words of one commentator, the scheme 'did not die of poverty, however, but of prosperity. The land of Icaria Speranza acquired great value. It was, therefore, decided by the members to divide it among themselves, to be exploited in a truly individualistic way'.[9] As for the Old Icarians, they almost succeeded in taking their utopia into the twentieth century, but financial difficulties and a declining population finally forced a dissolution in October 1898.

The Spirit of Fraternity

> If we are asked: What is your *science*? – We reply, *Fraternity*. What is your *principle*? – *Fraternity*. What is your *doctrine*? – *Fraternity*. What is your *theory*? – *Fraternity*. What is your *system*? – *Fraternity*. Yes, we maintain that *Fraternity* is everything . . .[10]

Cabet frequently described his theory of fraternal communism as a science, yet in fact the scientific character of his writings is very weak indeed. The theory of communism is rarely related to systematic and extended argument, and principles are usually put forward with the bare minimum of rational justification. What justification there is generally assumes the uninspiring form of numerous references to other thinkers, illustrated by selected (often poorly selected) quotations, as for example in the second part of *Journey to Icaria*, chapters XII and XIII, where Cabet's views on equality and community are 'proved' by supporting statements drawn from nearly every major figure in the history of western philosophy (together with quotations from certain thinkers, Napoleon Bonaparte for instance, whose claim to be included in such a list of great philosophers is, to say the least, doubtful). Cabet was greatly influenced, in particular, by his reading of More's *Utopia*. When he chose the novel as a vehicle for the presentation of his own theories, he confessed that it was after studying More's book during his exile in England that he first began to take the idea of establishing communism (or 'community') seriously. Before then he had tended to regard communism as an unrealistic ideal.[11] It is interesting to note that although in the quotation from *Journey to Icaria* at the head of this section (the quotation on fraternity's importance) Cabet defended the scientific status of his theory, in a later work, *The True Christianity According to Jesus Christ*, he admitted that his novel could not really be regarded as a scientific work:

> We preferred description and representation to scientific and metaphysical discussion because the first form is more striking, more palpable, more interesting, more intelligible, more within the grasp of readers who are not accustomed to exact reasoning.[12]

If there was any 'exact reasoning' behind Cabet's advocacy of communism, it was the reasoning which guided his historical studies during the 1830s, particularly those undertaken in England, studies which culminated in both *Journey to Icaria* and the *Popular History of the French Revolution from 1789 to 1830*. It is difficult to imagine two such different works, yet the conclusions put forward with such conviction in the utopian novel stemmed directly from the author's perception of history as revealed in his analysis of the French Revolution. If the latter was intended as a 'popular history', the novel took the process of popularisation even further. In a booklet of 1840, entitled *Why I Am a Communist (Comment je suis communiste)*, he explained how, in studying and writing about history, he had been struck by the prevalence of social disorder and revolution, and the widespread misery this had produced. In searching for the cause of disorder and revolution – and hence of unhappiness – he had discovered the importance of inequality, 'the truly original and primordial cause of all vices and all evils in all societies since the world began'. Inequality had always produced the same vices and evils, and would continue to do so 'until the end of the world if it was allowed to continue for ever'.[13] Inequality, he pointed out, was in part a matter of government and the constitutional arrangement of authority. Historically one could see that such forms of government as aristocracy and despotism were expressions of inequality. So equality therefore called for an end to aristocracy and despotism, and the institution of popular democracy in their place. The French Revolution had actually embodied this tendency with its emphasis on the rights of man, the sovereignty of the people, and the principles of liberty, equality, and fraternity. But the French Revolution had *not* attacked the economic and social dimensions of inequality. Its strategy had been based on the incorrect assumption that the establishment of a democratic republic was all that was needed, and that this alone would provide everyone with food, give everyone a job of work to do, and promote universal peace, prosperity, and happiness. Cabet believed that his own major contribution as a student of history was to have revealed that inequality was to be found not only in the structure of government, but also in education; in the provision of food, clothing, housing, and furnishings; and in work. Many people had written about inequality in government, but who had yet demonstrated what full economic and social equality required? It was this line of investigation which had guided Cabet through his historical research, and had convinced him of the need for a descriptive account of how a society based on full equality would have to be organised:

> I soon saw that equality demanded an extension of agricultural and manufacturing production, an economy, order, and distribution based on intelligence and reasoning, things which do not exist and which cannot exist today. Soon I was led to education in common, work in common, to the necessity for concentration in huge workshops and stores, to the unlimited spread of machines, to the exploitation of the land in common, to the sharing of its fruits and products, in a word to *Community.*[14]

It can be seen that most of these preconditions were related to the large increases in economic production made possible by new technology. Equality, as Cabet defined it, was almost unimaginable in a predominantly agrarian society; nor was it really feasible in a small country with few resources. It must be an equality of abundance. The account of Icaria which appeared in 1840 was thus a description of a large (although decentralised), powerful, industrialised nation-state – the France or England of a future golden age of mechanisation.

When asked how the demand for full equality could be justified in moral terms, Cabet pointed to the fact that 'nature has given to all men the same desire to be happy, the same right to *existence* and *welfare*'.[15] If all men desired happiness, then surely, Cabet argued, the happiness of each individual man was as important as the happiness of all others, and hence the means of achieving happiness must be made available to everyone, a principle which was reinforced when one observed that man could not possibly satisfy his physical needs without recourse to the materials furnished for the whole of humanity by nature. In this sense, nature did not belong to individual persons but to mankind as a collective entity. This did not mean that all members of society must be treated in exactly the same way – for instance, the sick would obviously need more medical services than the healthy, and the elderly and the very young might legitimately claim extra care and attention – but all persons had an inalienable right to equal consideration qualified only by the unavoidable variation in their particular circumstances at any given time. A difficulty did arise, however, when it came to relating welfare benefits to the various contributions which different people made to society through their labour. Did Cabet's enthusiasm for the most absolute equality possible extend as far as rewarding citizens equally even though some people worked harder than others? Cabet's answer was that all men in good health had an equal duty to contribute to the common good by labouring to the best of their ability. Such a duty would be enforced under Icarian communism, although the persuasiveness of the Icarian moral code, taught to children in the home and the school, would presumably make physical compulsion unnecessary. (Also, the worst jobs would be done by machines, not people, and hence all human labour would be a source of positive satisfaction. This idea of attractive industry was probably taken from Fourier.) On the front page of *Journey to Icaria* the fundamental moral law was announced in prominent letters: 'To each according to his needs ... From each according to his powers.' This law reminds one of the earlier Saint-Simonian principles, 'from each according to his ability, to each ability according to its work' and 'ranking according to ability, reward according to work', although Cabet's formulation, with its explicit attention to need, is more egalitarian and less hierarchical than the Saint-Simonians' 'law of peaceful labour'.[16]

The concern for equality could also be defended by reference to the moral teachings of early Christianity. This perspective was not given much emphasis in *Journey to Icaria*, but it was very much to the fore in *The True Christianity According to Jesus Christ*. In that work Cabet put forward what at first sight would appear to be a relativist view of social morality, pointing out that the concept of morality referred to a society's traditions, customs, and manners, and consequently one might reasonably expect different societies to have different moral codes. (Polygamy, for example, was regarded as moral in some countries but not in others.) When it came to comparing different moral codes, obviously the only way to decide on their respective merits was to have some more universal standards by which to judge them. Cabet suggested that 'of all moralities the best is that which conforms most to nature, the interest of the individual, and the interest of society'.[17] As in the earlier quotation, one notes the prominence of the idea of nature as a source of moral virtue; and whereas Cabet previously brought in the notion of happiness as the goal towards which social behaviour ought to aim, he now put it in the slightly different terminology of a man's *interest*, the interest of society being the sum total of all such individual interests. It was Christianity's great achievement, he argued, to have presented man with a moral code fulfilling all these requirements. There were thus good rational grounds for embracing Christianity as a social doctrine. In addition Cabet was quite willing to make use of the more orthodox argument that if Jesus was the Son of God, His morality was bound to be perfect.

The next step was for Cabet to show that Christianity was in effect a doctrine of communism. This was a crucial point in the development of the Icarian philosophy, for it was this which distinguished it from earlier versions of New or True Christianity, in particular the version associated with Saint-Simon. Much of Saint-Simon's interpretation of Christianity, especially its emphasis on the concept of brotherly love ('treat your neighbour as you would want him to treat you'), is adopted by Cabet. However, whereas Saint-Simon found nothing in Christianity to justify the replacement of private property by common ownership, Cabet saw Christianity as a direct attack on such private property rights, mainly because of the way in which Christ commanded the rich to give up their wealth to the poor (a commandment which clearly lends itself to various interpretations). Furthermore, it was claimed, the actual organisation of early Christianity was itself based on a primitive form of communism. This was a model which the True Icarian-Christians of the modern world were morally required to copy. Cabet believed that he had already succeeded, in his utopian novel, in showing how communism could be applied to a modern industrialised society. By the late 1840s he was ready to provide the world with a practical example of communism in action. Ever since his own period of residence in England, he had felt that it was that country which afforded the best opportunity for such a practical experiment, with France and the United States as the next choices. In the end, however, circumstances dictated that the first Icarian community should be established in America.

Icaria Revisited

Journey to Icaria can still be read and enjoyed as a utopian novel. It is indeed one of the most delightful of all utopian novels, although one suspects that its length (600 pages in the fullest edition) is likely to deter all but the most patient readers (just as it also seems to have deterred translators). However, the book is no ordinary example of utopian fiction. For it was written as a 'philosophical and social novel' (this sub-title was added for the second edition of 1842), and as such its underlying intention was extremely serious, namely, to convince the reader of the desirability of actually founding a real Icarian society on French soil or, for that matter, in any other Western country where support was forthcoming.

Significantly, the first positive attractions of Icaria to be mentioned by Cabet are essentially material and environmental. Icaria is about as big as France or England in terms of geographical area, but the number of inhabitants is equal to the combined populations of those two countries. Icarians live in superb villages and towns, all adorned with classical monuments, and everywhere there are beautiful houses and gardens, and delightful countryside. The roads, rivers, and canals are equally magnificent. Icarian industry is fully mechanised and very productive. There is an abundance of every kind of tree, fruit, flower, and animal. Everyone is physically attractive and charming. Reason, justice and wisdom prevail. Crime is unknown. Life is peaceful, pleasurable, full of joy and happiness. These benefits, it is argued, stem from the Icarians' unique social and political organisation, which is based on the principle of absolute equality 'in every sphere where this equality is not materially impossible',[18] and which was inaugurated in 1782, the year in which the great revolutionary leader Icar led his people out of civil war and into the system of community. (Elsewhere Cabet estimated that the realisation of the new system would take from twenty to fifty years depending on circumstances, in particular on the capacity of the educational system to train a new generation of citizens.[19]) In this system, which was fully established by 1812, land and capital are owned collectively by the people, and everyone shares equally in the products of farming and industry. This method of distribution makes money unnecessary, since there is no such thing as buying or selling, and it ensures that everyone is provided with the necessities of life, in particular food, clothing, and housing. Each year an adjustment of production to needs is made through an economic plan for the entire nation. Public education is available for all, a combination of general elementary instruction and special vocational training geared to each individual's chosen profession.

The government of Icaria operates in accordance with the concept of popular sovereignty: the people as a whole reserve the right to approve or reject the proposals of their representatives in the national legislature (a single-chamber assembly of 2,000 deputies elected for two-year terms) and those of the executive (a President plus fifteen other ministers, also elected for two-year terms). The country is divided into 100 provinces and 1,000 communes, each commune being represented by two deputies in the national legislature, and each commune and province having its own executive and assembly for discussion of local and regional issues, and for the detailed administration of national laws. Each provincial assembly has 120 members, representatives of the ten communes within its territory. Communal assemblies, however, do not consist of representatives, since all citizens (this means all adult males: women and children are not eligible) are permitted to participate directly in local decision-making, meeting every ten days to implement provincial and national regulations, and to manage the specifically internal affairs of the communes. In all of Icaria's 1,101 assemblies specialist committees and sub-committees, dealing with constitutional affairs, education, agriculture, industry, and other policy areas, carry out the detailed investigations which are essential if law-making is to be both rational and democratic.

The exclusion of women from full citizenship in Icaria is curious, since Cabet frequently called for the granting of equal rights to males and females. In *The True Christianity According to Jesus Christ* he insisted that

> As much as Jesus, and more emphatically than any other reformer, our communism calls for the enfranchisement of women, the recognition of her natural rights, her equality, her education; above all our communism demands justice for all women, respect and filial love . . . for all elderly women, brotherly friendship for all young women, fatherly affection and protection for all little girls, even more so than for their brothers.[20]

Despite the fact that Icaria is apparently regarded by its female inhabitants as an idyllic paradise (since all women are 'cherished and protected in their spring and summer, cherished and respected in their autumn and winter, always calm and happy'[21]), female suffrage is not sanctioned. Cabet in fact never allowed women to vote or participate in any assemblies in his communitarian schemes in the United States. His greatest concession to women was to grant them a modest consultative role, as for example in the 1851 constitution of the Nauvoo community in Illinois (Article 120).

One of the largest sections in Cabet's detailed account of Icarian life is that dealing with religion (chapters XX and XXVII in part one of *Journey to Icaria*). This is not surprising, for by 1840 Cabet had come to regard religion as a very important political institution, an institution which alone had the power to create and maintain a true sense of unity and solidarity among men. During the 1840s Cabet became convinced that the religion of the future could be regarded as a form of Christianity – the *true* Christianity (this was the title of his book of 1846), but such an idea was merely hinted at in *Journey to Icaria*, the primitive communism of Christ and his disciples being presented (very sketchily) as a model for Cabet's own doctrine of community. In the description of Icarian religious practices, however, Christianity is not even mentioned. At first sight it appears that in Icaria there is complete religious toleration: everyone would seem to be free to join the sect of his or her own choosing. But in reality this toleration is much more limited, for the Icarian educational system ensures that certain types of religious sect are unlikely to flourish. Children are taught nothing about religion until the 'age of reason', that is, sixteen or seventeen. Then, in the space of one year, a philosopher (*not* a priest) introduces them to all existing religious systems and their teachings, and each young man or woman can then decide which system seems the best. Inevitably, Icarian philosophy's own scientific-rational framework, rooted in an opposition to superstition and supernatural belief, dominates the learning process. Thus we are told by one Icarian that they have 'replaced the expressions *God, Divinity, Religion, Church, Priest,* by new expressions so perfectly defined that they give rise to no ambiguity'.[22] Religion is presented to children as a moral and philosophical code whose purpose is to show men how to live together as brothers. Among the Icarians, in fact, there is a striking religious consensus which is held to be the result of education, reason, and discussion. A kind of religion of humanity prevails which involves each individual praising the Supreme Being according to his own inclinations. It is a religion which does without elaborate ceremony and ritual. Temples exist for common worship, but it is believed that true worship finds expression in the home and in social relations, particularly in the justice and fraternity underlying Icarian communism. Ceremony and ritual are regarded as bad because they are associated with an authoritarian priesthood. The Icarian religion has its priests, but they 'have no power, not even spiritual power'; they are no more than 'preachers of morality, religious instructors, advisers, guides, friendly comforters'.[23]

It can be seen that Cabet considers the Icarian religious system to be libertarian and democratic. It is the counterpart in the spiritual sphere of the popular sovereignty which characterises the law-making process. Unlike Saint-Simon, Cabet does not urge the establishment of a spiritual *power* (which would be elitist and hierarchical), even though in other respects the views of the two thinkers on religion's importance as a source of social morality are very similar. There is an ambiguity here, for Cabet regards religion as a basis for unity in society, yet that unity is supposed to emerge naturally out of an initial diversity of religious belief. Would such diversity give way so easily to a generally accepted religion of humanity? This seems a reasonable question to ask. The answer, for Cabet, centres on the role of education, for it is the influence of education which would seem to be mainly responsible for the Icarians' religious transformation. If (to take the example mentioned earlier) the Icarian philosophers are allowed to control the vocabulary of religious instruction in the name of science and reason, then does this not in fact amount to a somewhat authoritarian act? The prohibition of all religious discussion until the age of sixteen or seventeen also seems authoritarian, and one wonders how such a rule could ever be enforced. If, as Cabet suggests, man's religious instinct is so strong, could it possibly be kept dormant for so long?

The fervent philosophical rationalism of Cabet's views on religion in *Journey to Icaria* is interesting, but it really represents only one phase – a fairly brief one at that – in the development of Cabet's thought. *The True Christianity*, written six years after the novel, is an attempt to show how modern science and the Christian concept of God can be reconciled. In Icaria the very word 'God' is redundant, but in *The True Christianity* it is the focus of attention. Communist society is seen as the Kingdom of God, because it is a stage of social perfection and brotherly love, the reign of God on earth. And the scientific aspect of God is also emphasised: God, after all, must know everything, and since science is knowledge, then the Kingdom of God is also the Kingdom of Science. In *Journey to Icaria* Cabet explains that he sees

Christ's teachings as having a communistic basis. This argument is taken much further in *The True Christianity*, although even in this work the force of argument is sometimes very weak indeed. For example, as evidence that Christ recognised the virtues of association as a guiding principle of social organisation, Cabet quotes the following well-known passage from Saint Matthew's Gospel: 'For where two or three are gathered together in my name, there am I in the midst of them.'[24] Equally vague is a section where Cabet tries to convince the reader that Christ advocated community of goods: 'Jesus', Cabet points out, 'did not say: Give your goods to one poor man or to a few poor men, but *to the poor*, that is, to all poor people.' And this, it is asserted, amounts to a commandment that all goods originally belonging to the rich should be given up to form a fund held in common by the poor.[25]

Two more features of *The True Christianity* are particularly interesting. First, there is the same reluctance to authorise the institutionalisation of religion through a priesthood and formalised ritual that was noted earlier in the discussion of *Journey to Icaria*. In fact, this reluctance is even more pronounced in the later work, for example, where Cabet insists that 'in the Kingdom of God, in the New Jerusalem, there are no longer any priests or kings'.[26] In *Journey to Icaria* there *were* priests, although it was emphasised that they were mere 'preachers of morality'. In *The True Christianity*, however, priests have been completely eliminated from the vision of future society, and religious devotion is seen to emanate from the individual's heart without the intervention of any external authority. Secondly, although there are many implicit criticisms of Catholicism, Protestantism, and other forms of established Christianity in Cabet's analysis, these criticisms are rarely made explicit. There is certainly nothing like the angry, mocking attack against Christian Churches which Saint-Simon made in his *New Christianity*.

Cabet's interpretation of Christianity was always a strongly ascetic one. He subscribed to a very strict moral code, and loathed the selfish pursuit of pleasure as much as Fourier praised it. Nor was he willing to sanction any modification to the institution of marriage or to family life in general, a fact which he constantly emphasised to those of his critics who equated communism with the holding of women, as well as property, in common. In Cabet's view the ethical commandments of Christianity demanded moral restraint and great moderation in eating, drinking, sexual relations, tobacco smoking, and other pursuits associated with the satisfaction of man's physical urges. Besides, such habits were considered to be so obviously detrimental to health that they were also criticised for purely medical reasons. Cabet, like Saint-Simon, regarded the medical profession as having an especially important role to play in furthering social progress, and he frequently put forward the view that the best measure of progress was the gradual improvement in man's physical and mental condition brought about through the application of medical knowledge. In a section on doctors in *Journey to Icaria* (chapter XIII in part one) Cabet (whose own first choice of career, it will be remembered, was medicine) describes the regulation of public health in great detail and with obvious delight. The emphasis is on preventive medicine, for example through regular examinations and the extensive use of vaccination. But other methods are much more controversial, notably the suggestion that if a couple are thought likely to have disabled or seriously ill children, they should not be allowed to get married. Thus what would now be regarded as a kind of eugenics is deliberately sanctioned. Everything possible is done to promote man's medical understanding. The dissection of corpses and the performance of post-mortem examinations, widely rejected for religious reasons in Cabet's day, are defended for their scientific value. On the same grounds the cremation of the dead, it is argued, is preferable to burial. The result of all this is the gradual elimination of disease and disability, a power to which Cabet sets no limits:

> While the genius of education can teach stammerers to talk with ease, the deaf and dumb to hear everything with their eyes and say everything with their fingers, and the blind to see everything through touch, surgery can actually restore speech to the dumb, hearing to the deaf, sight to the blind, and their limbs to the many unfortunates who have lost them: so that in Icaria today there are so to speak no more blind, deaf, dumb or toothless persons, etc.![27]

Cabet considered it necessary to spell out in some detail how the Icarian utopia was to be governed, and how authority was to be distributed and exercised. In this respect he seems to have inherited Saint-Simon's interest in constitutions and legislative procedures, an interest which was no doubt stimulated by his own experience in the legal profession and in the world of politics in France. This emphasis also grew out of the conviction embraced by Cabet in the 1830s that a large national society such as France could begin to be transformed into a land of perfect harmony if appropriate constitutional arrangements were made. (He always stressed, however, that constitutional changes must be accompanied by the necessary social measures.) Furthermore, a fairly detailed blueprint was seen by Cabet to be absolutely essential in order to respond to the common criticism directed at socialist thinkers at this time: that in trying to demolish one social and political order, that based on individualism, the typical socialist did not really have a clear idea of any viable alternative. He emphasised, however, that he was putting forward only one possible scheme for the achievement of community, and that this was not necessarily the best. Other thinkers would no doubt be able to suggest improvements and variations on the basic model.

While Owen and Fourier were primarily concerned with the creation of small-scale communities, and could therefore regard national politics as somewhat unimportant, Cabet deliberately wrote his *Journey to Icaria* to show that it was realistic to aim at the reorganisation of an entire nation-state through direct political action. This was in fact one of the few truly distinctive conceptions put forward in Cabet's book, although he acknowledged that his thinking on this issue had been influenced by his reading of More's *Utopia* – 'the first work in which one finds community applied to *an entire nation*, and to *a large nation*'.[28] When, in 1848, the initial party of sixty-nine Icarians set sail for New Orleans to commence the colonial emigration, Cabet was still arguing that his ultimate aim was to found a large Icarian nation of several million persons as portrayed in his novel, and that this first experiment was to be regarded chiefly as an inspirational model. Once in America, however, Cabet was compelled by the sheer force of circumstances to recognise that his grand theories of national transformation must give way to theories of how best to organise very small associations, associations which were not even as big as the communes described in *Journey to Icaria.* He thus found himself drawn increasingly, in some ways reluctantly, into precisely the same kind of communitarian movement normally associated at this time with the Owenites and the Fourierists. (As will be seen in the next chapter, Wilhelm Weitling eventually found himself in exactly the same position.) Cabet had always been critical of small, isolated communitarian experiments. One important reason he gave for early Christianity's failure to establish communism on earth was that its religious communities were always so small, and thus amounted to what was in effect a new kind of exclusive individualism, that is, the negation of communism. This was precisely the same dilemma facing the herald of True Christianity in America: how could small Icarian communities avoid sinking into a state of splendid isolation from the rest of society? Furthermore, in *Journey to Icaria* Cabet had emphasised the importance of extensive industrialisation and mechanisation as necessary conditions for the attainment of full equality. It is difficult to see how such a requirement could ever be fulfilled in a very small community deprived of the advantages of large-scale production.

Whereas Owen, in the 1820s, came to the conclusion that it ought to be easier to establish a community in the United States than in the Old World, since America offered the opportunity to build a completely new social environment (and hence it was more likely to promote the formation of good character), Cabet, at the end of the 1840s, was not at all optimistic about the chances of success:

> The founding of Icaria in America, on the other side of the seas, two or three thousand leagues away, in a new climate, in a waste region where all would need to be created, side by side with men of an alien tongue, would be a more costly and difficult enterprise than it would have been in France.[29]

On the other hand, the United States offered some crucial political advantages, especially in terms of the liberties guaranteed by the American Constitution. A scheme of association could be regarded as a more realistic proposition in that country inasmuch as the fundamental right to associate was recognised and given legal protection. Cabet also believed that there was a much better chance that communism would spread in America than anywhere else, through the amalgamation of previously separate communist associations, and also the acceptance of communism by some of the many associations which were based originally on private ownership of property, that is, on individualism. (On this point it is interesting to note that Cabet was quite willing to encourage the establishment of Fourierist Phalanxes, 'convinced that they would soon convert themselves into communities'.[30])

According to the constitution which governed the community at Nauvoo, Illinois, Cabet's original intention was to transform this first association into a city and then into a constituent state within the American federal union (Article 8). 'In the meantime', Article 9 emphasised, 'it is obedient to the laws of the State of Illinois'.[31] Cabet did not explain how constitutional withdrawal from Illinois was to be achieved prior to the setting up of a State of Icaria, yet he obviously considered this to be a thoroughly realistic proposition. The chief reasons for the failure of the Nauvoo experiment, and indeed of all subsequent Icarian developments after that, were summarised in the previous section of this chapter, and there is no need to repeat them here. However, one striking feature of this practical phase of Icarianism does deserve to be mentioned, and that is the sustained effort made by Cabet to base Icarian organisation on the principles he had already stated in his theoretical writings, particularly in *Journey to Icaria*. The constitution drawn up at Nauvoo was in many ways a summary of the features of the Icarian system described in Cabet's novel, even though the actual conditions which existed at Nauvoo might reasonably have been regarded as unsuitable for such an immediate application of the philosophy of fraternal communism. This attempt to govern life in the Icarian Community according to a pre-existing (and very detailed) blueprint caused considerable difficulties, since it led to a degree of regulation by the executive, and particularly by Cabet as President, which many people found intolerable.

In the imaginary Icaria of Cabet's novel the basic framework of social and political organisation was instituted by a benevolent and popular dictator, Icar:

> The immortal Icar, convinced that the cause of so many revolutions lay not only in the vices of *political organisation*, but even more importantly in those of *social organisation*, undertook with courage the *radical reform* of that twofold organisation (which in reality is only one organisation), and substituted that which is responsible for our present happiness.[32]

In the real Icaria in America Cabet undoubtedly saw himself in the role of 'the immortal Icar', and could think of no reason why his authority as law-giver should ever be in doubt as long as it operated on the basis of popular support through the institutions of democratic responsibility which had been established. This proved to be a serious miscalculation, and it was not long before a substantial number of citizens chose to reject Cabet's leadership. In *Journey to Icaria* there was no mention of such an eventuality; it was always assumed by its author that popular enthusiasm for the Icarian system and its architect, once created, would be reinforced as the benefits of Icarianism became obvious. In reality, however, the most fundamental of all political problems – that is, how to manage opposition and conflict – became supremely important, and it was a problem to which Cabet could only see one solution: the division of Icaria into two separate communities. Unity and solidarity had been proclaimed as two of Icaria's most significant features, yet they had proved impossible to maintain, even on a very small scale, for more than a few months.

6
Wilhelm Weitling

Life and Work

Wilhelm Christian Weitling was born on 5 October 1808 at Magdeburg, an ancient German city which since 1806 had been occupied by French armed forces and incorporated in the Napoleonic Empire. His mother, Christine Weitling, was an unmarried housemaid who had fallen in love with an officer in the French artillery, Guillaume Terijon, the boy's father. Christine had little money, and her son's formal education was consequently limited to a few years at the local elementary school, although the Catholic Church, into which he was introduced at an early age, also did much to stimulate his mind.

After leaving school, he was apprenticed to a tailor, and at eighteen he set out as a journeyman, hiking from town to town in search of employment. During 1830-32 he worked in Leipzig, where he lived with August Schilling, who shared his emerging interest in socialist and communist ideas. Weitling is known to have submitted several articles on social and political questions to the *Leipziger Zeitung* at this time (they were all rejected), and his biographer, Carl Wittke, suggests that he might have participated in the revolutionary upheaval in Saxony in 1830.[1]

Between 1832 and 1837 Weitling worked successively in Dresden, Vienna, Paris, and Vienna again. He was particularly impressed by Paris, and in 1837 he returned there in the hope of furthering his understanding of the doctrines expounded by the various socialist and communist sects now established in the French capital. He became one of the leaders of a secret society, the League of the Just (*Bund der Gerechten*), composed mainly of German *émigrés* but also including some Swiss, Scandinavian, and Hungarian members. In 1838 he undertook the task of preparing a theoretical work for the League, setting out a programme of action. The resulting short book, *Mankind As It Is and As It Should Be (Die Menschheit, wie sie ist und wie sie sein sollte)*, advocated a workers' revolution leading to the establishment of a new order based on the egalitarian principles of early Christianity. In particular, communism – in the sense of communal ownership of property – and democratic institutions of government were seen to be essential preconditions of a just society.

In May 1839 the League participated in an abortive revolutionary uprising in Paris. The leaders, who included Louis Auguste Blanqui and Armand Barbès, were imprisoned, and Weitling himself was fortunate to escape. The following year he was on his way to Switzerland to inform the workers there of the League's communist programme. Switzerland was a centre of revolutionary activity, chiefly because of its liberal press laws, but Weitling found that specifically communist propaganda had not yet made any real impact. So he set about establishing communist workers' clubs, and within eighteen months had founded seventeen societies – thirteen German and four French – comprising some 1,300 individual members. He also inaugurated a journal known originally as *The Cry of German Youth for Help (Der Hülferuf der deutschen Jugend)* but subsequently entitled *The Young Generation (Die junge Generation)*.

December 1842 saw the appearance, in a secretly published edition of *Guarantees of Harmony and Freedom (Garantien der Harmonie und Freiheit)*, which is undoubtedly Weitling's single most important work and a landmark in the development of German socialism. (Marx was later to describe it as the 'incomparably brilliant début of the German worker'.[2]) The book was an attempt by Weitling to present his communist theories in a straightforward language which ordinary workers could easily understand. In the first section he outlined the evolution of modern society, showing how the gradual establishment of private property rights and the increasing power of money had led to class antagonisms and the enslavement of human labour. The second section set out to show that freedom could only be attained by restoring the balance or harmony between man's needs and his physical and intellectual capacities which had once existed in a long-lost 'golden age'. This implied the necessity for some overall scientific regulation of production and consumption, which in turn demanded the abolition of private property and its replacement by communism. Like Saint-Simon, Weitling drew a distinction between the government of society through the exercise of force and the administration of society through the application of knowledge. The eventual triumph of administration over government, predicted with such confidence by Saint-Simon, was also regarded as inevitable by Weitling. He had no doubts, either, about the most effective method of inaugurating the required changes: 'During the transition dictatorship is necessary to establish the new organisation.'[3] (The dictatorship would be popular, though, and in this restricted sense it could be described as democratic.)

Communism had always been regarded by Weitling as a new religion based on an ethical system which derived ultimately from the teachings of Christ, and this subject was the central theme of his next work, *The Poor Sinner's Gospel (Das Evangelium des armen Sünders)*. The book was due to be published in Zurich in the summer of 1843, but, as Weitling himself explained:

> When half the printing had left the press I was arrested at night in the open street and the plates and the rest of the manuscript were confiscated. I was imprisoned for fifty weeks, banned, released, banned again and deported to England. The confiscated plates were *destroyed*.
>
> But a friend managed to rescue most of the manuscript. In order to help me and also make its publication possible, he sold it while I was in prison to Mr Jenni in Bern.[4]

Increasingly Weitling seemed to see himself in the role of a persecuted communist Messiah, and he set sail for England in the summer of 1844 confident in the expectation that the British working class would welcome his gospel of salvation. He knew that communist doctrines had already had some success in Britain due to the efforts of Robert Owen, for whom he frequently expressed admiration; and his own ideas had also aroused some interest through reports in a paper published first as *The Promethean* and then as *The Communist Chronicle* (edited by Goodwyn Barmby, founder of the Universal Communitarian Society). But he had to contend with vehement opposition during his seventeen-month stay in London, not least from a group of moderate German communists, led by Karl Schapper and Heinrich Bauer, who rejected his revolutionary approach and his views on religion.

Disappointed with the reception his ideas had received in London, Weitling moved to Brussels in February 1846. Within a short time he found himself immersed in a new conflict over the validity of his theories. This time his opponent was Karl Marx, who two years previously had praised Weitling's *Guarantees of Harmony and Freedom*, but who now saw the author as the representative of a backward-looking, sentimental approach to communism which might appeal to the more skilled artisans, but which would never inspire the new factory proletariat. Even more importantly, Marx completely dismissed Weitling's belief that communism could be established directly without a preparatory stage of capitalist industrialisation and 'bourgeois' democracy. A small circle of communists was now meeting in Brussels to prepare a draft party programme, and Marx realised that no progress could be made until one of the two alternative approaches was rejected. He accordingly threw himself into a heated and protracted argument the final outcome of which was never in doubt: Marx's intellectual superiority persistently revealed the shallowness of his adversary's conceptions, and by early 1847 the Marxian strategy had been adopted. It won formal approval at a congress of the League of the Just in London (the League's new headquarters) in June 1847, and the organisation, now calling itself the Communist League, found itself for the first time with a coherent revolutionary strategy.

Some months previously, while the quarrel with Marx was still going on, Weitling decided to leave Europe for the United States, and with financial assistance from the New York Social Reform Association (*Sozialreform Verein*) he was able to reach America in January 1847. He immediately started to travel around the country, establishing contacts with groups of German workers, and forming new organisations, including a League of Emancipation (*Befreiungsbund*) and, in the wake of the revolutionary upheavals in Germany in 1848, the Philadelphia Workingmens' Association (*Arbeitverein*).

The German Revolution drew Weitling back across the Atlantic. He arrived in Paris in June 1848 and found the French capital immersed in its own revolutionary crisis. He quickly moved on to Germany, where he began to distribute revolutionary pamphlets and address public meetings. In August and October he attended national workers' congresses in Berlin. Also in October he inaugurated a newspaper, *Der Urwähler*, in which he advocated a communist system based on extensive state control through a new Ministry of Social Economy. After its fifth issue *Der Urwähler* was forced to close due to lack of subscriptions. Towards the end of 1848 Weitling left Berlin, where it was becoming increasingly difficult to avoid Government persecution, and moved to Hamburg. For a while he was able to continue his propaganda efforts, but in August 1849 the police ordered him to leave the city.

Weitling was never to set foot on German soil again. He spent the remaining twenty-one years of his life in America attempting to convert workers, especially the large number of German immigrants, to the communist cause. Shortly after settling in New York he started another newspaper, *Die Republik der Arbeiter*, and revived the League of Emancipation as the Workingmen's League (*Arbeiterbund*), an organisation which at the height of its success is thought to have had some 4,000 members.[5] The newspaper achieved moderately good results in terms of the size of its readership, but Weitling never managed to make it financially viable. Under the circumstances he did well to keep it going for as long as five years (January 1850 to July 1855). In the paper Weitling frequently related his own theories of communism to the practical results achieved in America's numerous communist 'colonies' or communities. Weitling was able to visit some of these communities (including the Icarian town at Nauvoo, Illinois) on lecture tours in the early 1850s, and this encouraged him to go ahead, in 1851, with the development of a new utopian experiment at Communia, Iowa, a settlement which had first been established four years earlier by another group of German communists. Such an approach represented a clear departure from the state-centred model of communism which he had usually advocated in relation to the German situation, but in the context of conditions in America the communitarian philosophy seemed perfectly appropriate – indeed, one might even say conventional. It was certainly far from original, and for this reason it is not surprising to find that American commentators frequently saw Weitling as a man who was simply following in the footsteps of earlier pioneers. The New York *Herald*, for example, once described him as 'a sincere convert and disciple of the system of Icarian socialism'.[6]

By 1855 both the Workingmen's League and the Communia colony had virtually collapsed as a result of factionalism, financial disorders, and widespread disillusionment with Weitling's authoritarian style of leadership. 'If all had followed me as the children of Israel followed Moses out of Egypt, I would have succeeded' – so the disappointed prophet declared in his *Workers' Catechism (Der Katechismus der Arbeiter*, 1854).[7] Yet it was perfectly clear by now that Weitling could never hope to command such a high degree of working-class respect, not even among the German immigrants. Weitling himself recognised this fact, and he accordingly decided that the time had come to give up the life of a political activist and to devote more attention to his private affairs. In 1854 he married a German girl, Dorothea Caroline Louise Toedt, just twenty-two years old, who had arrived in America two years earlier. The couple set up home in New York City, and Weitling resumed his work as a tailor.

The Weitlings had a large family (five sons and one daughter), and the father took a great interest in his children's education and upbringing. During the last years of his life he also found time to work on numerous scientific schemes and inventions, including a particularly fascinating project for a new universal language, and he became a keen astronomer. Generally speaking, he was always able to resist the temptation to become actively involved in politics. He was asked to serve on the executive committee of a new Social Party (*Soziale Partei*), founded in New York in 1868, but he refused, pointing out that his circumstances prevented him from attending meetings, and that 'my thirty years' activity have proved to me that means and ends of a good cause are never achieved by parliamentary procedures, but are actually injured thereby'.[8]

Weitling's financial situation deteriorated steadily during the 1860s. The family's income was never high, and they usually had to borrow money to meet their expenses. Weitling also tended to spend too much on attempting to develop and promote his scientific investigations and inventions, and not surprisingly by the late 1860s he was actually bankrupt. His health was gradually getting worse too. In 1868 he severely injured his toe, and it subsequently became infected and had to be amputated. According to Wittke, Weitling was also suffering from diabetes.[9] On 25 January 1871, following a stroke, he died. Just a few hours earlier he had made a rare public appearance at a meeting organised by the Workers' International of New York.

The Primacy of Need

The foundation of Weitling's analysis of social organisation is a theory of human needs. According to this theory every individual is motivated in his behaviour by certain all-important needs which derive from his physical and mental urges. It follows that the key question to be asked of any form of social organisation is whether or not it allows these needs to be satisfied. In his *Guarantees of Harmony and Freedom* Weitling put forward a classification of needs divided into three major groups:

> 1. The need for acquistion. The satisfaction of this need is called: acquisition, possession, wage, property, earnings, etc. A person whose need is satisfied is called: owner, proprietor, purchaser, lord, master, etc. Should the satisfaction of this need be achieved through the violent or cunning suppression of other men's need and the use and expropriation of their capacities, then that is called: robbery, theft, bankruptcy, usury, fraud, taxation, and sometimes: wage, earnings, profit, etc.
>
> 2. The need for pleasure. The satisfaction of this need is called: health, prosperity, happiness, honour, glory, enjoyment, etc. A person whose need is satisfied is

> called: prosperous, happy, contented, pleased, one who enjoys the good life, etc. Should the satisfaction of this need be achieved through the violent or cunning suppression of other men's need and the use and expropriation of their capacities, then that is called: luxury, extravagance, excess, opulence, gluttony, etc.
>
> 3. The need for knowledge. The satisfaction of this need is called: understanding, wisdom, talent, learning, etc. Should the satisfaction of this need be achieved through the violent or cunning suppression of other men's need and the use and expropriation of their capacities, then that is called: tyranny, fraud, falsehood, etc.[10]

Weitling was struck by the fact that many other socialist thinkers seemed to overlook the significance of these various needs, and he singled out for particular criticism in this respect the Saint-Simonian and Fourierist schools of thought, which, he argued, tended to overemphasise the criterion of functional ability or capacity as a basis for social organisation. The Saint-Simonian principle, 'from each according to his ability, to each ability according to its work', sums up well the kind of approach Weitling was anxious to reject, not because he regarded ability as unimportant in allocating work, but because he considered it to be of much less importance than need as a basis for allocating social benefits. For the same reason Fourier's notion of rewarding each worker in the Phalanx according to his contribution of capital, labour, or talent was regarded as no better. Weitling was in fact moving in the direction of the Marxist principle, 'from each according to his ability, to each according to his needs' (although he never actually used these exact words). What he was trying to do above all else was to show how, in future, a new harmony between capacities and needs could be achieved.

In an article on socialism published in November 1842 in *The Young Generation*, Weitling criticised the Saint-Simonians and Fourierists for departing from the principle of full equality. The Saint-Simonians had made the mistake of elevating talent to the level of a privilege 'just like the mightier physical or mental strength of a person', while the Fourierists had made a two-fold blunder by advocating the reward of capital as well as talent.[11] Only in the writings of the principal communist thinkers (such as Owen, Babeuf, and Buonarroti) could a system based on full equality of needs be found, since the communists alone had succeeded in identifying the chief obstacle which must be removed before equality could be achieved: private property. In terms of the very broadest conception of communist theory, therefore, Weitling did not claim to be a great innovator, but saw himself as the successor to various eminent founding fathers in Britain and France. However, he was, he believed (and with obvious justification), a pioneer of communism in Germany, and as such he never doubted that he had a particularly decisive and formative role to perform. Furthermore, he did have some new things to say when it came to describing in detail how needs ought to be catered for within the context of a communist system.

He started by identifying three areas of social activity – three capacities or types of ability – each being a source of satisfaction for one of the three categories of basic human needs. (Capacities, in the Saint-Simonian sense, were thus regarded as significant only inasmuch as they were the instruments by which needs could be satisfied.) Economic production made it possible to satisfy man's acquisitive appetite; the process of consumption gave rise to the range of pleasures and enjoyments which constituted man's sense of well-being; and knowledge found expression in a society's administrative system (like Saint-Simon, Weitling preferred the idea of administration to that of government, since the latter term suggested repressive regulation and the use of coercion). The foundation of any particular society was its administrative system, since it was this system which embodied man's scientific knowledge and understanding (especially his social understanding); next in order of priority came production; and then consumption. The key to social advancement, therefore, was really to be found in the development of science, a development which enabled man to achieve successive improvements in the system of administration, and hence in the balance of human needs and capacities. For Weitling progress in the sciences was 'the single, irrevocable, fundamental law of society'.[12] He qualified this view, however, by carefully distinguishing between a number of different scientific disciplines, some of them much more useful than others in terms of their social applications:

> Among the many sciences which have been cultivated are several which are often more harmful than useful to society. There are other quite useless sciences which, nevertheless, cannot be dispensed with prior to the establishment of a better social order. During the reign of sensual needs in society many a useless science has taken root and found sustenance in bad social organisation.
>
> . . . Necessary sciences are those without which progress would come to a halt, thus leading to the disintegration of society.
>
> Useful sciences are all those whose ideas promote social well-being.
>
> Acceptable sciences are those which through both their ideas and the realisation of those ideas furnish society with comfort, pleasure, and maintenance.
>
> All remaining by-products are unnecessary sciences or arts.[13]

Weitling held that social well-being was promoted chiefly by three sciences whose advancement would provide the basis for the administration of communist society: the sciences of healing, physics, and mechanics (the latter being taken to mean the theory and practice of production). But 'the science of all sciences'[14] was philosophy, which brought all the particular sciences together in one co-ordinated system of knowledge characterised by a total harmony of all ideas. Hence the study of philosophy 'embraces the whole physical and spiritual nature of man, his bodily and spiritual weaknesses and ailments, and the knowledge of their elimination and extirpation'.[15] In other words, it is the philosopher who is able to take a general view of the relationship between human capacities and needs, and who is in a position to show how the right balance (or harmony) may be established beween them.

It can be seen, then, that Weitling, who came from a poor social background, lacked a good education, and who certainly could not claim to be trained in any particular, specialised science, nevertheless regarded himself as a philosopher capable of commenting on fundamental questions concerning social organisation. He did so from the perspective of the moralist armed with insights into human nature and social justice, insights which, in this case, were derived from his practical experience among working-class men and women, his knowledge of the Bible and the teachings of Christianity, and his study of the works of other socialists and communists who had convinced him of the ethical virtues of their systems. Weitling's Christian millenarianism is particularly interesting, since he obviously absorbed it directly from his early experience in German working-class communities and fraternal societies. Millenarianism, far from being new, had well established roots in Germany going back to the Middle Ages. In Weitling's case, therefore, the absorption of millenarianism *preceded* his first serious encounter with the socialist thought of Saint-Simon, Owen, Fourier, and others. This meant that by the time he came to set out his own ideas in systematic form for the first time, in *Mankind As It Is and As It Should Be* (1838), he was already predisposed towards an interpretation of socialism in terms of a millenarian transformation. This places him in a rather different situation from, say, Saint-Simon and Cabet, whose versions of socialism as a New Christian religion were developed at a much later stage in their authors' careers.

Weitling's view of history reflected the influence of traditional German millenarianism as much as that of nineteenth-century socialist doctrines. Historical development was seen to be divided into three major phases: an ancient 'golden age' of primitive communism, the age of private property and competitiveness in social relations, and, finally, the future restoration of universal social well-being under a new communist system. We are thus offered a cyclical theory of historical change, a theory which stipulates that the terrestrial paradise of the future represents a return to a state of happiness which has already existed in a previous long-lost age. Whereas Saint-Simon urged men to look to the future for a vision of the golden age, Weitling did something rather different by attempting to reconcile this outlook with the more orthodox Christian conviction that true happiness had already been enjoyed by man in his original, primitive state. Paradise had been lost, but it could assuredly be regained.

Weitling undoubtedly relied a great deal on ideas drawn from the works of other socialists. It must be remembered that his first major work, *Guarantees of Harmony and Freedom*, appeared in 1842, by which time Saint-Simon and Fourier were both dead, the organised Saint-Simonian school had ceased to exist, Owen was in his seventy-first year, and Cabet was fifty-four, having completed *Journey to Icaria* at the end of the previous decade. Weitling was thus able to make use of an existing socialist literature in a way which was not open to his predecessors. To a certain extent, therefore, his own theories were bound to be derivative, although the combination of Christian millenarianism and socialist doctrine did produce what was in many ways a unique synthesis whose significance should not be underestimated. Furthermore, this uniqueness was firmly consolidated by Weitling's growing attachment to the revolutionary fervour of Babouvism.

The Revolutionary Necessity

In this study of utopian socialism Weitling stands out as the only one of the thinkers under discussion to have recommended revolution as the appropriate means of achieving social transformation. Others – Saint-Simon, some of the Saint-Simonians, and Cabet – did believe that under certain circumstances revolution was likely to occur, but they were confident they could avoid it. Weitling, by contrast, longed for revolution and sought to pave the way for it. He articulated many of the same values as the other thinkers, and thus helped to link British and French ideas with German socialism in its initial phase; but he articulated these values within a framework of revolutionary theory, thereby furnishing an equally important link between early socialism and Marxism.

Weitling's own social background certainly contributed something to the development of his enthusiasm for revolutionary change. He was untypical of early socialist theorists inasmuch as he actually belonged to the working class himself, and was not an intellectual. His belief that the working class must secure liberation through its own revolutionary action, and not through the efforts of bourgeois philanthropists or benevolent governments, undoubtedly stemmed in part from his own class position. It is not a belief one would expect to find so readily put forward in the works of the other thinkers, given that their social background was generally that of the middle or 'bourgeois' class (Saint-Simon's origins, of course, were higher still), and even though they expressed great and sincere concern for the plight of the mass of ordinary workers in society. For this reason there has been a tendency in certain parts of the literature to see Weitling as the first (and perhaps the only) 'authentic' voice *of* (rather than *for*) the working class in its approach to socialism in the nineteenth century. To take just two examples:

> If he has a place in history, it is because he was the first real proletarian (besides the weak Pierre Leroux) who proved to be a revolutionary writer, and the only proletarian who ever built a consistent and complete utopian system of communism. (Hans Mühlestein)[16]

> The works of Wilhelm Weitling . . . stand out amid the communist utopias of the 1840s . . . because he was himself a member of the working class and therefore a better exponent of its attitude at the time than were theorists belonging to the privileged classes. (Leszek Kolakowski)[17]

Both these illustrative quotations are in fact misleading, and for various reasons. Mühlestein's description of Weitling as a proletarian is open to question, since by occupation Weitling was a journeyman tailor, an artisan rather than a proletarian in the more modern sense. Kolakowski refers to him in more general terms as a member of the working class, which is more accurate; but to say that because of this he was a better exponent of the attitudes of the working class than other, more privileged theorists is really quite an incoherent statement, since, as was made clear in the introduction to this book, the working class at this time was certainly not a homogeneous whole characterised by one particular set of attitudes which can be expressed in the writings of an individual thinker. Weitling's background was that of the artisan, more particularly that of the German journeyman worker, and in no sense could he be regarded as a representative of the full range of working-class attitudes to be found among different occupational groups and in different countries (with their varying levels of economic development). The point also needs to be re-emphasised that Weitling's doctrine drew quite freely on the insights of his predecessors, that is, of thinkers who did *not* belong to the working class, a fact which casts further doubt on the suggestion that Weitling's doctrine may be viewed as necessarily more representative of working-class attitudes than any other socialist doctrines in the early nineteenth century.

We can be sure that Weitling's background did stimulate in his mind certain thoughts concerning the need for workers to liberate themselves through their own efforts. These initial thoughts were later confirmed by his analysis of French revolutionary thinking and practice as represented, in particular, by the Babouvist tradition. One must take some care, however, to define precisely what Weitling had in mind when he used the concept of revolution. In particular, the crucial question of whether he thought revolution must involve violence has to be answered. 'There will always be revolutions', he wrote in his most systematic analysis of this issue, 'but they will not always be bloody.'[18] He advocated a workers' rising, a *coup d'état*, as the necessary method of laying the foundations for communism, and saw this transition in terms of a major upheaval. Such an upheaval was unavoidable, he argued, because communism would never be established in any other way, certainly not through the voluntary action of the existing ruling classes. The *coup d'état* would be an act of theft – the theft by the workers of the power which resided in the hands of their oppressors. In a society based on true equality theft could never be tolerated, but under present conditions of inequality the *coup d'état* was an act of perfectly justifiable theft, the last such act which would ever occur during the course of human history. 'Stealing is . . . the test of a social organisation',[19] asserted Weitling, contrasting the way in which, under existing circumstances, many people were forced to steal in order to live with future communist society, where theft would be unnecessary and, in any case, impossible, since the basic needs of everyone would be satisfied through collective provision.

Weitling did not doubt that a workers' revolution might involve violent conflict. One only has to consider his persistent admiration for the Babouvists' conspiratorial strategy, his own work for the League of the Just, especially in helping to plan and co-ordinate its part in the Paris uprising of May

1839, and his enthusiastic support for the French and German revolutions of 1848. All this points to the inescapable conclusion that he recognised the need, in certain situations, for the use of force. At the same time, however, he hoped that the workers' great strength (based on their large numbers, the advantages of combination, and efficient conspiratorial organisation) would enable them to gain control of society quickly and without much bloodshed. This was really the main point behind his remark that a revolution did not have to be bloody.

The transition to communism was to be carried out by a popular (and therefore democratic) dictatorship.[20] In this way the foundations of the new system of administration, production, and consumption would be established in a thoroughly scientific and efficient manner. Weitling seems to have envisaged his ideal communist society as one with a population of several million persons. He was thus advocating communism on the scale of nation-states, very much as Cabet did in his *Journey to Icaria*, rather than on the scale of very small communities such as those recommended by Owen and Fourier. In later life, of course, he did become interested in small-scale communitarian experiments in America, but, as with Cabet, this represented a clear departure from the original model. In the case of both thinkers the small-scale community was intended to be simply the initial stage in the process of creating a much larger communist association.

In his very first book, *Mankind As It Is and As It Should Be* (1838), written for the guidance of the League of the Just, Weitling provided the reader with an outline constitution for administering a communist society. The new society was to be a League of Families (*Familienbund*), and this League was to be divided up into a large number of territorial provinces, each consisting of about 10,000 families. Every province would be further sub-divided into ten units of 1,000 families each, and these smaller units (*Familienvereine*) would form areas of local administration. Each locality and province would have its own elected board to manage the area's administrative affairs, and at the central level a congress, consisting of one representative chosen by each provincial board, would be instituted. This congress would in turn choose a senate, which would operate as the supreme legislative authority for the entire society, and also a three-person executive council, including one representative of each of the major branches of science (healing, physics, and mechanics), whose job it would be to show how scientific knowledge could best be applied to the solution of social problems, and to supervise the judging of regular competitions which would be held to encourage scientific inventiveness. Women would have the same political rights as men, and would thus be able to vote and stand for office, with the one exception that in the initial stages of communism no woman would be eligible for the three-person council. The main priority was that no economic and social distinctions should emerge to separate office-holders from ordinary citizens: 'After a social upheaval no man can be trusted to rule who is not prepared to live at the same material level as the poorest and most humble members of the community.'[21]

In addition to these institutions representing groups of families there would also be a complex network of functional organisations representing the major occupational categories, and given special responsibility for dealing with matters relating to the production of goods and services. What this amounted to in fact was a scheme for industrial and professional democracy, with small groups of farmers, workers, and teachers forming themselves into three major structures, and electing their own immediate superiors who would in turn choose chiefs at successively higher tiers of administration, right up to the central level.

The first set of institutions, based on groups of families, would have the responsibility of defining the main requirements of society; and the second set, based on functional organisations, would respond by deciding on the best methods of satisfying those requirements. The link between the two would be provided by the senate and its ministerial departments, which would oversee the whole process of decision-making, and would supervise the implementation of policies by appointing regional directors in charge of economic planning, one director for each group of ten provinces (equivalent to a population of about a million). Weitling's constitution thus attempted to reconcile the needs for expertise and popular participation, and it also attempted to show how, in future, the administrative system (which, as pointed out earlier, was regarded by Weitling as the most fundamentally important feature of any society) could enable man to achieve a new harmony between productive work (the sector corresponding to functional, occupational organisation in Weitling's scheme) and consumption (the latter's requirements being expressed through the system of family groupings).

Like all the other utopian socialists, Weitling had his own list of basic consumer needs which he wished to see satisfied in future society, although, as his draft constitution made clear, in matters of detail he was willing to give some discretion to representative institutions. Because he was a communist, he rejected private ownership of property as a title to any reward, and was thus left with two possible methods of allocating benefits: collective, planned provision through the public authorities, and/or an element of consumer choice through the expenditure of income earned through work. In actual fact he placed his emphasis firmly on the first method, although he did allow some scope for the second. The absolute necessities of life, he argued, must be made available for the whole of society through a general social plan, a plan which would obviously demand a certain structure of employment. But, once these necessities were provided, 'luxuries' could be produced by workers deciding for themselves what jobs to do, and the credit earned by these workers (recorded in terms of labour-hours) could be exchanged directly for other 'luxury' products made by their fellow workers. A Bank of Exchange would be instituted to issue labour notes (money in the orthodox sense would be abolished), and to help preserve a certain amount of individual consumer choice in an otherwise centrally planned economy.

'Under communism all people will have the same resources for bringing up their children and for their own development.'[22] This was to be the chief principle underlying the public provision of necessities in communist society. Food, clothing, housing and sanitation, a pleasurable environment, health care, education, useful and satisfying employment were all to be recognised as necessities of life, and basic standards would accordingly be safeguarded by the state. Like most of the other utopian socialists, Weitling enjoyed filling in the details of what everyday life in the new society would be like. He frequently stressed the central importance of family life, and was much more of a traditionalist in this respect than Owen and Fourier, although he did call for the emancipation of women from household drudgery, and he acknowledged the need to free marriage from all economic and social restrictions, while at the same time making divorce easier. Each family would have its own private living accommodation and garden, but kitchens, storehouses, and orchards would be communal. Children would remain at home until they were six years old, when they would depart for the start of their communal education.

On the subject of work and its organisation Weitling was greatly influenced by the ideas of Fourier. From the latter he took up the notion that in future society, in order to make work satisfying, no one should be restricted to one particular job. This was especially important, he believed, for industrial workers, who should be able to change from one task to another every two hours. As far as possible everyone should have the chance to do both physical and mental work. Women should have the same employment rights as men, but an effort should be made to give them the lighter physical work; and it was considered desirable for women to have their own separate occupational associations. Huge industrial armies (again the influence of Fourier is apparent) were to be set up for the training of all fit persons between the ages of fifteen and eighteen. (One of the attractions of service in the industrial army was that extra labour credits would be earned.) In the long term Weitling looked forward to a time when work would be 'organised rationally with the full use of machinery', and when the working day would accordingly be reduced to less than five hours: 'this will leave everyone time for other things such as writing and study'.[23]

When he came to deal with the issue of religion in communist society, Weitling adopted a similar strategy to that proposed by Cabet. Both thinkers were anxious to defend the virtues of their systems in terms of Christian morality, and this inevitably led them to stress the importance of teaching the Christian moral code to all citizens from an early age. However, neither thinker was interested in a very formal, ritualistic religion, and Weitling was quite happy to leave such practical matters to the decision of each individual. He did not personally approve of an established church hierarchy, but if certain people wished to keep such a structure, they would be allowed to do so as long as this did not divert them from their broader allegiance to the ethics of communism:

> Religious people under communism can keep all that they now hold dear in their religion. Communism only insists that they must not do this at the expense of others who do not want religion. Communist rule does not require religious or legal doctrines, it merely teaches that morality propounded at the beginning of this book which is necessary to the nature of communism; this morality does not contradict any religious doctrine. The practice of religion is a matter of choice, and as long as work is done, there is no reason why leisure time should not be spent on it.
>
> . . . People can keep their bishops, priests and jesuits so long as these people work like others, and teach their doctrines with the interests of believers in mind and not out of self-interest.[24]

The prescribed moral code would teach men to understand the ethical superiority of communism over the existing form of social organisation. These ethical arguments in favour of communism were always emphasised by Weitling, and although he believed in the historical inevitability of achieving communism in the future, such a view was never regarded by him as the real basis of his doctrine. The moral conviction was much more important. In this context, too, Weitling warned of the need to keep alive a perpetual sense of future social progress, even under communism. Communism was the best possible societal system he could envisage, but he recognised that it would always be capable of further improvement: 'Mankind will never attain the highest ideal of perfection, since this would mean a halt to our spiritual progress.'[25] It is interesting to note, indeed, that even in his very first book, *Mankind As It Is and As It Should Be*, Weitling alerted his readers to the dangers of imagining that under communism further change would be impossible:

> We do not claim that we are setting out the most perfect ideal of social reform. This would be to accept that the fountain of knowledge has been completely

> drained. Every generation, like every individual, has its own idea of perfection. Man can certainly draw nearer and nearer to perfection, but he will never attain it completely in this life.[26]

In recent years it has become fashionable to criticise utopian thinkers for wishing to place man in a situation of what might be called social immobility, that is, one in which man's social evolution has finally come to a halt. Thus, to take just one example, Ralf Dahrendorf has asserted that all utopias

> have had one element of construction in common: they are all societies from which change is absent. Whether conceived as a final state and climax of historical development, as an intellectual's nightmare, or as a romantic dream, the social fabric of utopia does not, and perhaps cannot, recognise the unending flow of the historical process.[27]

As far as the utopian socialists are concerned, this criticism seems to overlook the fact that all of them have some notion of continuing development within the general framework of their ideal societies. In the writings of Weitling, in particular, there is an explicit recognition of what Dahrendorf calls 'the unending flow of the historical process'. In this respect, at least, one might say that Weitling injected a realism into his conception of social progress which can still come as quite a surprise to those critics of utopianism who are convinced that all utopian visionaries are prophets of a changeless world.

Notes

Introduction

1. Leo A. Loubère, 'The Intellectual Origins of French Jacobin Socialism', *International Review of Society History*, vol. IV, 1959, p. 422. See also Bernard H. Moss, 'Parisian Producers' Associations (1830-51): The Socialism of Skilled Workers', in Roger Price (ed.), *Revolution and Reaction. 1848 and the Second French Republic*, London, 1975, pp. 73-86; and the same author's *The Origins of the French Labor Movement 1830-1914. The Socialism of Skilled Workers*, Berkeley, California, 1976, ch. 2.
2. Arthur Louis Dunham, *The Industrial Revolution in France 1815-1848*, New York, 1955, p. 203.
3. See the writings by Bernard H. Moss referred to in note 1 above; also his 'Parisian Workers and the Origins of Republican Socialism, 1830-1833', in John H. Merriman (ed.), *1830 in France*, New York, 1975, pp. 203-21.
4. The *compagnonnages* originated under the guild system in the fifteenth century as associations of skilled journeymen (*compagnons*). Although their general significance was declining by the nineteenth century, they persisted in certain trades.
5. 'The word "association" is being applied in our time only to narrow combinations that embrace but one type of interest' – so the leading Saint-Simonians complained in 1829. Instead they put forward the goal of 'universal association' – 'the association of all men on the entire surface of the globe in all spheres of their relationships'. Georg G. Iggers (trans. and ed.), *The Doctrine of Saint-Simon: An Exposition. First Year, 1828-1829*, 2nd ed., New York, 1972, p. 58.
6. Malcolm I. Thomis, *The Town Labourer and the Industrial Revolution*, New York, 1974, p. 194.
7. The *sociétés de secours mutuel* were essentially friendly societies providing their members with financial aid in cases of illness or death.
8. Both Fourier and Weitling welcomed an industrial society as a society based on productive labour, but they nevertheless detested the idea of traditional occupations being superseded by factory-based manufacturing. For Fourier agriculture (and, more specifically, horticulture) should remain the key occupation. Weitling, even though he recognised the need for greater mechanisation, still considered it to be imperative to protect the position of handicraft.

9. Rosabeth Moss Kanter, *Commitment and Community. Communes and Utopias in Sociological Perspective*, Cambridge, Massachusetts, 1972, pp. 54-5.
10. This newspaper also issued fervent defences of the institution of private property in response to the Saint-Simonians, who, although they were not communists, wished to abolish the right of inheritance.
11. See, for example, Albert Brisbane, *Association, or, A Concise Exposition of the Practical Part of Fourier's Social Science*, New York, 1843, p. 4. Fourier himself described Owen's notion of economic communism as 'so pitiful that it is not worthy of refutation'. Charles Gide (ed.), *Design for Utopia. Selected Writings of Charles Fourier*, intro. by Frank E. Manuel, New York, 1971, p. 128, quoting from *The New Industrial and Societary World.*
12. See Robert C. Bowles, 'The Reaction of Charles Fourier to the French Revolution', *French Historical Studies*, vol. 1, 1958-60 p. 355.
13. Some useful material on this point may be found in E.P. Thompson, *The Making of the English Working Class*, rev. ed., Harmondsworth, 1968, ch. 15, esp. pp. 668-70.
14. For example: David H. Pinkney, *The French Revolution of 1830*, Princeton, New Jersey, 1972; Roger Price, *The French Second Republic. A Social History*, London, 1972; Jacques Godechot (ed.), *La Révolution de 1848 à Toulouse et dans la Haute-Garonne*, Toulouse, 1948; Fernand Rude (ed.), *La Révolution de 1848 dans le département de l'Isère*, Grenoble, 1949; Fernand Rude, *L'Insurrection lyonnaise de novembre 1831. Le Mouvement ouvrier à Lyon de 1827-1832*, preface by Edouard Dolléans, 2nd ed., Paris, 1969; Robert J. Bezucha, *The Lyon Uprising of 1834. Social and Political Conflict in the Early July Monarchy*, Cambridge, Massachusetts, 1974; Maurice Agulhon, *Une Ville ouvrière au temps du socialisme utopique. Toulon de 1815 à 1851*, 2nd ed., Paris, 1977. The general hypothesis which emerges from these studies is that the chief participants in the upheavals of this period were artisans or newly proletarianised workers suffering the most severe consequences of socio-economic transition. The case of the silk-workers (*canuts*) of Lyons is the best documented.
15. Rude, *L'Insurrection lyonnaise de novembre 1831*, pp. 697-711.
16. Some modern critics of utopianism (e.g. F.A. Hayek, J.L. Talmon, K.R. Popper) go even further and persistently equate utopianism and totalitarianism.
17. This was, in particular, one of the main points at issue in the continual disputes between Saint-Simonians and Fourierists.
18. Robert Alun Jones and Robert M. Anservitz, 'Saint-Simon and Saint-Simonism: A Weberian View', *American Journal of Sociology*, vol. 80, 1975, pp. 1095-1123.
19. See Kanter, op. cit., pp. 129-36.
20. For this notion of utopian commitment I am indebted to Kanter (op. cit.).
21. Rudolf Heberle, *Social Movements*, New York, 1951, p. 70.
22. Christopher H. Johnson, 'Etienne Cabet and the Problem of Class Antagonism', *International Review of Social History*, vol. XI, 1966, pp. 403-43; 'Communism and the Working Class before Marx: The Icarian System', *American Historical Review*, vol. 76, 1971, pp. 642-89; *Utopian Communism in France. Cabet and the Icarians, 1839-1851*, Ithaca, New York, 1974.
23. Johnson, *Utopian Communism in France*, pp. 145-9. Unfortunately, Johnson himself is not entirely consistent in his overall assessment of Icarianism as a social movement. On the one hand he sees Icarianism as 'the first mass movement to accept the total overthrow of the emerging capitalist society' (p. 299); but on other occasions he tends to qualify this judgment.

Thus: Icarianism 'takes a place beside a wide variety of *transitional* social movements that arise in the earlier and more traumatic stages of industrialisation but are inherently incapable of becoming viable mass movements in the modern industrial context' (p. 16).

24. Ibid., pp. 153-68. Johnson's analysis is here very useful, but it occasionally leads to confusion owing to a lack of precision in the terminology employed. In particular, the Icarian movement is said to be neither proletarian nor petty-bourgeois. How, then, are we to characterise it? Is the idea of an 'artisan movement' sufficiently clear?
25. Ibid., p. 160.
26. Heberle, op. cit., p. 14.
27. Iggers, op. cit., p. xxiv.
28. Ibid., p. xxiv.
29. The 'generational consciousness' at this time throughout western Europe but especially in France was truly remarkable. As Feuer has written: 'Generational consciousness, in the sense of involving an antagonism, first came into existence when the hopes of the French Revolutionary era were unfulfilled, and those of the Restoration period were de-authoritised in the eyes of the young. Thus arose "the generation of 1830".' Lewis S. Feuer, *The Conflict of Generations*, London, 1969, p. 35.
30. See Johnson, *Utopian Communism in France*, pp. 13 and 156 (footnote).
31. Quoted by Johnson, ibid., p. 207.
32. Furthermore, Fourierism never put forward any coherent religious creed, nor did it ever form a deliberately organised sect. Religion was encouraged, but no dogmatic beliefs were defined. As with other aspects of the Fourierist doctrine, a considerable degree of freedom was thought desirable.
33. An excellent account is provided by J.F.C. Harrison, *Robert Owen and the Owenites in Britain and America. The Quest for the New Moral World*, London, 1969, pp. 195-232.
34. See Thompson, op. cit., pp. 857-87; E.J. Hobsbawm, *The Age of Revolution*, London, 1962, p. 210. Harrison (op. cit., pp. 213-14) concludes that Owenism constituted a mass movement only in 1833-4, the period during which the Owenites succeeded in capturing the trade union movement.
35. For example Henryk Katz, 'Social Movements – an Essay in Definition', *Polish Sociological Bulletin*, no. 1, 1971, p. 65.
36. Thompson, op. cit., p. 894.
37. Ibid., pp. 869-70.
38. Henry Pelling, *A History of British Trade Unionism*, Harmondsworth, 1963, pp. 42-3.
39. Hobsbawm, op. cit., p. 221.
40. A comprehensive analysis of this issue is provided by P.H. Noyes, *Organization and Revolution*, Princeton, New Jersey, 1966. See also Edward Shorter, 'Middle-Class Anxiety in the German Revolution of 1848', *Journal of Social History*, vol. 2, 1968-9, pp. 189-215.
41. There are brief comments in *The Communist Manifesto*, part III, section 1 (c). Engels' *On the History of the Communist League* offers more detail.
42. Maldwyn Allen Jones, *American Immigration*, Chicago, 1960, pp. 110-11.
43. See Herbert G. Gutman, *Work, Culture, and Society in Industrializing America*, New York, 1976, ch. 1.
44. Karl J.R. Arndt, *George Rapp's Harmony Society 1785-1847*, Philadelphia, 1965, p. 6.
45. My thoughts on this question of how realism, in the sense of practicability, is to be understood have been greatly clarified by reading an excellent article

by H.J.N. Horsburgh: 'The Relevance of the Utopian', *Ethics*, vol. 67, 1957, pp. 127-38.

Chapter One. Henri Saint-Simon

1. His full name and title: Claude-Henri de Rouvroy, comte de Saint-Simon. Most biographers state that he was born in Paris, but documentary evidence exists to show that Berny was the actual birthplace. See Mathurin Dondo, *The French Faust. Henri de Saint-Simon*, New York, 1955, p. 10.
2. *Letters to an American*, in Henri Saint-Simon, *Selected Writings on Science, Industry and Social Organisation*, trans. and ed. Keith Taylor, London, 1975, p. 162. (In subsequent notes the abbreviation *S.W.* is used to refer to this book.)
3. *Letters to an American*, in *S.W.*, p. 163.
4. *Lettres au Bureau des Longitudes. Préface*, in *Oeuvres de Claude-Henri de Saint-Simon* (in 6 vols.), Paris, 1966, vol. I, pt. 1, p. 67. (In subsequent notes the abbreviation *Oeuvres* is used to refer to these volumes.)
5. Today such proposals may strike the reader as somewhat ridiculous. It must be remembered, though, that various attempts had already been made in France to institute new religious cults – for example, Robespierre's 'Cult of the Supreme Being', and the Theophilanthropic movement. The Religion of Newton was another 'cult of reason' and was totally in keeping with revolutionary ideology.
6. The list is reproduced in Alfred Pereire, *Autour de Saint-Simon. Documents originaux*, Paris, 1912, pp. 4-9, and makes fascinating reading. It contains the names of 134 subscribers of various sums ranging from 100 to 1,000 francs, giving a total subscription of 24,400 francs. Included in the list are the names of the Minister of Finance (Roy), four peers, and twenty-four deputies. Most of the other contributors were prominent businessmen.
7. Saint-Simon introduced the term 'industrial' (*'industriel'*), used as a noun, at the beginning of the Bourbon Restoration to refer to any person – employer or employee – engaged in any productive activity, whether in the strictly 'practical' sphere (agriculture, manufacturing, commerce, finance) or the more 'theoretical' sphere (science and art). From about 1820 onwards he modified this usage and usually used the term to refer only to the 'practical' workers. In other words the scientists and artists became 'non-industrials'. The modern English equivalent for *'industriel'* is 'industrialist', but this word tends to be applied nowadays only to entrepreneurs in the manufacturing sector, and so does not really correspond to Saint-Simon's much broader conception. For this reason I have preferred to use 'industrial' throughout the present study.
8. He was 'considered only as a clever *original*', as John Stuart Mill, who met him in 1821, put it in his *Autobiography*, London, 1873, p. 61. The meeting took place in the house of Jean-Baptiste Say. The accuracy of Mill's view is confirmed by contemporary French sources, e.g. the *Biographie nouvelle des contemporains*, Paris, 1824, pp. 374-5, which emphasises Saint-Simon's originality, with particular reference to *The Organiser*, but offers no systematic analysis of his doctrine.
9. *Introduction to the Scientific Studies of the 19th Century*, in *S.W.*, pp. 88, 90.
10. The French word *'organisation'* can mean both 'organisation' and 'organic structure'. (Hence *'organisé'* may mean either 'organised' or 'organic'.) In the *Memoir on the Science of Man* Saint-Simon used the term *'organisation'* to refer to the organic structure of man and other animals. See *S.W.*, pp. 114-15.

11. *The Reorganisation of European Society*, in S.W., p. 136.
12. *L'Organisateur*, in *Oeuvres*, vol. II, pt. 2, p. 72.
13. See Peyton V. Lyon, 'Saint-Simon and the Origins of Scientism and Historicism', *Canadian Journal of Economics and Political Science*, vol. XXVII, 1961, pp. 55-63.
14. *Letters from an Inhabitant of Geneva to His Contemporaries*, in *S.W.*, p. 75.
15. *Memoir on the Science of Man*, in *S.W.*, p. 112.
16. See, for example, W.M. Simon, 'Ignorance is Bliss: Saint-Simon and the Writing of History', *Revue internationale de philosophie*, vol. 14, 1960, pp. 357-83.
17. *Introduction to the Scientific Studies of the 19th Century*, in *S.W.*, p. 94.
18. Prospectus for *L'Industrie*, vol. III, in *S.W.*, p. 170.
19. *De la Réorganisation de la société européene*, in *Oeuvres*, vol. I, pt. 1, p. 158.
20. *The Political Interests of Industry*, in *S.W.*, p. 181.
21. Although this precise expression was never actually used by Saint-Simon, it does sum up his moral outlook, which was basically utilitarian in the Benthamite sense. Whether this was due to the direct influence of Bentham's ideas is not definitely known. But the supposition does seem reasonable in view of the widespread popularity enjoyed by Bentham in France during the first quarter of the nineteenth century. Cf. W. Stark, 'The Realism of Saint-Simon's Spiritual Program', *The Journal of Economic History*, vol. V, 1945, pp. 24-42 *passim*. See also J.-B. Duvergier, *De la Législation*, in *Opinions Littéraires, philosophiques et industrielles*, Paris, 1825. In this illuminating but hitherto neglected essay the relationship between the ideas of Bentham and Saint-Simon is discussed in some detail.
22. For an explanation of this term see note 7.
23. *Letters to an American*, in *S.W.*, p. 165.
24. *Nouveau Christianisme*, in *Oeuvres*, vol. III, pt. 3, p. 164.
25. *Letters to an American*, in *S.W.*, p. 168.
26. The conception's originality must not be exaggerated, however. The idea of a transition from arbitrary government to scientific administration was almost certainly derived, at least in part, from Bacon's argument that a truly scientific society can dispense with power politics. This belief was transmitted to Saint-Simon both through his own reading of Bacon's work and also through the influence of the Encyclopaedists, who were great admirers of Bacon and were largely responsible for introducing his ideas into France. (In *Novum Organum* Bacon predicted that the progress of the arts and sciences would result in the replacement of dominion over man by 'the empire of man over things'. Quoted by Benjamin Farrington, *Francis Bacon. Philosopher of Industrial Science*, London, 1951, p. 7.) It also seems likely that Saint-Simon's advocacy of a new system of expert administration owed something to the influence of the classical political economists, both English and French, and Jeremy Bentham, who shared Saint-Simon's faith in 'the professional ideal of a functional society based on expertise and selection by merit'. (Harold Perkin, *The Origins of Modern English Society 1780-1880*, London, 1969, p. 320.)
27. *Deuxième Correspondence avec messieurs les industriels, Du Système industriel*, pt. 1, in *Oeuvres*, vol. III, pt. 1, pp. 131-2.
28. F.A. Hayek, *The Road to Serfdom*, London, 1944, p. 18.
29. Lyon, op. cit., p. 62.
30. F.M.H. Markham, 'Saint-Simon. A Nineteenth-Century Prophet', *History Today*, vol. IV, 1954, p. 547. Cf. the same author's introduction to Henri

de Saint-Simon, *Social Organization, The Science of Man and Other Writings*, New York, 1964, pp. xlviii-xlix.

31. Giovanni Sartori, *Democratic Theory*, New York, 1965, p. 389.
32. Leonard Schapiro, *Totalitarianism*, London, 1972, p. 89.
33. H.G. Schenk, 'Revolutionary Influences and Conservatism in Literature and Thought', in *The New Cambridge Modern History*, vol. IX, ed. C.W. Crawley, Cambridge, 1965, p. 112.
34. Walter M. Simon, 'History for Utopia: Saint-Simon and the Idea of Progress', *Journal of the History of Ideas*, vol. XVII, 1956, p. 329.
35. J.L. Talmon, *Political Messianism. The Romantic Phase*, New York, 1960, pp. 35-70 *passim*.
36. See further ch. 4, especially pp. 148-58, and the illuminating article by Georg G. Iggers: 'Le Saint-Simonisme et la pensée autoritaire' (in English), *Économies et sociétés*, vol. IV, 1970, pp. 673-91. Iggers quite rightly points out (p. 673, note 3) that 'the major studies dealing with Saint-Simonian affinities to totalitarianism have first appeared in the English language', reflecting the fact that 'the major centre of research into the nature of totalitarianism has been the English-speaking world'. It is certainly interesting to note that French commentators have not demonstrated the same preoccupation.
37. See, in particular, his statements on the subject in *S.W.*, pp. 210 (*The Organiser*) and 229 (*The Industrial System*, pt. I).
38. *Letters to an American*, in S.W., p. 165.
39. Ibid., p. 165.
40. *Fragments on Social Organisation*, in *S.W.*, p. 266.
41. *Address to Philanthropists*, in S.W., p. 224.
42. 'The essence of my life's work', Saint-Simon declared shortly before his death, 'is to afford all members of society the greatest possible opportunity for the development of their faculties.' Quoted by Frank E. Manuel, *The New World of Henri Saint-Simon*, Notre Dame, Indiana, 1963, p. 365.
43. See, for example, *Letters from an Inhabitant of Geneva to His Contemporaries*, in *S.W.*, p. 81.
44. *Catéchisme des industriels, 4e cahier*, in *Oeuvres*, vol. V, pt. 1, p. 25.
45. *Catéchisme des industriels, 3e cahier*, in *Oeuvres*, vol. IV, pt. 2, p. 4.
46. *Considérations sur les mesures à prendre pout terminer la révolution, Du Système industriel*, pt. 1, in *Oeuvres*, vol. III, part 1, p. 122.
47. *Lettres sur les Bourbons, Du Système industriel*, pt. 1, in *Oeuvres*, vol. III, pt. 2, p. 81.
48. The actual term 'capitalist' ('*capitaliste*') was used by Saint-Simon to mean 'financier' or 'money-lender'. This is, of course, a much more restricted definition than that employed by Marx.
49. *Fragments on Social Organisation*, in *S.W.*, p. 265.
50. In France this could only be done, in Saint-Simon's view, through reforms of the taxation system, since only the country's chief taxpayers were given the vote. See *S.W.*, ch. 14 *(Views on Property and Legislation).*
51. *Sketch of the New Political System*, in *S.W.*, p. 206.
52. *Fragments on Social Organisation*, in *S.W.*, pp. 262-3.
53. *Comparison of the English and French Political Systems*, in *S.W.*, p. 255.
54. See *S.W.*, ch. 14 *(Views on Property and Legislation)* and also the footnote, ibid., p. 151.
55. See, for example, Anthony Giddens, *The Class Structure of the Advanced Societies*, London, 1973, pp. 23-4, 64, 135-6, 287.

Chapter Two. Robert Owen

1. Robert Owen, *The Life of Robert Owen Written by Himself. With Selections from His Writings and Correspondence* (in 2 vols. numbered I and IA), London, 1857-8, vol. I, p. 4.
2. Ibid., vol. I, p. 19.
3. Ibid., vol. I, p. 46.
4. Ibid., vol. I, pp. 56-7.
5. Ibid., vol. I, p. 57.
6. Ibid., vol. I, p. 81.
7. Owen marked the occasion with *An Address Delivered to the Inhabitants of New Lanark, on the First January 1816, at the Opening of the Institution for the Formation of Character.*
8. G.D.H. Cole, *The Life of Robert Owen*, 3rd ed., new intro. by Margaret Cole, London, 1965, p. 177.
9. 'I have from that day to this considered that day the most important of my life for the public:- the day on which bigotry, superstition, and all false religions, received the death blow.' Owen, *The Life of Robert Owen Written by Himself*, vol. I, p. 162.
10. Cole, op. cit., p. 307.
11. *A New View of Society*, in Robert Owen, *A New View of Society and Other Writings*, intro. by G.D.H. Cole, London and New York, 1927, pp. 16, 45. (In subsequent notes this book is referred to as *Writings.*)
12. William Hazlitt, *Political Essays, with Sketches of Public Characters*, London, 1819, p. 98. (Hazlitt went on to say that Owen's ideas 'are not only old, they are superannuated, they are dead and buried, they are reduced to mummy, they are put into the catacombs at Paris, they are sealed up in patent coffins, they have been dug up again and anatomised, they have been drawn, quartered and gibbetted, they have become black, dry, parched in the sun, loose, and rotten, and are dispersed to all the winds of Heaven!' Ibid., p. 98.)
13. Graham Wallas, *The Life of Francis Place 1771-1854*, 4th ed., London, 1925, p. 64, quoting from the Place manuscripts.
14. Robert Dale Owen, *Threading My Way. An Autobiography*, New York, 1874, p. 90.
15. It is interesting to note that when John Stuart Mill, Thomas Carlyle, and other British thinkers became interested in the concept of historical development after about 1830, it was under the direct influence of French – not British – sources, and, in the case of Mill and Carlyle, the chief source was Saint-Simonism. Mill acknowledged this influence in his *Autobiography*, London, 1873, p. 163: 'The writers by whom, more than by any others, a new mode of political thinking was brought home to me, were those of the Saint-Simonian school in France. . . . I was greatly struck with the connected view which they for the first time presented to me, of the natural order of human progress; and especially with their division of all history into organic periods and critical periods. . . .'
16. *An Address to the Working Classes*, in *Writings*, p. 149.
17. *A New View of Society*, in *Writings*, p. 63.
18. *The New Moral World*, no. 11, 10 January 1835, p. 84.
19. *The New Moral World*, no. 1, 1 November 1834, p. 1.
20. *The New Moral World*, no. 1, 1 November 1834, p. 6. In issue no. 2 (8 November 1834) this method was described as 'the most natural, the most easy, and decidedly the best' (p. 10).
21. Robert Owen, *The Book of the New Moral World, Containing the Rational System of Society, Founded on Demonstrable Facts, Developing the*

Constitution and Laws of Human Nature and of Society, pt. I, London, 1842, p. xvii.
22. *A New View of Society*, in *Writings*, p. 73.
23. Cole, op. cit., p. 209.
24. Robert Owen, *The Revolution in the Mind and Practice of the Human Race or The Coming Change from Irrationality to Rationality. With a Supplement 1849*, London, 1849, pp. 74-5.
25. Robert Owen, *The Book of the New Moral World . . .*, pt. III, London, 1842, p. 48.
26. Ibid., p. 47.
27. *Report to the Committee for the Relief of the Manufacturing Poor*, in *Writings*, p. 158.
28. Ibid., p. 158.
29. Ibid., p. 164.
30. *Report to the County of Lanark*, in *Writings*, p. 259.
31. Ibid., p. 265.
32. J.F.C. Harrison, *Robert Owen and the Owenites in Britain and America. The Quest for the New Moral World*, London, 1969, p. 56.
33. *Report to the County of Lanark*, in *Writings*, pp. 265-6.
34. Ibid., p. 287.
35. Harrison, op. cit., p. 180.
36. *Report to the County of Lanark*, in *Writings*, p. 260.
37. Ibid., p. 267.
38. Ibid., p. 278.
39. Ibid., p. 289.
40. Owen, *The Revolution in the Mind and Practice of the Human Race*, p. 119.
41. Ibid., p. 124.
42. Ibid., p. 131.
43. Robert Owen, *An Address to the Socialists on the Present Position of the Rational System of Society*, London, 1841, p. 11.

Chapter Three. Charles Fourier.

1. Quoted by Charles Pellarin, *The Life of Charles Fourier*, 2nd ed., trans. Francis Geo. Shaw, New York, 1848, p. 35.
2. See ibid., pp. 64-5.
3. Quoted ibid., p. 66.
4. Letter dated 7 June 1831. Quoted ibid., p. 108.
5. Cf. Roland Barthes, *Sade, Fourier, Loyola*, trans. Richard Millers, London, 1977, pp. 3-10.
6. See Jonathan Beecher and Richard Bienvenu (trans. and eds.), *The Utopian Vision of Charles Fourier. Selected Texts on Work, Love, and Passionate Attraction*, Boston, Massachusetts, 1971, pp. 215-24 (in subsequent notes the abbreviation *S.T.* is used to refer to this book.); and Mark Poster (ed.), *Harmonian Man. Selected Writings of Charles Fourier*, with new translations by Susan Hanson, Garden City, New York, 1971, pp. 75-114.
7. *Theory of the Four Movements and the General Destinies*, in *S.T.*, p. 215.
8. Ibid., pp. 215-16.
9. Poster, op. cit., p. 19.
10. Frank E. Manuel, *The Prophets of Paris*, Cambridge, Massachusetts, 1962, p. 212.
11. *Industrial and Scientific Anarchy* provides a summary statement of this view. See *S.T.*, pp. 122-8.
12. Ibid., pp. 127-8.

13. *S.T.*, pp. 128-9, quoting from one of Fourier's manuscripts first published in 1851.
14. *Industrial and Scientific Anarchy*, in *S.T.*, pp. 125, 124.
15. *S.T.*, p. 114, quoting from one of Fourier's manuscripts, first published in 1853.
16. *Theory of the Four Movements and the General Destinies*, in *S.T.*, pp. 114-15.
17. *S.T.*, pp. 161-2, quoting from a manuscript first published in 1848 (in *La Phalange*).
18. *S.T.*, p. 162, quoting from one of Fourier's manuscripts first published in 1851.
19. *Theory of the Four Movements and the General Destinies*, in *S.T.*, pp. 195-6.
20. *Theory of Universal Unity*, in *S.T.*, pp. 179-83.
21. Ibid., pp. 235-6, 238.
22. 'The annual profits are divided into three unequal portions and distributed in the following manner: 5/12 to manual labour, 4/12 to invested capital, 3/12 to theoretical and practical knowledge. According to his abilities, each member can belong to any or all of these categories.' Ibid., p. 250.
23. Ibid., pp. 274-5.
24. *The New Industrial and Societary World*, in *S.T.*, p. 279.
25. Ibid., p. 284.
26. Ibid., p. 317.
27. *The New Amorous World*, in *S.T.*, p. 332.
28. See above, p.102-3. Extracts in English translation are included in both *S.T.* and Poster, op. cit.
29. *The New Amorous World*, in *S.T.*, p. 337.
30. *Theory of Universal Unity*, in *S.T.*, p. 249.
31. See above, note 22.
32. *Theory of Universal Unity*, in *S.T.*, p. 298.
33. Ibid., p. 252.
34. *The New Amorous World*, in *S.T.*, p. 377.
35. See above, p. 102.
36. *Theory of Universal Unity*, in *S.T.*, p. 237.
37. *Theory of the Four Movements and the General Destinies*, in *S.T.*, p. 326.

Chapter Four. The Saint-Simonians

1. Comte, naturally enough, did not regard himself in any sense as a Saint-Simonian, but he was willing to contribute to the journal as it offered him an opportunity to expound his own views.
2. He had, after all, worked with Saint-Simon from 1817 to 1824, during which time he made no secret of his intellectual debt to 'the master': 'Intellectually, I certainly owe a lot to Saint-Simon', he told one close friend in 1824, '. . . he contributed powerfully to launching me on the philosophical course which I have clearly created for myself today, and which I will follow unhesitatingly all my life.' (Letter to Valat, quoted by Georges Weill, *Saint-Simon et son oeuvre*, Paris, 1894, p. 207.) And in the preface to his *System of Positive Politics*, published as the third book of *The Industrials' Catechism* in 1824, he praised Saint-Simon at some length, 'so that if my works seem to merit some approval, it may go to the founder of the philosophical school of which I am honoured to be part'. (*Oeuvres de Claude-Henri de Saint-Simon*, vol. IV, Paris, 1966, pt. 2, p. 9.)
3. F.A. Hayek, *The Counter-Revolution of Science. Studies on the Abuse of Reason*, New York, 1955, p. 152.

4. Georg G. Iggers (trans. and ed.), Introduction to *The Doctrine of Saint-Simon: An Exposition. First Year, 1828-1829*, 2nd ed., New York, 1972, p. xxiv. (In subsequent notes this book is referred to as *Exposition I.*)
5. Letter from Duveyrier to Enfantin, 10 February 1832. Quoted by Richard K.P. Pankhurst, *The Saint-Simonians, Mill and Carlyle,* London, 1957, p. 63.
6. Louis Blanc, *The History of Ten Years 1830-1840* (in 2 vols.), London, 1845, vol. I, p. 562.
7. *Oeuvres complètes de Saint-Simon*, 2 pts. in 1 vol., Paris, 1832. Despite its title this volume is far from being a complete edition of Saint-Simon's works.
8. Emile Durkheim, *Socialism*, trans. Charlotte Sattler, ed. Alvin W. Gouldner, New York, 1962, p. 235.
9. Alexander Gray, *The Socialist Tradition. Moses to Lenin*, 2nd, corrected, impression, London, 1947, pp. 163-4.
10. *Exposition I*, p. 48.
11. Ibid., p. 51.
12. Theodore Zeldin, *France 1848-1945*, vol. I, Oxford, 1973, ch. 16: 'The Genius in Politics'.
13. *Exposition I*, p. 233.
14. Ibid., p. 52.
15. See above, pp. 51-4.
16. Comte himself, in his later thought, came to advocate a new religion, a 'Religion of Humanity' based on a doctrine of positivist humanism, and thoroughly hierarchical in organisation. It is difficult to reconcile this with his earlier complaints against the Saint-Simonian religion.
17. *Exposition I*, p.65.
18. Ibid., p. 67.
19. Ibid., p. 73.
20. *Prédication XX* (by Abel Transon), in *Oeuvres de Saint-Simon & d'Enfantin* (in 47 vols.), Paris, 1865-78, vol. XLIV, pp. 8-9. (In subsequent notes the abbreviation *St.-Sim. & Enf.* is used to refer to these volumes.)
21. See introduction, note 5.
22. *Prédication XXXIV*, in *St.-Sim. & Enf.*, vol. XLIV, pp. 410-11.
23. *Exposition I*, p. 72.
24. Ibid., pp. 195-6.
25. Ibid., p. 58.
26. *Le Globe*, 18 February 1832. Quoted by Georg G. Iggers, *The Cult of Authority. The Political Philosophy of the Saint-Simonians*, 2nd ed., The Hague, 1970, p. 95.
27. *Exposition I,* p. 107.
28. *Exposition de la doctrine Saint-Simonienne. Deuxième Année*, in *St.-Sim. & Enf.*, vol. XLII, pp. 163-4.
29. Isaac Pereire, *Leçons sur l'industrie et les finances*, Paris, 1832, p. 34.
30. *Exposition I*, p. 141.
31. Iggers, *The Cult of Authority*, p. 73.
32. For an examination of this whole complex issue see the article by Georg G. Iggers listed in ch. 1, note 36.
33. Preface to *St.-Sim. & Enf.*, vol. I, p. XIII.

Chapter Five. Etienne Cabet

1. Jules Prudhommeaux, *Icarie et son fondateur Etienne Cabet. Contribution à l'étude du socialisme expérimental*, Paris, 1907, p. 3.
2. 'He appeared constricted, overwhelmed, even frightened when he took the

floor. He was totally inept as an orator and generally uncreative as a legislator.' Christopher H. Johnson, *Utopian Communism in France. Cabet and the Icarians, 1839-1851*, Ithaca, New York, 1974, p. 31.

3. Ibid., p. 37.
4. See above, pp. 20-1.
5. Johnson, op. cit., p. 238, quoting from *Le Populaire*, 9 May 1847.
6. Ibid., p. 264, quoting from *Le Populaire*, 25 February 1848.
7. For an English version of the constitution see Etienne Cabet, *History and Constitution of the Icarian Community*, trans. Thomas Teakle, *Iowa Journal of History and Politics*, vol. 15, 1917, pp. 214-86. (Reprinted in book form, New York, 1975, with original pagination.)
8. Prudhommeaux, op. cit., p. 510.
9. Sylvester A. Piotrowski, *Etienne Cabet and the Voyage en Icarie. A Study in the History of Social Thought*, Washington, D.C., 1935, pp. 136-7.
10. *Voyage en Icarie*, 5th ed., 1848, in *Oeuvres d'Etienne Cabet* (in 4 vols.), vol. I, Paris, 1970, p. 567. (In subsequent notes this work is referred to as *Icarie*.)
11. *Icarie*, pp. 547-8.
12. Etienne Cabet, *Le Vrai Christianisme suivant Jésus-Christ*, Paris 1846, p. 635. (In subsequent notes this work is referred to as *Vrai Christianisme*.)
13. Etienne Cabet, *Comment je suis communiste*, Paris, 1840, p. 5. A brief summary of the same argument was included in the preface to *Icarie* (pp. i-ii).
14. Ibid., pp. 6-7.
15. *Icarie*, p. 35.
16. See ch. 4, p. 148.
17. *Vrai Christianisme*, p. 235.
18. *Icarie*, p. 35.
19. Cabet, *Comment je suis communiste*, pp. 12-13.
20. *Vrai Christianisme*, p. 624.
21. *Icarie*, p. 297.
22. *Icarie*, p. 169.
23. *Icarie*, p. 172.
24. *Vrai Christianisme*, p. 153.
25. *Vrai Christianisme*, pp. 226-7.
26. *Vrai Christianisme*, pp. 297-8.
27. *Icarie*, p. 120.
28. *Icarie*, p. 480.
29. Cabet, *History and Constitution of the Icarian Community*, pp. 220-21.
30. Etienne Cabet, *L'Ouvrier; ses misères actuelles; leur cause et leur remède; son futur bonheur dans la communauté; moyens d'établir (The Worker. His Present Misfortunes . . .)*, 3rd ed., Paris, 1846, p. 44.
31. Cabet, *History and Constitution of the Icarian Community*, p. 254.
32. *Icarie*, p. 308.

Chapter Six. Wilhelm Weitling

1. Carl Wittke, *The Utopian Communist. A Biography of Wilhelm Weitling, Nineteenth-Century Reformer*, Baton Rouge, Louisiana, 1950, p. 8.
2. Writing in *Vorwärts* in 1844. Quoted by Franz Mehring, *Karl Marx. The Story of His Life*, trans. Edward Fitzgerald, London, 1936, p. 84.
3. Wilhelm Weitling, *Garantien der Harmonie und Freiheit*, ed. Fr. Mehring, Berlin, 1908, p. 127. (In subsequent notes this book is referred to as *Garantien*.)

4. Wilhelm Weitling, *The Poor Sinner's Gospel*, trans. Dinah Livingstone, foreword by David McLellan, London, 1969, p. xvi. (In subsequent notes this book is referred to as *Gospel*.)
5. Wittke, op. cit., p. 205.
6. Quoted ibid., p. 194.
7. Quoted ibid., p. 234.
8. Quoted ibid., p. 290.
9. Ibid., p. 313.
10. *Garantien*, pp. 123-4.
11. *Die junge Generation*, November 1842, in *Der Hülferuf der deutschen Jugend; Die junge Generation, 1841-1843*, selections reprinted Leipzig, 1972, p. 192.
12. *Garantien*, p. 207.
13. *Garantien*, pp. 131-2.
14. *Garantien*, p. 132.
15. *Garantien*, pp. 132-3.
16. Hans Mühlestein, 'Marx and the Utopian Wilhelm Weitling', trans. Henry F. Mins, *Science and Society*, vol. XII, 1948, p. 113.
17. Leszek Kolakowski, *Main Currents of Marxism. Its Rise, Growth and Dissolution*, vol. I, trans. P.S. Falla, Oxford, 1978, p. 211.
18. *Garantien*, p. 227. Chapter 18 of this book is vital for an understanding of Weitling's theory of revolution.
19. *Gospel*, p. 186.
20. See above, p. 188.
21. This point was made by Weitling in *Gospel*, p. 186.
22. *Gospel*, p. 138.
23. *Gospel*, p. 138.
24. *Gospel*, pp. 184-5.
25. *Garantien*, p. 118.
26. Wilhelm Weitling, *Die Menschheit, wie sie ist und wie sie sein sollte*, Munich, 1895, p. 27. (This is a reprint of the book's second edition, Bern, 1845, and the volume also includes a reprint of Weitling's *Nachtrag zu: Das Evangelium eines armen Sünders*, New York, 1847.)
27. Ralf Dahrendorf, 'Out of Utopia: Toward a Reorientation of Sociological Analysis', *American Journal of Sociology*, vol. LXIV, 1958-9, p. 115.

Bibliography

A truly comprehensive bibliography on the subject of utopian socialism would itself extend to the length of this book, so immense is the existing literature (although at the same time some individual thinkers – Cabet and Weitling, in particular – have still not received anything like sufficient attention). The list which follows has the more modest purpose of assisting the English-speaking student in further research, and in general is restricted to the most important books and articles in English which have appeared since 1900. There are a few references to earlier works where I have judged them to be especially useful.

Utopian Socialism in General

Texts

Fried, Albert and Sanders, Ronald (eds.). *Socialist Thought. A Documentary History*, Edinburgh, 1964.

Manuel, Frank E. and Manuel, Fritzie P. (eds.). *French Utopias. An Anthology of Ideal Societies*, New York, 1968.

Negley, Glenn and Patrick, J. Max (eds.). *The Quest for Utopia. An Anthology of Imaginary Societies*, New York, 1952. Reprinted College Park, Maryland, 1971.

Salvadori, Massimo (ed.). *Modern Socialism*, New York and London, 1968.

Commentaries

Armytage, W.H.G. *Heavens Below. Utopian Experiments in England 1560-1960*, London, 1961.

Beales, H.L. *The Early English Socialists*, London, 1933.

Benevolo, Leonardo. *The Origins of Modern Town Planning*, trans. Judith Landry, London, 1967.

Berki, R.N. *Socialism*, London, 1975.

Bestor, Arthur E., Jr. 'The Evolution of the Socialist Vocabulary', *Journal of the History of Ideas*, vol. IX, 1948, pp. 259-302.

Bowle, John. *Politics and Opinion in the Nineteenth Century. An*

Historical Introduction, London, 1954.
Briefs, Goetz A. 'The Rise and Fall of the Proletarian Utopias', *Review of Politics*, vol. 1, 1939, pp. 31-50.
Buber, Martin. *Paths in Utopia*, trans. R.F.C. Hull, London, 1949.
Cole, G.D.H. *Socialist Thought. The Forerunners 1789-1850 (A History of Socialist Thought*, vol. I), London, 1953.
Cornu, Auguste. 'German Utopianism: "True Socialism" ', trans. Henry F. Mins, *Science and Society*, vol. XII, 1948, pp. 97-112.
Goodwin, Barbara. *Social Science and Utopia. Nineteenth-Century Models of Social Harmony*, Hassocks, 1978.
Gray, Alexander. *The Socialist Tradition. Moses to Lenin*, London, 1946 (2nd, corrected, impression 1947). Reprinted New York, 1968.
Gruner, Shirley M. *Economic Materialism and Social Moralism. A Study in the History of Ideas in France from the Latter Part of the 18th Century to the Middle of the 19th Century*, The Hague, 1973.
Hardy, Dennis. *Alternative Communities in Nineteenth Century England*, London, 1979.
Heilbroner, Robert L. *The Worldly Philosophers. The Great Economic Thinkers*, rev. ed., London, 1969.
Hertzler, Joyce Oramel. *The History of Utopian Thought*, New York, 1923. Reissued 1965.
Kolakowski, Leszek. *Main Currents of Marxism. Its Rise, Growth, and Dissolution*, vol. I, trans. P.S. Falla, Oxford, 1978.
Lasky, Melvin J. *Utopia and Revolution. On the Origins of a Metaphor, or Some Illustrations of the Problem of Political Temperament and Intellectual Climate and How Ideas, Ideals, and Ideologies Have Been Historically Related*, Chicago, 1976; London, 1977.
Lichtheim, George. *The Origins of Socialism*, London, 1969.
Lichtheim, George. *A Short History of Socialism*, London, 1970.
Loubère, Leo. *Utopian Socialism. Its History since 1800*, Cambridge, Massachusetts, 1974.
Mannheim, Karl. *Ideology and Utopia. An Introduction to the Sociology of Knowledge*, trans. Louis Wirth and Edward Shils, preface by Louis Wirth, London, 1936.
Manuel, Frank E. *The Prophets of Paris*, Cambridge, Massachusetts, 1962.
Manuel, Frank E. and Manuel, Fritzie P. *Utopian Thought in the Western World*, Oxford, 1979.
Morton, A.L. *The English Utopia*, London, 1952.
Mumford, Lewis. *The Story of Utopias. Ideal Commonwealths and Social Myths*, intro. by Hendrik Willem van Loon, London, 1923.
Plekhanov, G. *The Development of the Monist View of History*, trans. Andrew Rothstein, London, 1947 (also included in Plekhanov's *Selected Philosophical Works*, vol. I, London, 1961).
Rosenau, Helen. *The Ideal City. Its Architectural Evolution*, 2nd ed., London, 1972.
Talmon, J.L. *Political Messianism. The Romantic Phase*, New York, 1960.
Taylor, Keith. 'Politics as Harmony. Utopian Responses to the Impact

of Industrialism, 1830-1848', *Alternative Futures,* vol. 2, no. 1, Winter 1979, pp. 60-75.

Tod, Ian and Wheeler, Michael. *Utopia*, London, 1978.

Tonnesson. K.D. 'The Babouvists: From Utopian to Practical Socialism', *Past & Present*, no. 22, July 1962, pp. 60-76.

Wilson, Edmund. *To the Finland Station. A Study in the Writing and Acting of History*, rev. ed., London, 1972.

Henri Saint-Simon

Texts

Ionescu, Ghita (ed.). *The Political Thought of Saint-Simon*, trans. Valence Ionescu, London, 1976.

Saint-Simon, Henri Comte de. *Selected Writings*, trans. and ed. F.M.H. Markham, Oxford, 1952. Reissued under the title *Social Organisation, The Science of Man and Other Writings*, New York, 1964.

Saint-Simon, Henri. *Selected Writings on Science, Industry and Social Organisation*, trans. and ed. Keith Taylor, London and New York, 1975.

Commentaries

Bernstein, Samuel. 'Saint-Simon's Philosophy of History', *Science and Society*, vol. XII, 1948, pp. 82-96. Reprinted with revisions in the same author's *Essays in Political and Intellectual History*, New York, 1955.

Booth, Arthur John. *Saint-Simon and Saint-Simonism. A Chapter in the History of Socialism in France*, London, 1871. Reprinted Amsterdam, 1970.

Dondo, Mathurin. *The French Faust. Henri de Saint-Simon*, New York, 1955.

Durkheim, Emile. *Socialism and Saint-Simon*, trans. Charlotte Sattler, ed. Alvin W. Gouldner, London, 1959. Reissued under the title *Socialism*, New York, 1962.

Grossmann, Henryk. 'Evolutionist Revolt Against Classical Economics. I. France: Condorcet, Saint-Simon, Sismonde de Sismondi', *Journal of Political Economy*, vol. LI, 1943, pp. 381-96.

Gruner, Shirley M. 'Political Historiography in Restoration France', *History and Theory*, vol. VIII, 1969, pp. 346-65.

Hart, David K. 'Saint-Simon and the Role of the Elite', *Western Political Quarterly*, vol. XVII, 1964, pp. 423-31.

Hayek, F.A. 'The Counter-Revolution of Science', *Economica*, vol. VIII (New Series), 1941, pp. 9-36 (Part I), 119-50 (Part II), 281-320 (Part III). Reprinted in *The Counter-Revolution of Science. Studies on the Abuse of Reason*, New York, 1955.

Ionescu, Ghita. 'Saint-Simon and the Politics of Industrial Societies', *Government and Opposition*, vol. 8, 1973, pp. 24-47.

James, M.H. 'A Bibliographical Mistake in the Study of Henri de Saint-Simon', *Political Studies*, vol. XX, 1972, pp. 202-5.

Jenks, Leland Hamilton. 'Henri de Saint-Simon', in *Essays in Intellectual History* (various authors), dedicated to James Harvey Robinson by his former seminar students, New York, 1929.

Jones, Robert Alun and Anservitz, Robert M. 'Saint-Simon and Saint-Simonism: A Weberian View', *American Journal of Sociology*, vol. 80, 1975, pp. 1095-1123.

Larrabee, Harold. 'Henri de Saint-Simon at Yorktown. A French Prophet of Modern Industrialism', *Franco-American Review*, vol. II, 1937, pp. 96-109.

Lyon, Peyton V. 'Saint-Simon and the Origins of Scientism and Historicism', *Canadian Journal of Economics and Political Science*, vol. XXVII, 1961, pp. 55-63.

Manuel, Frank E. 'From Equality to Organicism', *Journal of the History of Ideas*, vol. XVII, 1956, pp. 54-69.

Manuel, Frank E. *The New World of Henri Saint-Simon*, Cambridge, Massachusetts, 1956. Reissued Notre Dame, Indiana, 1963.

Manuel, Frank E. 'The Role of the Scientist in Saint-Simon', *Revue internationale de philosophie*, vol. 14, 1960, pp. 343-56.

Manuel, Frank E. *Freedom from History and Other Untimely Essays*, London, 1972. (Includes reprints of the articles 'From Equality to Organicism' and 'The Role of the Scientist in Saint-Simon'.)

Markham, F.M.H. 'Saint-Simon. A Nineteenth-Century Prophet', *History Today*, vol. IV, 1954, pp. 540-47.

Polinger, Elliot H. 'Saint-Simon, the Utopian Precursor of the League of Nations', *Journal of the History of Ideas*, vol. IV, 1943, pp. 475-83.

Simon, Walter M. 'History for Utopia: Saint-Simon and the Idea of Progress', *Journal of the History of Ideas*, vol. XVII, 1956, pp. 311-31.

Simon, Walter M. 'Ignorance is Bliss: Saint-Simon and the Writing of History', *Revue internationale de philosophie*, vol. 14, 1960, pp. 357-83.

Stark, W. 'Saint-Simon as a Realist', *Journal of Economic History*, vol. III, 1943, pp. 42-55.

Stark, W. 'The Realism of Saint-Simon's Spiritual Program', *Journal of Economic History*, vol. V, 1945, pp. 24-42.

Taylor, Keith. 'Henri de Saint-Simon: Pioneer of European Integration', *European Community*, June 1972, pp. 22-3.

Taylor, Keith. 'Saint-Simon and the Conquest of the Future', *Futures*, vol. 9, 1977, pp. 58-64.

Robert Owen

Texts

Morton, A.L. *The Life and Ideas of Robert Owen*, London, 1962; Berlin, 1969.

Owen, Robert. *A New View of Society and Other Writings*, intro. by G.D.H. Cole, London and New York, 1927.

Owen, Robert. *A New View of Society and Report to the County of Lanark*, ed. V.A.C. Gatrell, Harmondsworth, 1970.

Owen, Robert. *The Book of the New Moral World, Containing the Rational System of Society, Founded on Demonstrable Facts, Developing the Constitution and Laws of Human Nature and of Society* (in 7 pts.), 1842-4, reprinted New York, 1970.

Owen, Robert. *A New View of Society or Essays on the Formation of the Human Character Preparatory to the Development of a Plan for Gradually Ameliorating the Condition of Mankind,* 2nd ed., 1816, reprinted with intro. by John Saville, London, 1972.

Owen, Robert. *The Revolution in the Mind and Practice of the Human Race or The Coming Change from Irrationality to Rationality. With a Supplement 1849*, 1849, reprinted Clifton, New Jersey, 1973.

Owen, Robert. *A Development of the Principles and Plans on Which to Establish Self-supporting Home Colonies*, 1841, reprinted New York, 1975.

Owen, Robert. *Report to the County of Lanark, of a Plan for Relieving Public Distress, and Removing Discontent, by Giving Permanent, Productive Employment to the Poor and Working Classes*, 1821, reprinted New York, 1975.

Silver, Harold (ed.). *Robert Owen on Education*, London, 1969.

Commentaries

Butt, John (ed.). *Robert Owen. Prince of Cotton Spinners. A Symposium*, Newton Abbot, 1971.

Cole, G.D.H. *The Life of Robert Owen*, 3rd ed., London, 1965.

Cole, Margaret. *Robert Owen of New Lanark*, London, 1953. Reissued New York, 1969.

Davies, R.E. *The Life of Robert Owen. Philanthropist and Social Reformer. An Appreciation*, London, 1907.

Garnett, R.G. *Co-operation and the Owenite Socialist Communities in Britain, 1825-45*, Manchester, 1972.

Haworth, A. 'Planning and Philosophy: The Case of Owenism and the Owenite Communities', *Urban Studies*, vol. 13, 1976, pp. 147-53.

McCabe, Joseph. *Robert Owen*, London, 1920.

Miliband, Ralph. 'The Politics of Robert Owen', *Journal of the History of Ideas*, vol. XV, 1954, pp. 233-45.

Oliver, W.H. 'Robert Owen and the English Working-Class Movements', *History Today*, vol. VIII, 1958, pp. 787-96.

Podmore, Frank. *Robert Owen. A Biography* (in 2 vols.), London, 1906. Reprinted (in 1 vol.), New York, 1968.

Pollard, Sidney and Salt, John (eds.). *Robert Owen. Prophet of the Poor. Essays in Honour of the Two Hundredth Anniversary of His Birth*, London, 1971.

Rennard, T.A. *Robert Owen*, Exeter, 1937.

Charles Fourier

Texts

Beecher, Jonathan and Bienvenu, Richard (trans. and eds.). *The Utopian*

Vision of Charles Fourier. Selected Texts on Work, Love, and Passionate Attraction, Boston, Massachusetts, 1971; London, 1972.

Gide, Charles (ed.). *Selections from the Writings of Fourier*, trans. Julia Franklin, London, 1901. Reissued under the title *Design for Utopia. Selected Writings of Charles Fourier*, intro. by Frank E. Manuel, New York, 1971.

Poster, Mark (ed.). *Harmonian Man. Selected Writings of Charles Fourier*, with new translations by Susan Hanson, Garden City, New York, 1971.

Commentaries

Barthes, Roland. *Sade, Fourier, Loyola*, trans. Richard Miller, London, 1977.

Bowles, Robert C. 'The Reaction of Charles Fourier to the French Revolution', *French Historical Studies*, vol. I, 1958-60, pp. 348-56.

Clarke, I.F. 'Charles Fourier: The Prophet and His Laws', *Futures*, vol. 5, 1973, pp. 244-7.

Riasanovsky, Nicholas V. *The Teaching of Charles Fourier*, Berkeley, California, 1969.

Zeldin, David. *The Educational Ideas of Charles Fourier (1772-1837)*, London, 1969.

The Saint-Simonians

Texts

Iggers, Georg G. (trans. and ed.). *The Doctrine of Saint-Simon: An Exposition. First Year, 1828-1829*, 2nd ed., New York, 1972. An extract is included in John B. Halsted (ed.), *Romanticism. A Collection of Documents*, London, 1969, pp. 176-88.

Commentaries

Booth, Arthur John. *Saint-Simon and Saint-Simonism. A Chapter in the History of Socialism in France*, London, 1871. Reprinted Amsterdam, 1970.

Butler, E.M. *The Saint-Simonian Religion in Germany. A Study of the Young German Movement*, Cambridge, 1926.

Carlisle, Robert B. 'Saint-Simonian Radicalism: A Definition and a Direction', *French Historical Studies*, vol. 5, 1967-8, pp. 430-45.

Carlisle, Robert B. 'The Birth of Technocracy: Science, Society, and the Saint-Simonians', *Journal of the History of Ideas*, vol. XXXV, pp. 445-64.

Durkheim, Emile. *Socialism and Saint-Simon*, trans. Charlotte Sattler, ed. Alvin W. Gouldner, London, 1959. Reissued under the title *Socialism*, New York, 1962.

Hayek, F.A. 'The Counter-Revolution of Science', *Economica*, vol. VIII (New Series), 1941, pp. 9-36 (Part I), 119-50 (Part II), 281-320 (Part III). Reprinted in *The Counter-Revolution of Science. Studies on the Abuse of Reason*, New York, 1955.

Iggers, Georg G. 'Elements of a Sociology of Ideas in the Saint-Simonian Philosophy of History', *Sociological Quarterly*, vol. 1, 1960, pp. 217-25. Reprinted (with revisions) in Gunter W. Remmling (ed.), *Towards the Sociology of Knowledge. Origin and Development of a Sociological Thought Style*, London, 1973, pp. 60-67.

Iggers, Georg G. *The Cult of Authority. The Political Philosophy of the Saint-Simonians*, 2nd ed., The Hague, 1970.

Jones, Robert Alun and Anservitz, Robert M. 'Saint-Simon and Saint-Simonism: A Weberian View', *American Journal of Sociology*, vol. 80, 1975, pp. 1095-1123.

Etienne Cabet

Texts

Cabet, Etienne. *History and Constitution of the Icarian Community*, trans. Thomas Teakle, *Iowa Journal of History and Politics*, vol. 15, 1917, pp. 214-86. Reprinted New York, 1975.

Icarien Committee (of London). *Community of Icarie*, London, no date. (Almost certainly published in 1847, this pamphlet includes various texts by Cabet concerning the emigration proposals of that year.) Reprinted in *Cooperative Communities: Plans and Descriptions. Eleven Pamphlets 1825-1847*, New York, 1972.

Commentaries

Hausheer, Herman. 'Icarian Medicine: Etienne Cabet's Utopia and Its French Medical Background', *Bulletin of the History of Medicine*, vol. 9, 1941, pp. 294-310, 401-35, 517-29.

Johnson, Christopher H. 'Etienne Cabet and the Problem of Class Antagonism', *International Review of Social History*, vol. XI, 1966, pp. 403-43.

Johnson, Christopher H. 'Communism and the Working Class before Marx: The Icarian System', *American Historical Review*, vol. 76, 1971, pp. 642-89.

Johnson, Christopher H. *Utopian Communism in France. Cabet and the Icarians, 1839-1851*, Ithaca, New York, 1974.

Piotrowski, Sylvester A. *Etienne Cabet and the Voyage en Icarie. A Study in the History of Social Thought*, Washington, D.C., 1935.

Shaw, Albert. *Icaria. A Chapter in the History of Communism*, New York, 1884. Reprinted Philadelphia, 1972.

Wheeler, Wayne and Others. 'Icarian Communism. A Preliminary Exploration in Historiography, Bibliography, and Social Theory', *International Review of Modern Sociology*, vol. 6, 1976, pp. 127-37.

Wilhelm Weitling

Texts

Weitling, Wilhelm. *The Poor Sinner's Gospel*, trans. Dinah Livingstone, foreword by David McLellan, London, 1969.

Commentaries

Clark, F.C. *A Neglected Socialist. A Paper Submitted to the American Academy of Political and Social Science* (A.A.P.S.S. Publications No. 144), Philadelphia, Pennsylvania, 1895.

Mühlestein, Hans. 'Marx and the Utopian Wilhelm Weitling', *Science and Society*, vol. XII, 1948, pp. 113-29.

Wittke, Carl. 'Marx and Weitling', in Milton R. Konvitz and Arthur E. Murphy (eds.), *Essays in Political Theory Presented to George H. Sabine*, Ithaca, New York, 1948, pp. 179-93. Reissued Port Washington, New York, 1972.

Wittke, Carl. *The Utopian Communist. A Biography of Wilhelm Weitling, Nineteenth-Century Reformer*, Baton Rouge, Louisiana, 1950.

Index